The Claim to Christianity

Politics abhors a religious vacuum and so, over recent years, in an atmosphere of alleged secular neutrality, the far-right have used Christianity to legitimise their agenda. It is easy to condemn or dismiss this; much harder to understand and respond to it. But that is what Hannah Strømmen and Ulrich Schmiedel attempt here. Discomforting in some places, provocative in others, intelligent and well-researched throughout, *The Claim to Christianity* is a serious contribution to the growing literature on our new age of religion and politics.

Nick Spencer, Senior Fellow, Theos

This book looks set to cause a storm in our churches in Britain, advocating a new liberation theology which confronts the new, and ancient, racism against Islam, Muslims, and many of our other old prejudices such as Antisemitism and against travellers. It sets up a challenge to churches – that they cannot seek to be neutral moderators of unpleasant politics, but must rather engage with and encourage personal relationships which seek to break down racist propaganda and hatreds. This will be no small task, as the Church of Norway has acknowledged in Christianity's entanglement in such politics. The authors reveal the shockingly dark layers beneath the veneer of Christian niceties – how the Bible is read matters, taking sides in the face of persecution matters. Only after wrongs are confronted can we begin the much-needed task to repair divisions.

Bonnie Evans-Hills co-author of Engaging Islam from a Christian Perspective

I cannot think of a more insightful book about the rise of the Islamophobic far right. Taking the UK, Germany and Norway as case studies, the authors show that laying claim to Christianity is at the heart of today's 'new racism'. Writing as Christians, they combine a powerful critique of the way the church has responded to the far right with a challenge to fellow Christians: claim Christianity back. You do not, however, have to be either a Christian or a theologian to benefit from reading this timely and illuminating book.

Bryan Klug, St Benet's Hall, Oxford

Strømmen and Schmiedel develop important insights into populism on the left and right in contemporary political discourses of religion. While many close readings of political and religious statements stay at the level of analysis, this book is practice-oriented. Both critical and constructive, it is a timely response to the political catastrophes created by struggles over the meaning and identity of Christianity. Theologians, political scientists, religious activists, and policy makers will benefit from reading it.

Fatima Tofighi, University of Religions (Qom, Iran)

With *The Claim to Christianity* we have got a substantial and critical analysis of the Far Right theology in Europe. It is crystal clear that the fear for Islam plays a crucial role. The book gives faceted reflections on how the churches in Germany, Great Britain and Norway have responded differently to the challenge of the Far Right. It is a timely and important book.

Martin Lind, Bishop Emeritus, Lutheran Church of Great Britain

The Claim to Christianity

Responding to the Far Right

Hannah Strømmen
and
Ulrich Schmiedel

scm press

© Hannah Strømmen and Ulrich Schmiedel 2020

Published in 2020 by SCM Press
Editorial office
3rd Floor, Invicta House,
108–114 Golden Lane,
London EC1Y 0TG, UK
www.scmpress.co.uk

SCM Press is an imprint of Hymns Ancient & Modern Ltd
(a registered charity)

Hymns Ancient & Modern® is a registered trademark of
Hymns Ancient & Modern Ltd
13A Hellesdon Park Road, Norwich,
Norfolk NR6 5DR, UK

All rights reserved. No part of this publication may be reproduced,
stored in a retrieval system, or transmitted,
in any form or by any means, electronic, mechanical,
photocopying or otherwise, without the prior permission of
the publisher, SCM Press.

The Authors have asserted their right under the Copyright, Designs and
Patents Act 1988 to be identified as the Authors of this Work

British Library Cataloguing in Publication data

A catalogue record for this book is available
from the British Library

978-0-334-05923-3

Contents

Acknowledgements vii

1. Introduction: Claiming Christianity — 1
2. Cementing the Clash: Religion in the European Far Right — 15
3. The Terrorist Right — 38
4. The Populist Right — 66
5. The Hard Right — 92
6. Challenging Churches: From Complacency to Critique — 119
7. Conclusion: Reclaiming Christianity in Response to the Far Right — 146

Notes — 162
Index of Biblical References — 199
Index of Names and Subjects — 200

Acknowledgements

There is no way of telling exactly when a book begins. This book began at the Center of Theological Inquiry (CTI) in Princeton, New Jersey. CTI's commitment to theology that matters inspired us – *twice*. Conversations with colleagues during two interdisciplinary inquiries, on 'religion and migration' and 'religion and violence', spurred us on to write this book for what academics like to call 'a wider audience'. First and foremost, we thank the Director of CTI, William Storrar. Will might not agree with all of what we have written here, but we wouldn't have written it without him. We are also grateful to Joshua Mauldin and Jamie Basher for academic and administrative support during our stays in Princeton. Thanks are due to the team at SCM Press, particularly David Shervington, who started supporting the book even before we sat down to write it. We are also grateful to Christopher Pipe and Lesley Staff for their eagle-eyed copy-editing of our manuscript.

Many colleagues read through the book or chapters of the book. We are hugely indebted to their careful and constructive comments, both where we have agreed and where we have disagreed with them. In particular, we would like to thank James Crossley, Marijn de Jong and Marije de Jong Marijs, Bonnie Evans-Hills, Werner G. Jeanrond, Jörg Lauster, Johanna Gustafsson Lundberg, Tommy Lynch, Mattias Martinson, Mark Mason, Lukas David Meyer, Joshua Ralston, Sebastian Schirmer, Sturla Stålsett, Øyvind Strømmen, Jayne Svenungsson, and Tobias Tanton. Hanna Barth Hake and Steinar Ims answered our inquiries about the Church of

Norway's confirmation class resources. We are also grateful to the participants at conferences and colloquia at Emory University, Kings College London, the University of Bamberg, the University of Cambridge, the University of Chester, the University of Toronto, and particularly the University of Lund, where we presented an almost-final version of our reflections in a multi-disciplinary research seminar. After so much scrutiny, there shouldn't be any mistakes in this book. Those that remain are no doubt our own.

Our students continue to keep us on our toes. Discussions with them have helped us to think and re-think the significance of theologies for politics and of politics for theologies. We look forward to thinking and re-thinking with them again. We thank our families for encouraging us to engage with tricky topics like the one we tackled in this book. We dedicate this book to the friends we made at CTI.

Hannah Strømmen and Ulrich Schmiedel
Chichester and Edinburgh, March 2020

I

Introduction: Claiming Christianity

Is Europe a battlefield? As some would have it, a battle is raging across Europe, over soil and symbols. It is the battle of Islam against Christianity and of Christianity against Islam, fought with words and with weapons. The survival and salvation of Europe are at stake. This battle scenario is sketched in countless speeches and statements by far-right figures across Europe. The Norwegian Police Security service has recently raised the threat levels of far-right inspired terror, expressing concern over growing numbers of far-right sympathisers.[1] Germany's domestic intelligence agency cautions that monitoring far-right militants is more and more challenging.[2] The Head of the Police in the UK warns that the threat of violence from the far right is rising fast and furiously.[3] Meanwhile, far-right parties inside parliaments and far-right protesters outside parliaments have gained ground by propagating the idea of a battle for Europe.[4] Claims to Christianity are central in the battle that the far right perceives and propagates. Our book is about these claims.

Political scientists point out that definitions of the far right are problematic. Far-right parties are riddled with conflicts, change their political positions over time, and rarely achieve or even seek to achieve coherence in their rhetoric.[5] Are there shared traits and tendencies between the Alternative for Germany (*Alternative für Deutschland*), the Austrian Freedom Party (*Freiheitliche Partei Österreichs*), the British National Party, the Danish People's Party (*Dansk Folkeparti*), the Dutch Party for Freedom (*Partij voor de Vrijheid*), the Italian National Alliance (*Alleanza Nationale*) and the Italian League (*Lega*, previously *Lega Nord*), the National Rally (*Rassemblement National*, previously *Front National*), the Norwegian Progress Party (*Fremskrittspartiet*), the Belgian Flemish Interest (*Vlaams Belang*, previously *Vlaams Blok*), the Sweden Democrats (*Sverigedemokraterna*), and the True Finns (*Perussuomalaiset*)?[6] What, if anything, do far-right parties and far-right protesters have in common?

We use the concept 'far right' because it can cover moderate far-right parties inside parliaments, less moderate far-right protesters outside parliaments, and far-right terrorism that operates online and offline, sometimes hidden and sometimes not so hidden. In our understanding and use of 'far right', what unites these parties and protesters is that they propagate a narrative for which a clash of cultures is central – a clash in which Islam competes with Christian culture and Christianity competes with Islamic culture for territorial and theological dominance over Europe. In the far right, this clash of cultures comes with a return of identity politics in the name of the nation. While nationalisms and neo-nationalisms were for a while seen as a remnant of the past, political scientists characterize the current turn to identity as a consequence of globalization. Globalization, they contend, causes a crisis of identity.[7] Globalization makes for unsettled and unsettling times.[8] What is it about globalization that is so threatening to the far right?

Whatever else globalization means, it means that more and more people with different and diverse ways of life, religious and non-religious, come into more and more contact with each other. We encounter each other day after day; sometimes these encounters are convivial and sometimes these encounters are conflictive. But the far right seeks to separate the insider from the outsider, suggesting that the welfare of the one competes with the welfare of the other. For the far right, the identity of the nation must be clear and confined, hence the intensified focus on national identity on the political scene. In far-right

INTRODUCTION: CLAIMING CHRISTIANITY

rhetoric, the nation itself is clearly circumscribed: 'natives' are insiders warranting privilege and protection, 'non-natives' are outsiders not warranting privilege and protection. The far right promotes what has been called 'an ethnocentric conception of politics', centring its ambitions and actions on one people and one people only, a people characterized – sometimes implicitly and sometimes explicitly – by its ethnicity.[9] The protection of this people is put at the forefront of the political agenda.[10] Pluralization is resisted.[11] Crucially, 'the people' thus defined are always seen positively and 'the non-people' thus defined are always seen negatively. By definition, then, 'the other' – the one who confronts us with difference – is a problem. All troubles can be blamed on this other.[12]

In spite of the significance of the identity of the nation, the notion of the people in the European far right is in fact both national and international. It is strikingly European. Islamophobia is the flag under which far-right parties and far-right protesters across Europe unite. The Muslim is the example or the epitome of the other who confronts us with difference. The far right stresses the significance of culture in order to draw a distinction between European and non-European cultures, identified with Islam. This distinction enables them to 'other' Islam, to portray all Muslims as aliens. Presenting Islam as a threat to security creates a contrast between non-Muslim friend and Muslim foe in which all Europeans come to stand together. Terrorism in the name of Islam, such as the attacks of 9/11 in the US and of 7/7 in the UK, reinforces this narrative of enmity.[13] Cooperation across European borders is enabled and enforced by the common foe who needs to be fought.[14] Of course, Islam is not the only enemy of the far right. The antisemitism of the far right hasn't disappeared. The far right is targeting both people whom it considers to be of a different colour and people whom it considers to be of a different culture. But targeting Islam as a threat brings the far right across Europe together, despite their propagation of national identities.[15]

The presence of the far right in Europe is not new. There have been multiple attempts to create and consolidate far-right networks across the continent.[16] But what lurks behind the current rhetoric of culture is a 'new racism'. In *The Crisis of Multiculturalism in Europe*, historian Rita Chin characterizes the discriminatory distinction drawn between European and non-European cultures in the clash of cultures as 'new racism'.[17] She pinpoints its emergence in the 1970s and 1980s, when the far right shifted from racialized to non-racialized rhetoric in response to immigration into Europe. While there are continuities and discontinuities between 'racism' and 'new racism', the concept of new racism allows us to capture Islamophobia as a type of racism that reacts to Muslimness or to perceived Muslimness.[18] We will return to the definition and the discussion of new racism in the next chapter. What is crucial here is that it's not so much about blood or biology, but about culture. At the core of culture lies religion. The concept of the clash of cultures – Christianity against Islam, Islam against Christianity – is a consequence of the strong shot of religion in this culture-cocktail. Despite regional and national differences, this new racism runs through the ideas and the ideologies of the contemporary far right.

Although academics and analysts have spoken of the demise or even the death of religion, claims to religion as cultural inheritance or cultural identity are persistent. Samuel P. Huntington captured the narrative of a conflict between cultures in his concept of the clash of civilizations in the 1990s.[19] According to Huntington, the Cold War was a confrontation between global communism and global capitalism. After the end of the Cold War, the political scientist from Harvard University proposed, religion returned into politics as a volatile factor, both locally and globally. The Iron Curtain was gone. But a 'Velvet Curtain' was now drawn between religiously rooted cultures, with Western civilization on the one side and non-Western – Islamic – civilization on the other side.[20] 9/11 has been taken as evidence for Huntington's concept of a clash of civilizations.

INTRODUCTION: CLAIMING CHRISTIANITY

Yet many maintain that the clash of civilizations is more fiction than fact.[21] Nonetheless, Huntington's narrative has been used to fuel far-right propaganda. Far-right forces claim Christianity as the common cultural inheritance and the common cultural identity of Europe, a Europe that must be safeguarded against the invasion of Islam.

For the far right, Islam is opposed to Christianity and Christianity is opposed to Islam. Both in the past and in the present, the distinctions between the two religions are considered to have cut so deep that a reconciliation between the cultures that are rooted in these two religions is inconceivable. The migration of Muslims to European countries is seen as dangerous. The integration of Muslims into European countries is seen as dubious. The inter-faith conversation with Muslims is considered to be doomed before it has even begun. The battle over Europe will end either in the defeat and displacement of Islam as a consequence of the victory of Christianity or in the defeat and displacement of Christianity as a consequence of the victory of Islam. There can be neither compromise nor cooperation. The battle for Europe is antagonistic and apocalyptic. Only one culture can prevail.

The rise of the far right as a political phenomenon has been discussed both inside and outside the academy. Yet the role of religion in far-right politics is far from clear. Both prejudice and paranoia about Islam are well documented, but we know little about the claims to Christianity in far-right rhetoric. If Christianity is mentioned at all, it is dismissed by many academics and analysts. The far right, they argue, isn't interested in Christianity. Christianity is merely instrumentalized for popular appeal and political actions. Claims to Christianity, then, are not an interpretation of religion but an instrumentalization of religion. Christianity is a mere means to propagandistic and political ends. Christianity has been hijacked.

We are uneasy with these characterizations of far-right claims to Christianity, because they let us off the hook – the *theological* hook. If Christians and non-Christians who are concerned with Christianity characterize far-right claims to Christianity as a hijacking, they characterize themselves as *not* responsible for these claims. It's not 'true' Christianity, so those who are concerned with Christianity don't have to worry about it. They know that the 'true' Christianity is honest and hospitable while the 'untrue' Christianity is hijacked and hostile. If you aren't responsible, you don't have to respond. But what if it is not so clear what Christianity is? What if Christianity can be both hospitable and hostile? The track record of Christianity is mixed. Throughout history, Christians have attacked their Christian and their non-Christian neighbours. Conceptions of what Christianity is or should be and conceptions of what Christianity isn't or shouldn't be are embedded in the claims to Christianity that have characterized these attacks – that is, conceptions of the identity of Christianity.

Claims to Christianity have been made in conflicting and competing ways throughout history. Particularly since 9/11, we are used to hearing about a political or politicized Islam that produces terrorism. We are less accustomed, however, to hearing about political or politicized Christianity, especially in Europe. While terms such as 'Christianism' have been coined in parallel to 'Islamism',[22] they haven't gained currency in popular and public debates. Instead, one religion is characterized as benign – able to exist in a secular state – while the other religion is characterized as malign – unable to exist in a secular state. It appears to be accepted that Islam is more threatening than Christianity for democracies in Europe. Whether such views are a product of conscious or unconscious bias, they certainly appear to be supported by mainstream media. But what about Christianity? What if far-right claims to Christianity are tapping into theologies of violence that Christians have actually propagated? What if far-right claims to Christianity are tapping into theologies of violence that Christians have actually practised? And what if Christians are responsible for Christianity, regardless of whether it serves violent or non-violent ends? These 'what ifs' are what drew us into writing this book.

INTRODUCTION: CLAIMING CHRISTIANITY

Throughout this book, we approach the claims to Christianity in the contemporary far right from a theological angle. Theology is commonly characterized as the activity of trained theologians who engage in academic and arcane debates about doctrine. Since the Middle Ages, theologians have mocked each other for counting how many angels might fit on the point of a needle. But theology doesn't have to be about needless points. If Christianity is a 'lived religion', a religion practised by people inside and outside churches, then these people can also be called theologians.[23] We are keen to take Christianity seriously as a lived religion. The theologies of lived Christianity are important. They might not always be conscious, consistent or clear, but Christians all over the world orient their beliefs, behaviours and belongings in accordance with their understanding of what it means to be a Christian – which means, in accordance with their theology. They draw on themes and tropes from the traditions of Christianity in order to tackle the issues that face them today. Even if theologies are tacit because they are neither called nor conceptualized as 'theology', they are still theologies. Such theologies run through the ideas and ideologies of the far right.

Consider the parable of the Good Samaritan (Luke 10.25–37).[24] In the Gospel of Luke, Jesus is asked what one has to do to inherit 'eternal life'. He answers with the double commandment of love: love God and love your neighbour. 'And who is my neighbour?', he is probed. In response, Jesus tells the story of the Good Samaritan. A Jewish man, badly injured by a band of robbers, is lying on the street. Two men pass him by without helping. But the third man, a Samaritan – from a people who were in long-standing conflict with the Jews – stops. 'Moved with pity', the Samaritan assists the injured man without asking for reimbursement or reward. 'Which of these three, do you think, was a neighbour to the man who fell into the hands of the robbers?', Jesus asks. There is no need to spell out the answer. 'Go and do likewise.' Because of its context, the story has been taken to say a lot about Christianity: what it is about, what it isn't about, and what it could or should be. It can be read as one of Jesus' own interpretations of the double commandment of love. In *A Theology of Love*, Werner G. Jeanrond argues that the point of the parable is not to 'be' but 'to become a neighbour to others'.[25] Jeanrond points out that there is a difference between liking and loving – Christians are called to *love* the other.[26] The parable provokes Christians 'to widen the horizon of love'.[27] It is striking that the parable ends in a 'doing' rather than a 'describing' of faith. It ends in practice.

Subsequent chapters will show how this parable comes up again and again both in the rhetoric of the far right and in the responses to the rhetoric of the far right.[28] The Bible is used theologically – read and re-read until it makes sense for today – across the political spectrum.[29] Trained theologians might not like political readings of the Bible. Biblical scholars might say that they are historically implausible, that they are hermeneutically incorrect, or that they are wilfully wrong. But these readings are still there. The Bible, too, is 'lived'. Understandings of the Bible shape the theologies which move and motivate both Christians and non-Christians. They also move and motivate the far right in Europe. The theologies that run through the far right didn't appear out of nowhere. Their themes and topics are taken from the sprawling history of Christianity, consciously or unconsciously. Taken, and then turned or twisted. But theologies, the tacit ones and the not-so-tacit ones, are there. And they vie for attention and appeal on the European political stage. They are not arcane or abstract. They are acute.

Tackling the theologies of the far right in Europe, our book has three aims – to investigate, to interpret and to invite intervention. First, the investigation. Since Christianity is claimed by the contemporary far right, we aim to investigate the theologies that run through these claims to Christianity. What kind of Christianity is the far right claiming? What kind of Christianity is the far right disclaiming? And which themes and tropes are central to these claims? Far-right claims to Christianity

INTRODUCTION: CLAIMING CHRISTIANITY

have not gone unnoticed by churches. Therefore, we also investigate the responses to the rhetoric of the far right. What kind of Christianity do the churches claim in responding to the far right? What kind of Christianity do the churches disclaim in responding to the far right? And which themes and tropes are central to these claims?

Second, the interpretation. Since Christianity is claimed by the far right, we aim to interpret the theologies that run through these claims. It's not enough to investigate what is going on in far-right manifestos and far-right movements. The machinery of the far right needs to be taken apart in order for us to understand how the theological cogs hang together. What connects claims to Christianity in different cases and countries? What disconnects claims to Christianity in different cases and countries? And how have the responses by church representatives worked out? Have they been critical? Have they been complacent? Have they been complicit?

Third, the invitation to intervene. Since Christianity is claimed by the far right, we aim to invite you to intervene with claims and counter-claims. We doubt that there is one theology to tackle the rise of the far right across Europe. No theology can fit all cases and all countries. No theology can simply swoop in to save the day. But a lot is done to tackle the rise of the far right in practice, both inside and outside churches. We invite you to contribute to these efforts by exploring creative and collaborative ways of reclaiming Christianity from the clutches of the far right. Given the violence engendered by the far right, far-right ambitions and far-right activities need to be challenged.

Throughout this book, we argue that Christianity cannot be fixed in a freeze-frame shot. There is no battle for Europe, at least not a battle in which Christianity can be marshalled against Islam and Islam can be marshalled against Christianity, because both religions are complicated, complex and changing. As Muslim theologian Mahmoud Ayoub argues, they are both 'continuously self-reforming'.[30] However, there is a 'semantic struggle' for Christianity. We have borrowed the concept of the semantic struggle from a journalist who has studied the rise of the far right in Germany.[31] Liane Bednarz points out that far-right claims to Christianity are made by both Christians and non-Christians. She calls the Christians on the far right 'preachers of fear'. The issue, she contends, is the increasing and intensifying split among Christians.[32] Who will succeed in claiming Christianity? Who will determine and define what Christianity means? Will it be Christian preachers of fear? Or will it be Christian preachers of faith? The contrast between fear and faith that she seems to suggest might be a little too tidy, but we agree with her that there is a semantic struggle for Christianity. In this semantic struggle – a struggle for the *meaning* of Christianity – the identity of Christianity is at stake. Who can lay claim to Christian traditions? Who can't lay claim to Christian traditions? And who decides on what claims can and can't be made?

We advocate for both Christians and non-Christians to lay claim to Christianity, to call each other to take responsibility for 'our' religions. As philosopher Brian Klug puts it, 'What to make of it: that is the question for anyone who lays claim to it.'[33] We argue that the identity of Christianity is a project rather than a possession. The fact that Christianity can neither be fixed nor frozen is not a shortcoming but a strength in response to the far right, because it opens Christianity up to the other. As we go on to argue, openness to otherness calls for contact between Christians and non-Christians in the name of Christianity. Such contact offers us the opportunity to learn how to be critical and self-critical in order to encounter the other openly. Given the spread and the significance of Islamophobia across the far right, it is in collaboration rather than competition with Muslims that we can reflect on what Christianity stands for. Christianity, then, needs contact with Muslims.

Theologically, it is crucial to acknowledge that God cannot be confined by our concepts of God. God exceeds them. Hence, faith in God requires us to be critical and self-critical with any and all concepts of God.[34] The collaboration between Christians and non-Christians that can follow from such a combination of criticism and self-criticism frees churches to offer a challenging but convincing proposal for tackling the rise of the far right. Ayoub again: 'We must obey God as Muslims and as Christians, not as Muslims who are also Christians or Christians who are also Muslims. We are different, and it is God's will that we be different,' but nonetheless the insight 'that the best way to obey God is through care for our fellow human beings is essential to all three monotheistic faiths.'[35] Together, we can practise Christianity in collaboration with Islam.

In order to advance our argument, our book takes three steps that follow from the aims we outlined above. In the first step, we set the scene. Following up on Chapter 1, Chapter 2 outlines the trends and tendencies that characterize the rise of the far right across Europe. We cast the spotlight on the role of religion in the rhetoric of the contemporary far right. Here we will concentrate on the construction of the clash of cultures, including the formats and functions of the new racism that traps people in their religious inheritance and their religious identity. New racism is, we suggest, a theological trap. Islam is not the only enemy of the far right. But since Islamophobia is so central to both the far-right construal of Islam (in contrast to Christianity) and the far-right construal of Christianity (in contrast to Islam), we concentrate on 'the Muslim' as enemy of the far right.

In the following three chapters – Chapters 3, 4 and 5 that make up the second step taken in our book – we will zoom in on three cases of far-right claims to Christianity in order to tackle the theological trap of new racism. We analyse and assess the case of the terrorist right in Norway in Chapter 3, the case of the populist right in Germany in Chapter 4, and the case of the 'hard right' in the UK in Chapter 5.[36] Our aim in these three chapters is analytical rather than argumentative. We aim at understanding both the far right and the responses to the far right before we argue with them. One reason for our choice of Northern and Western Europe over Southern and Eastern Europe is that we've lived in the three countries that we discuss, so we are able to read the sources in the languages in which they were written.[37] The main reason for our focus, however, is that we are interested in cases where the claims to Christianity are camouflaged. The countries we have chosen are often taken as evidence for the secularization of Europe.[38] Whether we should or shouldn't call them secular,[39] it's a fact that they are countries where more and more Christians are turning their backs on their churches. Nonetheless, religion continues to play a role in the politics of these countries. In each of our three cases, we focus on how far-right figures and far-right forces construct the new-racist clash of cultures that identifies Islam as the enemy. We discuss how theological traps can be found both in the far right and in the church responses to the far right.

In the third step that our book takes, we draw our three cases together. Chapter 6 takes up the church responses outlined in Chapters 3 to 5 in order to reflect on the challenges and chances for creative and collaborative resistance to the far right. Christianity can be reclaimed from the far right when Christians and non-Christians come together for the sake of the 'other' – the neighbour, to come back to the parable of the Good Samaritan. Here we turn to psychologist Gordon Allport's analysis of how contact between people can corrode prejudice. Transposing his studies from the past to the present shows that both the mechanisms operative in racist prejudice and in the countering of racist prejudice are the same for racism and new racism. Of course, contact is not so simple that it lets racist and new-racist prejudices disappear in a puff of smoke. Yet if contact is indeed instructive for combating (new) racism, then wherever and whenever churches promote encounters with Muslims, Christianity is reclaimed in response to the far right. In Chapter 7, we sum up our argument by pointing to examples of such encounters.

As scholars of Christianity, we are approaching the con-

INTRODUCTION: CLAIMING CHRISTIANITY

temporary far right from a theological angle. While we're indebted to research by our colleagues in sociology, philosophy, political sciences and cultural studies, our interest is in the role religion plays. This interest is, without a doubt, risky. By studying the far right, we run the risk of giving credence and credit to the far-right views we cover. This may be less of a risk when it comes to far-right parties that are participating in democratic politics, although there have been debates about how the media coverage of such parties can normalize new-racist views. When it comes to far-right terrorists, however, it might be argued that we are giving them what they want: attention. But the fact is that far-right terrorists cannot be seen simply as an aberration. They are embedded in networks promoting worldviews which provoke violence. Such networks reach from the margins to the mainstream. They need to be studied so that we don't fall into their traps.

Studying a far-right spectrum that reaches from the margins to the mainstream is risky too. We are connecting non-violent and violent actors, arguing for continuity between them. There are many who would be offended by the association we see between moderate and less moderate milieux. It might seem unfair to locate democratic politicians and anti-democratic provocateurs on the same political spectrum. Of course, neither the personal nor the political opinions of people map neatly onto descriptors such as 'left' or 'right'. There is a lot between and beyond. Are we bound to misrepresent the forces and figures of the far right? We aren't saying that all are the same. We are saying that their ideas and their ideologies overlap. We have to problematize the role of religion in new racism in order to defuse the theological traps it sets up.

Finally, in studying the rise of the far right from a theological angle we run the risk of suggesting that theology is at the core of the far right. Such a suggestion can't be made convincingly in all cases. Scholars talk about the need to 'right-size' religion. It should not be magnified to such an extent that insignificant religious factors overshadow significant non-religious factors.

Nonetheless, magnification is sometimes necessary. Religion is not all the far right is about. But only by focusing on the theologies of the far right can we make sure that the claims to Christianity don't go unchallenged.

Combining interests in the scripture and the systematics of Christianity, we have researched the impact of contemporary Christianities on public squares and political spheres. As academics who have lived in a number of countries, we are undoubtedly what the far right loves to hate. We have attempted to remain open both to the views that we don't endorse (which was tricky) and to the views that we do endorse (which was not so tricky). But we are *not* neutral. We are *not aiming* to be neutral. Openness is not the same as neutrality. While taking the ideas and the ideologies of the far right seriously, we insist that they are dangerous. Not only in the countries and cases that we study have people been attacked and assassinated – killed – by the far right recently. Anyone, regardless of race or religion, can be turned into a target of far-right terror.[40] The far right needs to be rebutted and resisted.

Throughout this book, we aim to offer theological reasons and a theological rationale that can resist far-right claims to Christianity. The book is for anyone who is interested in the claims to Christianity in the European far right. It's not only for Christians, but Christians might find it particularly provocative. We do not envision readers to imbibe what we write, but readers who disagree and discuss with us in order to think through how to tackle the rise of the far right. Hence, each chapter ends with questions that prompt further thought about the theologies of the far right. There are no easy answers to any of them. We haven't finished thinking about them either. But whether you sit in the pews or stand in the pulpit of your churches (or have never set foot in a church at all), our book has done what we want it to do if it has shed light on the claims to Christianity currently taking place on the political stage, thus prompting creative and collaborative counter-claims. In the semantic struggle for Christianity, the issue is: what is Christianity?

2

Cementing the Clash: Religion in the European Far Right

Europe has seen a swing to the far right.[1] There is no one version of this swing, but across Europe the far right often operates with a theology, sometimes implicitly and sometimes explicitly. To recall: by 'theology', we mean invocations of themes, tropes and traditions from a religion that are interpreted in view of today's issues. The clash of cultures that runs through far-right rhetoric is cobbled together from theological arguments and theological assumptions. Racism lurks in its shadows.

In this chapter, we argue that the theology of the far right sustains racism. It's a theology that traps both believers and non-believers alike. For the far right, it's not people that have religions, but religions that have people.[2] Such racism can be called 'new racism' because it emphasizes religious difference more than racial difference. But new racism is in many ways not new. It draws on racist tropes and racist tendencies in the history of Christianity. Here we take stock of the theology of the far right across Europe, before concentrating on particular countries and particular cases in the following three chapters.

From Race to Religion

The emergence of what is sometimes dubbed the 'new far right' is often traced back to the 1980s.[3] What is 'new' about the new far right? The French National Rally is a very good example of the process of modernization that is associated with the new far right. National Rally is the first modern far-right party to achieve significant electoral success at the national and the supranational level in the European Union. Because of its success, it has functioned as a model for many parties to follow.[4] Under its founder, Jean-Marie Le Pen, National Rally (then National Front) brought together an array of people and positions on the extreme end of the far right, including antisemites. Immigration has been a central issue. Until the 1980s, the immigrant was identified by race. Since the 1980s, however, this identification has shifted. Immigrants are now increasingly identified by culture. Fear is stoked around the image of the immigrant from Muslim majority countries who cannot be integrated.[5]

Under the leadership of Marine Le Pen, the daughter of Jean-Marie Le Pen, the party has gone through a 'clean-up', eradicating its extremist and explicitly racist components, including its antisemitic elements. National Rally is now a well-oiled political machine pushing its key messages cleverly and consistently through its online and offline media presence, including its own WebTV.[6] In this shift, National Rally takes advantage of the slippage between extreme and less extreme right-wing positions, garnering support from voters who come from different strands of society.[7] The core characteristic of the new far right is its concentration on culture – and through culture, religion. Moving away from explicit emphases on race and racial difference, the move to culture is a move that sees culture as caught up in religion. For the far right, religion is wrapped into culture, like a hard core.

As mentioned in our introduction, the focus on religion as the core of culture was captured by political scientist Samuel Huntington's construct of the clash of civilizations. He posits that since the end of the Cold War, politics has been driven by conflicts between civilizations. A civilization, according to him, is marked by the cultural inheritances and cultural identities of people who share historical, territorial and linguistic characteristics. But what is central to the civilization – 'most important', he insists – is religion.[8] He suggests that the differences between civilizations are 'fundamental' even if they are 'seldom sharp'.[9] Europe, then, is built on the fuzzy fundament of Christianity.[10] Interactions between the peoples of different civilizations 'enhance the civilization-consciousness of people that, in turn, invigorates differences'.[11] These differences sustain animosities that stretch back 'deep into history'.[12] According to Huntington, religion is key for these animosities: 'Even more than ethnicity, religion discriminates ... among people'.[13] Through religion, people draw distinctions: you're in, you're out; you're part of us, you're not part of us. As people demarcate and define themselves by their religions, he proposes, we will come to see a political dynamic that pits religions against each other across the world.[14] He sees this dynamic play out in Europe. For Huntington, the 'Velvet Curtain of culture' is the single most significant dividing line in Europe.[15]

In Huntington's construct of the clash of civilizations, there is a marked attention to the West. It is crucial that he doesn't juxtapose 'the West' with 'the East'. Instead, the West is in conflict with Islam and Islam is in conflict with the West. What, then, is 'the West'? In 'The West and the Rest', sociologist Stuart Hall insists that 'the West' has no simple or single meaning.[16] The concept allows for the characterization and classification of societies into different categories, such as 'Western' and 'non-Western'. For Huntington, this classification is key. What runs through it is the idea that the West, while built on the fuzzy fundament of Christianity, is secular. Christianity is seen to have learnt *not* to meddle in politics: churches are separated from the state. Islam, however, hasn't learnt this lesson. As a consequence, Huntington suggests that the 'centuries-old military interaction between the West and Islam is unlikely to decline'.[17] Quite the contrary, it could become 'more virulent'.[18] Citing historian Bernard Lewis's account of Islam as an 'ancient rival against our Judeo-Christian heritage' – note the 'our' that puts Lewis into the

West rather than the Rest – Huntington calls the relationship with Islam a 'clash of civilizations'.[19] Huntington published his *Clash of Civilizations* in the 1990s. Since then, his argument has become popular. The clash of civilizations is 'contagious'.[20]

There are at least two major problems with Huntington's account of the civilizational clash. The first is his assumption that religion is the possession of a particular people that demarcates and differentiates them from other peoples. The second is the assumption that difference automatically leads to antagonism. Neither of these assumptions is acknowledged or analysed. But religions can be porous; difference can be accepted and appreciated. People who consider themselves religious don't necessarily define their identities in competition or conflict to others. Huntington pays too little attention to these possibilities. Christianity and Islam have developed through *both* conflict *and* cooperation with each other.[21]

Although a lot of evidence speaks against it, a stark and simplistic worldview in which the West is antithetical and antagonistic to Islam has prevailed in far-right rhetoric. The clash of civilizations is at the centre of the theology of the far right. Following the rhetoric of the far right in Europe, we refer to clashing cultures rather than clashing civilizations in order to point to the far right's reliance on the absolute difference between cultures that are rooted in religion.

The turn to culture is not a turn away from racism. In *The Crisis of Multiculturalism in Europe*, historian Rita Chin captures the turn to culture in the context of public debates and political discussions about immigration in the 1980s. As mentioned above, Chin speaks of 'new racism'. Comparing how a variety of European countries have coped with multiculturalism, she points to a 1982 speech by Alfred Dregger, then a prominent politician of the union of two conservative political parties, the Christian Democratic Union (CDU) and the Christian Social Union (CSU) in Germany. Concentrating on what he called the 'high culture' of 'the Turkish people', Dregger suggested that Europeans have been shaped by the high culture of Christianity, while non-Europeans have not been shaped by the high culture of Christianity – Turks have been shaped by the high culture of Islam. As he announced:

> Even in its more secular form the cultural impulses of ... high culture have a lasting effect on our peoples. This contributes, in addition to a pronounced national pride of the Turks, to the fact that they are not assimilable. They want to remain what they are, namely Turks. And we should respect this.[22]

While it sounds as if Dregger attributes equal value to both 'high cultures' – the Christian and the non-Christian – he actually argues against equality: the Turks are 'not assimilable', 'they' couldn't and shouldn't live among 'us', even if they wanted to. According to Chin, Dregger's speech 'marked the very first moment that religion was used to define an entire national group within European political discourse. The fact that this shift first occurred in Germany is not especially surprising: Turks were the largest group of "foreigners" in the Federal Republic'.[23]

Dregger's speech showcases the strategies that have been picked up across a number of European countries.[24] The far right hasn't changed them very much. The reference to religion continues the reference to race without having recourse to blood or biology. The other – in Dregger's case, the Turk – is essentialized. Her complex characteristics are reduced into one simple and straightforward core. This core comes to stand for the whole person. When someone is essentialized according to their religion, a theological trap is set up. Dregger's speech traps 'the Turk' in her religion. Even if she isn't a Muslim, she cannot get rid of the religion in which she was brought up. Whether secular or not secular, Turks are Muslims so they cannot be assimilated. Here, the theological trap has sprung shut. Religion – just like race – is something that is *not* chosen. Our religions choose us. As professor of communication Mehdi Semati argues, the clash of cultures – religious rather than racial difference – may define the terms of the debate. But the debate is one in which the other is essentialized.[25] Hence, religion fulfils the function of race. Islamophobia, then, is a type of racism that responds to Muslimness or perceived Muslimness.[26] Following Chin, we refer to Islamophobia as 'new racism' rather than 'racism' to point to the shift from racial to religious terminology.

However, it is crucial that the racist logic is seen in continuity rather than discontinuity with other forms of racism, past and present. Tying categories of religion to categories of race is in many ways not new.[27] Antisemitism through the ages has been a way to racialize people. Theologians such as J. Kameron Carter and Willie James Jennings have argued that the history of Christianity is implicated in constructions of race.[28] Jennings calls out the 'diseased social imagination' in Christianity, where theology has been caught up in projects and processes of colonial domination.[29] He laments the fact that powerful interpretations of Christianity have thwarted Christianity's 'power of joining, mixing, merging, and being changed by multiple ways of life to witness a God who surprises us by love of differences'.[30]

Of course, new racism hasn't replaced racism in the far right. Antisemitism hasn't disappeared. The essentialization of the other that works through race rather than religion is still alive. Religion and race can go hand in hand. Philosopher of religion Thomas Lynch argues that despite the controversy around speaking of Islamophobia as racist, it is appropriate because of the way rhetoric around religion frequently slips into a determination of the other through racial(ized) difference.[31] 'Muslimness' is linked to physical appearance.[32] If a Muslim is of a different colour or of a different culture, even though she grew up in Europe, she'll be asked: 'Where are you from?', 'No, where are you *really* from?'

We find the term 'new racism' helpful because it draws attention to the way culture-coded language (concentrating on religion) rather than colour-coded language (concentrating on race) is mobilized to essentialize 'the Muslim'.[33] The term 'new racism' highlights that the rhetoric of the far right is not avoiding racism. Racism is clouded or camouflaged.

New racism is a theological trap. It doesn't matter whether the other is trapped in the clutches of race or in the clutches of religion. What matters is that the other is trapped. This trap is racist, even if it is set up through religious rather than racial semantics. It's crucial to expose the patterns of thinking that set up the theological trap that essentializes others in ways that harm them. The point is not to label all of those who consciously or unconsciously think in these patterns as 'racist' or 'new-racist'. The point is to break the pattern – defuse the theological trap – so that we don't fall for it in the future.

The theology of new racism fulfils a function: it justifies inequality.[34] If 'the Turks', to return to Dregger, cannot be assimilated into our culture, then we don't have to offer them opportunities for integration. Here, the far right's racist essentialization of who we are and of who we aren't pays off. While one can continue to assume that all persons should be treated equally in the abstract – have the same rights and the same responsibilities – one actually treats the 'other' differently. This treatment is legitimized with reference to her otherness. Because she is a Muslim, she wouldn't know how to accept this responsibility or how to assert this right. Their culture has no idea about the way things are done here. Their rights and responsibilities should be restricted: they shouldn't be allowed to wear what they want. The burqa signifies a backward culture, we don't want that here. As a consequence of the racist legitimation of inequality through religion, we don't have to look for failures of multiculturalism with us: the failures are with them.[35]

The far right draws its new-racist logic from arguments about 'the right to difference'. Some claim that Europe is different from Islamic culture. Difference needs to be respected and retained. Dilution is feared. Some claim that Europe is different from and superior to Islamic culture. This difference and superiority needs to be respected. Dilution and decline are feared. But whether ethnopluralism (difference without European superiority) or ethnocentrism (difference with European superiority) is pushed, the outcome is the same: Muslims can exist in their own territories, but they cannot be included in the 'us', they cannot be our next-door neighbours.[36] Theology is central to the strategies and the successes of the far right. Since they are talking about religion rather than race, the proponents of the far right avoid charges of racism, garnering support from voters who would not consider themselves racist.[37] Nonetheless, Muslim minorities are ascribed a 'racialized identity that can't be escaped', as political scientist Farid Hafez puts it.[38]

The threat of Islam, couched in a cultural clash between insider and outsider, is central to the theology of the far right.[39] In order to alleviate this threat, the minority has to be excluded. Hence, politicians and pundits of the far right stoke fear to conjure up a common ground in their audience.[40] The politics of exclusion doesn't come naturally. It is fuelled. The fuel is what linguist Ruth Wodak has called a 'politics of fear'.[41] Mehdi Semati has likened this politics of fear to ghost stories. The public are 'spooked' by stories of 'brown men of Middle Eastern descent' entering their neighbourhoods.[42] Fearmongering is crucial because it allows the far right to present itself as a response to a threat. The far right, then, has to conjure up both the impression of a threat and the impression of them addressing the threat – but the threat has to be kept alive so that the need for the far right remains alive too. The far right is playing with fire.

Immigration has become one of the hottest debates across Europe. As sociologist of religion Gert Pickel argues, 'religion has gained importance as a means of identifying the other' in these debates.[43] The 'other' can take a number of forms, but the figure of the migrant who is Muslim has arguably attracted most attention. The securitization of migration – regarding the Muslim migrant as a security threat – rests on rhetoric about Islam as an anti-democratic alien culture.[44] According to political scientist Olivier Roy, the year 2015 in which many Muslims arrived in Europe was a watershed moment in the mainstreaming of such rhetoric about immigration.[45] This year triggered a significant anti-Muslim and anti-migrant backlash across Europe.[46] Terror attacks perpetrated in the name of Islam in a number of cities across Europe have prompted fear of 'Islamist' terrorists. The terrorist targeting of people has understandably caused concern about Islam. But the depiction of Islam in public and political debates has pushed the picture of Muslims as prone to violence.[47] Little is done to point to the millions of Muslims who practise their faith in a peaceful manner, who don't recognize themselves in crude and cruel stereotypes about them.

The presentation of Islam and 'Islamization' as problems for Europe connects far-right movements inside and outside the parliaments. While appeals to national unity and uniqueness are crucial for much far-right rhetoric, the idea of 'Europe' is centre-stage. The concentration on Europe allows for collaboration across countries through both ideological and institutional links. As extremism expert Thomas Grumke explains, the 'international of nationalists' is created.[48] Again, religion is crucial. In a speech in Rome in March 2011, the leader of the Dutch Freedom Party, Geert Wilders, spoke of immigration as a threat to Europe. Appealing to a common European culture, Wilders stated that Europe shares a common culture – Judeo-Christian culture. The account of a superior Judeo-Christian culture under siege is espoused by prominent far-right politicians across Europe. Crucially, the shift from 'the Christian' to 'the Judeo-Christian' reveals who the foe of the far right is: Islam.[49] In May 2019 the leader of the League, Matteo Salvini, gathered representatives from more than ten European far-right parties for a rally in Milan. The aim was to foster close collaboration in the European Parliament to push their joint agenda against Islam.[50] In targeting Islam as a problem, the far-right consider and characterize themselves as the champions of the culture of Europe.[51] This culture is under siege by Islam from both the inside and the outside. Given the history of Judaism in Europe, its pairing with Christianity is, as Wolfgang Benz, a historian who specializes in the study of antisemitism, accentuates, 'hypocritical'.[52] If approached from the angle of social-psychological research into the constitution and consequences of stereotyping, he argues, the current so-called criticism of Islam shares strategies with the racially and religiously fuelled othering of Jews past and present.[53]

At first glance it might look as if the antisemitism that marked the far right prior to its turn to culture has been replaced by Islamophobia. Many proponents and parties on the far right avoid explicit antisemitism. Some court the support of prominent Jewish figures, seeking to foster alliances with Jews in a joint effort against Muslims, particularly in relation to Israel. In late 2010, key figures from the Austrian Freedom Party, the Belgian Flemish Interest and the Sweden Democrats visited Israel to sign the 'Jerusalem Declaration'. The declaration announced their support of Israel as an important ally in the struggle against 'fundamentalist Islam'.[54] The declaration demonstrates the shift to a programme in which the threat of Islam is held up as common to Europe and Israel.[55] Antisemitism has, however, by no means disappeared from the far right.[56] The previous leader of the British National Party, Nick Griffin, is known for his denial of the Holocaust.[57] His appearance on the popular British TV programme 'Question Time' in 2009, watched by millions of viewers, caused huge controversy. More recently, the attack on a synagogue in Halle, Germany, on Yom Kippur on 9 October 2019, by a far-right inspired gunman exemplifies the on-going targeting of Jews in Europe. That same year, during the Jewish festival of Hanukkah, shops and a synagogue in London were targeted with antisemitic graffiti. The idea of a 'Judeo-Christian' culture in Europe masks the historical demonization of Jews in Europe in the name of Christianity, a demonization that has had consequences until today.

The new racism is an 'accepted racism' that plays out in the

Islamophobic rhetoric of the far right since the 1980s.[58] Since culture-coded racism (concentrating on religion) is considered more acceptable than colour-coded racism (concentrating on race), far-right parties in Europe have garnered at times significant electoral success. But even where far-right parties have not gained success, the rhetoric of the far right has been promoted by mainstream political parties, in moderate or less moderate forms. From the margins to the middle of the far right, we see instances of religion functioning as the new race.

The Theology of the Far Right

There are two keys to the theology of the far right: Islam and identity. They are linked. The far right's account of identity rests on its account of Islam and the far right's account of Islam rests on its account of identity. The theology at work in the far right assumes that both religions are strong, stable and static. There is no account of the sociological and theological variations of these two religions in different periods and in different places – let alone accounts of how they have cooperated and cohabited with each other throughout history. Instead, religions are considered to constitute the hard cores of cultures. They are like monuments. The theological assumption behind the 'monumentalization' of religion, as theologian Mattias Martinson argues, is that religion can be fixed and frozen, its essence can be put on show.[59] Although figures on the far right rarely offer definitions or descriptions of the essence of Christianity, they are all too confident to speak in its name – against Islam.

Islam

Already in the 1980s, heated debates about Islam surfaced in the UK during the Rushdie Affair, when Ayatollah Khomeini, the leader of the Islamic Republic of Iran, issued a fatwa on the author Salman Rushdie due to claims that his novel, *The Satanic Verses*, was blasphemous in its depiction of the Prophet Mohammed. Chin stresses that the fatwa 'treated all Muslims as accountable to Islamic law', regardless of their religious and non-religious differences.[60] She suggests that 'this was a highly unorthodox and unprecedented move – traditionally, Sharia law had applied only to states under Islamic authority' – that created the perception of Islam as a monolithic entity.[61]

In the Netherlands, the Dutch politician Pim Fortuyn published *Against the Islamization of Our Culture: Dutch Identity as a Foundation* in the 1990s, highlighting Islam as the prime problem for European culture. In the 2000s, the cartoon controversy, sparked by the pictures of the Prophet in the Danish newspaper *Jyllands-Posten*, was used to present Islam as a threat to the principle of free speech in Europe. The attacks on the French satirical magazine *Charlie Hebdo* in 2015 pumped new life into these presentations more recently.[62] While such critiques of Islam were by no means only raised by those on the far right, they have become weapons in the arsenal of the far right.

In addition to presenting Islam as a threat to values such as tolerance, terrorism has become increasingly and intensively linked with Islam. In the US, the terror attacks of 9/11 triggered the 'War on Terror' that has been seen as a war mainly targeting Muslims. Since 9/11 almost all parties on the far right have made Islam a central issue on their agenda.[63] In a speech after the *Charlie Hebdo* attacks, Salvini presented Muslims as internal enemies: 'there are millions of people around the world, including some living next door to us, who are ready to slit throats ... in the name of Islam'.[64] The association of Muslims with terrorism has been intensified by many media outlets.[65] While some attempts are made to distinguish between 'extremist' and 'non-extremist' Muslims, there is rarely an attempt to suggest that terrorists are not in fact Muslim or that radicalization might come from other sources than religious belief. Islam is associated with danger – a religion for fundamentalists and fanatics.

A malicious assumption about Islam has become common across Europe: the idea that an 'Islamic invasion' is taking place.[66] The far right is fuelled by a variety of figures supplying ideological material for its platforms and pamphlets. One set of ideas that has fuelled the far-right account of an 'Islamic invasion' or an 'Islamization' of Europe is the so-called Eurabia theory. Egyptian-British writer Bat Ye'or has popularized the term 'Eurabia'.[67] The idea is that political leaders in Europe, especially the European Union, are part of a conspiracy to turn Europe, and with Europe the West, into an Islamic colony.[68] The idea circulates across borders in slightly varying forms but without ever being critically tried or tested against evidence that might yield other conclusions.[69]

Ye'or characterizes Islam as a dangerous political force. But the worldview she presents is one divided along religious lines. She repeatedly states that Muslims have persecuted Jews and Christians throughout history. She suggests that this history is suppressed.[70] But it is not just a matter of a suppressed history. This history is continued by Islamic jihad today.[71] Therefore, the very survival of the Judeo-Christian people is at stake, of Jews and Christians who in her view share 'Biblical values'.[72] Ye'or recounts story after story of their persecution by Muslims to build her case that Islam is the enemy of the Judeo-Christian people. Unveiling this 'truth', Ye'or presents herself as a pseudo-prophetic figure 'on an explosive, dangerous, and lonely path', in a 'fight for truth'.[73] It is clear that Ye'or's Eurabia theory is theologically driven. She draws on biblical imagery to present herself as a prophet who presents the Judeo-Christian people as a biblical people. They are 'peoples of the Book'. Ye'or borrows the term 'peoples of the Book' from Islamic law, where it in fact signifies the protection rather than the persecution of Jews and Christians. Ye'or adopts the term to draw a distinction between peoples, using the Bible: biblical people against un-biblical people. The Qur'an is presented as violent. This theology is picked up and pushed to new audiences as a truth that must be told. Social anthropologist Sindre Bangstad points out that it would be an understatement to say that the work of Bat Ye'or fails to meet the basic standards of academic research when it comes to Islam.[74] But she mimics an academic style, giving her work a scholarly appearance.[75]

Another key figure in the thought-world of the far right is American author Robert Spencer. Spencer self-identifies as Roman Catholic. He is a prominent figure in what is known as the counter-jihad scene. Spencer founded the blog 'Jihad Watch' and co-founded the 'Stop the Islamization of America Organization', which has European branches and sub-branches. Counter-jihad is a set of ideas which is interpreted differently from context to context. It could be called a network, but it is a loose one without clear organization. Rather, it signals a shared set of ideas. In his study of online counter-jihadist networks, extremism expert Mattias Ekman identifies key themes in counter-jihadism. 'Stealth jihad' is one such theme. Spencer's *Stealth Jihad: How Radical Islam is Subverting America without Guns or Bombs* suggests that Muslim organizations are secretly infiltrating societies in order to change them.[76] Muslims are seen to pose a demographic threat to Europe. They migrate to European countries in large numbers. And Muslims are seen to have a higher birth rate than non-Muslims.[77] Thus, the Muslim take-over – the 'stealth jihad' – is imagined.

Islam is interpreted as a totalitarian political power with colonizing ambitions. The assumption is that *all* Muslims – sometimes explicitly, sometimes implicitly – operate with a unified totalitarian belief-system which grasps for power.[78] The grasp for power is aided and abetted by multiculturalism which is seen as a 'surrender to Islam', supporting the process of Islamization subcutaneously.[79] The failure of multiculturalism, as it has been announced by political leaders such as Angela Merkel, Nikolas Sarkozy and David Cameron, is used as validation for such views.[80] The assumption that Europe is 'under attack' – either through a sneaking or a striking invasion by Islam – might seem melodramatic, but it is widespread.[81] These ideas are just a click away. From there, they have, as Ekman argues, 'permeated into public discourse'.[82]

The idea of a clash of cultures is accompanied by a view of history in which Christianity has always been at war with Islam. The Crusades are a key feature in this construction of history. As political scientist David Art puts it, the past has become 'a field of political contention'.[83] With George W. Bush's reference to the 'War on Terror' as a 'crusade', the Crusades have come to the fore in public debate. Medieval historian Nicholas Paul discusses the way Bush's words heralded 'a new appropriation of the crusades among some white Europeans and Americans who saw themselves as locked in a global struggle against a resurgent and threatening Islam'.[84] After 9/11 there were some who argued that the attacks should be interpreted as an understandable response to European and American assaults on Muslim societies, harking back to the crusades. This argument was also turned around. Drawing on Huntington's *Clash of Civilizations*, violence was portrayed as rooted in Islamic culture. As a consequence, the crusades could be presented as a necessary struggle to stop the violent sprawl of Islam.[85] Theologically, the crusades are put forward as a paradigm for a Christianity in self-defence mode. Thus, tropes and themes tied to forms of medieval Christianity are interpreted in light of today's issues. The 'War on Terror' could be construed as a continuation of the battle against Islam.

One of the prominent intellectuals participating in this historical construction of the crusades is Thomas Madden, an American historian, former Chair of the History Department at Saint Louis University in St Louis, Missouri. Madden suggests that during the crusades the violence 'was all on the Muslim side. At some point what was left of the Christian world would have to defend itself or simply succumb to Islamic conquest. ... In other words, the Crusades were from the beginning a defensive war'.[86] In such accounts, both religions are essentialized:

one as necessarily non-aggressive, the other as necessarily aggressive. Both are tied to a history that dictates its violent trajectory, past and present.[87] The consequence of this essentialization is clear: Muslims are our eternal enemies. Theology is embedded in the figure of the crusader as the Christian defending the faith. *Deus vult*, 'God wills it' – the battle cry of the crusades.[88]

How are these ideas played out in far-right actions and activism? The far right centres the conflict with Islam on issues that are seen as embodying Muslim difference par excellence, reaching from mosques through minarets to meals. In Switzerland in 2009 a referendum banned the building of minarets. The minarets were defined as symbols of 'foreign culture'.[89] In an analysis of online platforms tied to the English far right, complaints about Islam as un-British are rife, including references to celebrations of British cuisine – a bacon roll with a cup of tea.[90] Muslims are seen as incompatible with what is understood to be Englishness or Britishness.[91] Brits eat bacon. Proposed solutions to the 'problems' of Islam range from stopping benefits through banning the burqa to burning down Sharia courts. Other suggestions include violence against Muslims.[92] In France, the Islamic headscarf debate continues to spark intense debate. The most shocking example of this was perhaps the image that circulated in the media in August 2016, showing a woman on a beach in Nice who is forced to remove some of her clothing while surrounded by a group of armed policemen.[93] The situation was a result of the burkini ban in France, which forbade Muslim women from wearing the 'burkini', designed to conform to the modesty standards of some Muslim women.

Across Europe, clothing such as the burkini and the burqa have come to stand for danger to European civilization. As journalist Mona Eltahawy argues in 'Too Loud, Swears Too Much and Goes Too Far' – criticisms that she takes as compliments – the equation of Islam with burqa and burqa with Islam makes it harder for Muslim women to resist misogyny:

> Muslim women are caught between a rock – an Islamophobic and racist right wing that is eager to demonize Muslim men, and to that end misuses our words and the ways we resist misogyny within our Muslim communities – and a hard place: our Muslim communities that are eager to defend Muslim men, and to that end try to silence us and shut down the ways we resist misogyny. Both the rock and the hard place are more concerned with each other than they are with Muslim women. ... Our bodies – what parts of them are covered or uncovered, for example – are proxy battlefields in their endless arguments.[94]

Altogether, then, difference is demonized: the idea of different religions, with different customs and different clothes, are seen as harbingers of danger.[95] According to Syrian Christian theologian Najib George Awad, these discussions demonstrate the 'unease with a "religious other"' in Europe that underlines 'serious scepticism about the possible reconciliation of this other's religiosity with the conventional secular values of European societies'.[96] Islam is perceived and portrayed as alien.

It could be argued that the far right presents Islam as a problem for Europe because it is public and political rather than personal and private. In what most would call a secular Europe, Islam is perceived to be threatening because it is a public and political religion. In this view, Islamophobia would actually be 'religio-phobia'.[97] But the far right is not in any straightforward way against religion. The category 'far right' covers a varied set of political views, some of which do and some of which don't dislike religion. From time to time, it gets more complicated: the idea that Christianity is supportive of secular principles and secular practices is by no means the invention of the far right, but has been the subject of much debate over the last decades.[98] Far-right figures exploit this slippage between secularity and Christianity. Where some people would perhaps otherwise be indifferent to religion, pitting Islam against the secularized Christian culture of Europe taps into anxieties about cultural change. As we will see in our discussion of concrete cases in the next three chapters, there are far-right politicians and far-right protesters positing that one religion should be theologically and territorially dominant: Christianity.

Identity

Claims to Christianity are prevalent in the far right across Europe. The Austrian Freedom Party, the Italian League, the French National Rally, the Dutch Party for Freedom, the Alternative for Germany, and the United Kingdom Independence Party have all claimed that the Christian identity of Europe is threatened by Islamization.[99] In Austria, for instance, both the far-right Freedom Party and the far-right Viennese Citizenship Initiative speak of Christianity as a criterion for the inclusion or the exclusion from the Austrian people.[100] Christianity is treated as 'natural' to Europe.[101] Christians in, non-Christians out. These claims to Christianity are recent in the history of the far right, emerging in the 1990s and the 2000s.[102] The League in Italy, for instance, was known for its use of neo-pagan symbols, but has since 2000 consistently cast itself as the saviour of the people in a culturally Catholic Italy, under threat from secular elites who support Muslims.[103] Only through a return to the Christian roots of its culture can Europe be saved and sustained.[104] The League calls for a 'new crusade' against Islam and Islamization.[105]

The process of secularization that led to the neutrality of the state towards religious and non-religious worldviews is often interpreted as compatible with Christianity. As Marine Le Pen argued about French *laïcité*: 'France is France. It has Christian roots. This is how it is. This is what makes its identity. It is laïque and we are attached to this identity. We won't allow the transformation of this identity'.[106] Roy points out that both Christianity and secularity are taken to be non-negotiable for French identity.[107] But if the theology of the far right is one in which Christianity is intimately and intricately linked with European culture, then this is not a paradox. Rather, it points to a theology in which Christianity is about cultural rather than personal identity – let alone faith. The interpretation of Christianity here is one that values Christianity as history and heritage. Christianity cannot be confined by churches.[108] It can be claimed by all Europeans, against or along with the churches.[109] Theology plays the part of marking the boundaries of this history and this heritage from the 'other': Islam. The multi-religious history of Europe is wiped out.

In its use and understanding of symbols, the theology of the European far-right is provocative and performative. It is a matter of standing for Christianity. Often the Christian symbols hint at a necessary violence against the enemy. For National Rally, the annual celebration of the Day of Joan of Arc has become a trademark.[110] The founder of the party, Jean-Marie Le Pen, likened her to Jesus when he stated that she didn't come to bring peace but a sword (Matt. 10.34).[111] In Italy, the Venetian League (*Liga Veneta*) organized the celebration of a mass in 2002 where they commemorated the anniversary of the 'Christian victory' against the Turks at Lepanto in 1571. The historical event was marked because it supposedly 'saved Europe from "the horrors of a Muslim invasion"'.[112] The mass was celebrated by a priest who had asked Umberto Bossi of the League to make the defence of 'our identity' against the 'Islamic invasion' a central issue in the party's political struggle.[113] Indeed, the League has taken on a strong anti-Islam agenda and identifies itself as a defender of Christian values.[114] In 2000, the party organized protests against the construction of a mosque in the outskirts of Lodi, a small town in Lombardy. After a march, the site intended for the mosque was 'polluted' with pig urine, followed by the 're-consecration' of the land by a priest who celebrated mass there.[115] It's crucial to note that a priest participated. In 2002 the party came out strongly in favour of a law making it obligatory to display crucifixes in all public offices. Considering the nature of the crucifix as a strong symbol of Christianity, the law was designed to strengthen Italian cultural identity by countering the presence of Muslims in Italy.[116] The photos of Salvini at the beach in the summer of 2019, proudly sporting a cross around his neck, were only the tip of the iceberg.[117]

One of the more contradictory points in the theology of the far right has to do with family politics.[118] On the one hand, Islam is lambasted for being misogynistic. This critique is used to argue that the integration of Muslims into European societies is impossible, because it would weaken the tolerant stance taken on LGBTQ+ rights.[119] On the other hand, many far-right statements about family politics conform to conservative values that appeal to the idea of a lost golden age where families consisted of at least one child, a father and a mother who spent most of her time at home and hearth. There is overlap with some churches here. In their critical stance on what they call 'gender ideology', prominent clergy spread ideas that have been latched onto by the far right in their own conceptions of a homeland in which gender roles are firmly fixed by Christianity.[120] A core concept for much far-right ideology is the 'traditional' family, made up of biologically defined roles for men and women.[121]

Altogether, then, Christianity spells out the identity of Europe in the theology of the far right. Of course, the far right didn't invent the idea that Europe is Christian. Christianity has been central to the history of Europe. Although scholars argue about the extent to which Europe has been Christian in the past and the present, there is no doubt that Europe is indebted to Christianity. Theologian Jörg Lauster captures how Christianity has formed and informed the culture of Europe. Christian theology can be traced from its academies, through its art, to its architecture.[122] Nor did the far right invent the idea that Islam is 'other' to Europe. Perceptions of Islam as backward, given to fanaticism and fundamentalism, have a long history in Europe. What the far right has done, however, is to push a theology in which both religions are strong, stable and static sides that are by definition enemies. Religion functions as a marker of belonging and non-belonging: Christians do belong here, non-Christians don't belong here. Belonging is theologized as rooted in religions that are confined, closed – and against each other. As in Huntington's construct of the clash of civilizations, the world is divided into cultures with hard religious cores. This clash has been mobilized politically. Any hint that the two religions mean different things in different places, in different periods and to different people is papered over.

Contesting the Clash

The far right is fuelled by a theology that traps both believers and non-believers in their religions so that references to religion can replace references to race. In Europe, the theology of the far right is not couched in the more familiar formulations of the religious right in the US. But as we have seen, it can nonetheless take pertinent and pungent forms, with repercussions for the politics of fear. Religion fulfils the same function in both building blocks of the theology of the far right: Islam and identity. Both religions form the hard cores of cultures in ways that mirror each other. They are static rather than dynamic, singular rather than plural.

In 'The West and the Rest', Hall condenses this mirroring into the concept of 'stereotypical dualism'.[123] Stereotyping means that 'several characteristics are collapsed into one simplified figure which stands for ... the essence of the people'.[124] Once the stereotype is constructed, it 'is split into two halves' – the positive Christian identity of the West and the negative non-Christian identity of the Rest, identified here with Islam.[125] As a consequence, all the differences within the two halves – the different characteristics that make up identity and the different characteristics that make up Islam – are collapsed. This collapse cements the clash of cultures. This clash is funnelled into a theological trap: the other cannot escape their religion. The stereotypical difference between the two religions – one religion is positive; one religion is negative – legitimates inequality. Such inequality can lead from calls for discrimination of the other to calls for decimation of the other: all rooted in a theology that runs through the far right's new racism.

Christianity signifies a people who share a collective and cultural identity. But because the theology of Christianity is one in which this identity must be kept pure, it is also precarious. The theological assumption is that Christianity cannot be dynamic because it would dissipate. Once dissipated, its people would disappear. With precarity come real or unreal enemies. The need for an enemy is thus naturalized as that which threatens the precarious identity of Christian Europe. Islam becomes the essential and the eternal enemy.

It is often argued that religion is a matter of belonging rather than believing for the far right. This argument is correct. Both religions are taken as markers and matters of identity. Faith in God is not a core component of the far right's conceptualization of religion. However, although correct, the argument is not comprehensive. What our short overview of the theology of the far right has brought out is that the identity that is at the core of the ideas and ideologies of the far right is itself a matter of belief. The Europe to which the far-right figures and far-right forces want to belong isn't there. This Europe has never been there. Although it can draw on cultural memory and material culture from the rich history of Christianity in Europe, it has to be imagined or invented.[126] 'Christian Europe' is, as theologian Jayne Svenungsson argues, a 'mythological conception' that draws borders and boundaries between insiders and outsiders.[127] The belief in the myth of Christian Europe is itself a motor and motivator for the far right. Hence, it might be more pertinent and more precise to characterize the theology of the far right as a theology of believing in belonging.

For the far right, believing in belonging is not against faith in God. Invocations of God are few and far between, but they are there. The far right calls for an alliance between faithful and faithless defenders of a culturally Christian Europe.[128] As we are about to see in the three chapters that follow, clergy and churches have sometimes consciously and sometimes unconsciously joined the alliance. Since a theology is at the centre of the ambitions and the actions of the alliance, the far right has to be confronted theologically. Such a confrontation requires us to ask questions such as:

> What makes a culture 'Christian' or 'non-Christian'? Should Europe have a Christian culture?
> How does theology contribute to new racism? How does theology combat new racism?
> Have you encountered new racism?

Once the theologies of the far right have been studied, a creative and collaborative theological response can follow. Such a response will have to contest the cementation of the clash that pits Christianity against Islam and Islam against Christianity. As theologian Johanna Gustafsson Lundberg argues: 'In navigating between various demands for clarity and consistency connected to identity, the refusal of a narrative structure where only two polemical positions are possible ... seems vital for the continuing conversations about how to live together in a pluralistic society.'[129] But before we can even start to articulate a response that refuses such a structure, we have to dig deeper into the theology of the far right.

3

The Terrorist Right

On 22 July 2011, a bomb exploded in the government quarter of Oslo, the capital of Norway. The bomb was planted in a van parked close to the office of the then Prime Minister, Jens Stoltenberg of Norway's Labour Party (*Arbeiderpartiet*). Eight were killed, many more were wounded. After leaving the bomb to go off, the attacker drove to the island of Utøya, about an hour from Oslo, where the youth organization of Norway's Labour Party held their annual summer camp. The attacker presented himself as a policeman to gain trust, but dropped this cover as he opened fire. When the shooting spree was over, he had killed 69 people – most of them under the age of 20. Again, many more were wounded. As the news of the attacks spread, speculation centred on the attacker as an Islamist terrorist. Eventually, however, it emerged that the terrorist was Anders Behring Breivik, a Norwegian man in his early thirties, who called himself a 'crusader' struggling to save Europe from Islam. The attacks of 22 July 2011 were aimed at the Labour Party of Norway because they were considered to be complicit in the 'Islamization' of Europe. Breivik divided the world into two camps caught in an antagonistic and apocalyptic battle. In this world, Islam is the foe – aided and abetted by the social and political 'elites'. As a result of the trial that ran over the course of 2012, Breivik was sentenced to the most severe punishment in the Norwegian penal system.

Prior to his attacks, Breivik posted a manifesto online: *2083: A European Declaration of Independence*.[1] The manifesto presents the attacker's ideological justification for the terror.

The views that come to the fore in the manifesto lie on the extreme ends of the far-right spectrum. Cobbling together texts from far-right writings, his manifesto of more than 1,500 pages demonstrates the way ideas spread across far-right networks. As biblical scholar Jorunn Økland argues, the point isn't what Breivik wrote himself, but to pay careful attention to what material is selected, what is celebrated and what is critiqued.[2]

Breivik is often identified as a 'lone wolf', but such identifications miss the evidence – 1,500 pages of evidence – that he belonged to a loose network of far-right forces and figures. While Breivik may have acted alone, he did not think alone. Far-right extremism expert Øyvind Strømmen argues that Breivik's worldview was indebted to an international far-right milieu.[3] His manifesto was written in English. His social media posts prior to the attacks were also in English. Breivik's attacks were aimed at an international audience.

Two of the figures that are cited again and again in the manifesto are Bat Ye'or and Robert Spencer, whose views we discussed in the previous chapter. Breivik's manifesto repeats the tenets of the Eurabia theory, propagating the view that political leaders in Europe, especially the European Union, are conspiring to turn Europe into a colony of Islam.[4] The central ideas of the manifesto are arguably at the core of the new far right in Europe.[5] Political scientists Jean-Yves Camus and Nicolas Lebourg suggest that Breivik can be seen as 'a representative of the "far right 2.0"' which works through the web.[6] He is also an example of the extreme outworking of the theories of the more mainstream far right. Social anthropologist Sindre Bangstad points to this mainstreaming.[7] As we will see in subsequent chapters, mainstream versions of Breivik's far-right script are in circulation.

In this chapter, we investigate the ideology of the attacker in order to lay bare the theology in the extreme ends of the contemporary far right. Terrorists such as Breivik take statements and slogans of far-right parties seriously,[8] supplement them with propaganda found on far-right platforms, and act on them.

There are of course differences between violent and non-violent actors on the right-wing spectrum. But there are also shared tenets and tendencies when it comes to the political rhetoric that promotes new racism. In these tenets and tendencies, we suggest, there is a theology at work. Claims to Christianity are made. We aim to show that two Christianities are at work in Breivik's world, a 'Culture Christianity' and a 'Crusader Christianity'. We argue that both are about the control of Christianity as a tradition that is opposed to anyone who is deemed an other or an outsider. The theology that lies behind these claims to Christianity supports the new racism directed at Muslims. Crucially, it also has the function of justifying violence. As the discussions in the Church of Norway after 22 July 2011 demonstrate, Christians are called to engage in the debate about violence done in the name of Christianity. In our account of the Church of Norway's response to 22 July 2011, we show that the Church proclaims a Christianity that challenges Breivik's claims head-on. The Church posits a more critical and self-critical Christianity that doesn't need to be fixed in a monolithic identity that counters others.

Before describing and discussing these competing claims to Christianity, it is crucial to be clear about what we are *not* suggesting. We aren't saying that the set of ideas that come to the fore in Breivik's claims to Christianity were solely or straightforwardly the cause of his terrorism. Explanations for violence are complex. Looking for such explanations requires sociological and psychological insights. But we must *also* analyse the theologies – tacit or not so tacit – that are part of motivations and justifications for terror. Psychological, sociological and theological factors are intertwined in complex ways. We focus on how far-right figures draw on theology to incite fear.[9]

Christian Terror

Breivik has identified himself as both Christian and non-Christian. In the manifesto, Breivik introduces himself as 'a supporter of a monocultural Christian Europe'.[10] He explains that he and his followers 'do not necessarily have a personal relationship with Jesus Christ and God. We do however believe in Christianity as a cultural, social, identity and moral platform. This makes us Christian.'[11] However, Breivik has also distanced himself from a Christian affiliation by, for instance, making claims to pagan traditions.[12] In any case, he has received commendations from some figures on the European far right. Mario Borghezio, a League politician who was a member of the European Parliament, praised Breivik's manifesto a few days after the attacks.[13] Live on Italian state radio, Borghezio proclaimed that he shared Breivik's opposition to Islam, including his call for a Christian crusade. He added that a significant number of Europeans share Breivik's views.[14]

It is clear from Breivik's manifesto that Christianity plays a role in his worldview. Most Christians will have heard enough to conclude that he was not a man of faith – a conclusion that may allow them to sleep at night. What is arguably more troubling than Breivik's personal faith or lack of faith, however, is how Christianity becomes embroiled in a worldview which is embraced by far-right terrorists. Breivik is an extreme example of the radicalization that can take place through far-right networks. While many might hold similar views to Breivik without turning terrorist, these views are pernicious in their designation of the struggle between identity and alterity that calls for a defence of Christian Europe.

Identity

For Breivik, 'the cross will be the symbol in which every cultural conservative can unite under in our common defence. It should serve as the uniting symbol for all Europeans whether they are agnostic or atheists'.[15] The central symbol of Christianity, then, marks the identity of Europe. Europe is Christian – Christian in a way that can be accepted by agnostics and atheists alike. This is what we call 'Culture Christianity'. The theology of Culture Christianity holds that Christianity forms and informs the culture of a continent.[16] Whether you have faith in God doesn't matter. What matters is that you endorse Christianity as cultural inheritance and cultural identity. Christianity can thus distinguish between insider and outsider. Culture Christianity ties Christianity to Europe, a vision of a pure Europe, devoid of diversity. Theology, then, influences politics: Christianity is the bulwark against multiculturalism.

Culture Christianity doesn't have to take the form of demonizing difference and diversity. Christianity has been crucial to the cultures of Europe past and present.[17] Many espouse some form of cultural Christianity without espousing far-right views. Culture Christianity is, however, used in order to cement notions of a superior cultural inheritance and a superior cultural identity of Europeans against an 'other' culture.

The Culture Christianity in Breivik's thought-world is connected to what social anthropologist Thomas Hylland Eriksen calls 'purity-ideology'.[18] The problem with the drive to purify by determining and distinguishing between what or who belongs (the pure) and what or who doesn't belong (the impure) is, as he points out, that there is no end to such a process.[19] The theology that drives this distinction must be relentlessly repeated to ensure continued purity. Culture Christianity as collective identity has become a popular refrain for far-right groups in Europe. To explore the central characteristics of this Culture Christianity, it's worth looking closer at a key far-right figure, Robert Spencer. Spencer's ideas and writings – which we discussed in the previous chapter – come up repeatedly in Breivik's manifesto, but he is also cited by less extreme figures on the far right. Although Spencer is American, he is influential in European far-right milieus, exemplifying how the far right moves effectively across national borders, particularly online. He assumes that the 'values' and 'moral principles' of Western countries are 'rooted in Christian premises', values and principles that are shared with Judaism but 'do not carry over into Islam'.[20] These principles are 'the foundation of Western secular culture'.[21]

The problem for Spencer is twofold. First, Islam is accused of being a totalitarian religion which is destroying Western culture, and persecuting Christians. Second, the West is failing to stand up against Islam. In *Religion of Peace? Why Christianity Is and Islam Isn't*, published in 2007, Spencer bemoans the 'lack of cultural self-confidence' marking the West, critiquing the way Christianity – 'upon which Western civilization is largely based' – is treated as equal to Islam.[22] Western bookstores 'groan' under an avalanche of anti-Christian books and attacks 'on Christian history and doctrine'.[23] He sees this as a pernicious 'effort to instil a sense of cultural shame in even non-Christian European and American youth – a shame that militates against their thinking the West is even worth defending'.[24] Spencer's theology spells out a Christianity that is about a particular and precarious cultural identity, one that is repressed or even reviled. For him, an identity-crisis is crippling the West.

These lamentations about the decline of the Christian West are developed in Breivik's manifesto to include a critique of contemporary churches, particularly the Church of Norway. Church leaders in Europe are deemed 'internationalists/multiculturalists', caring more for the 'other' than for the 'own' – which is to say, Christians (Manifesto, p. 1137). They are therefore deemed complicit in the downfall of Europe. In the theology of Breivik's manifesto, Culture Christianity is used as a stick to beat contemporary churches for what is seen as their betrayal of Europe. The Church of Norway is critiqued for not being enough about religious ritual. Instead it's about 'fighting for equal rights, making the world a better place, being kind to everyone and "spirituality"'.[25] It has become a 'Labour Party

Protestant Church', derided for being subjective, sentimentalist and historically revisionist.[26] The Church is, therefore, cut off from tradition.

Culture Christianity is about fanning the idea of a lost golden age through a return to tradition. Økland has demonstrated the way in which this return to tradition has partly to do with conservative views of gender.[27] Feminism has allegedly destabilized religious tradition by questioning its authority, particularly in regard to patriarchy. The Bible is implicated in the return to the traditions of cultural Christianity. For Breivik, the Bible must be brought back to the Middle Ages, with a return to the Latin version, the Vulgate, 'which represented a Christendom that propagated self-defence against the infidel Muslims'.[28] The contemporary Bible is described as 'modified', a piece of propaganda with a modern agenda, a 'pacifist, gender neutral Bible' that has lost touch with 'what God says'.[29] What has been lost according to the manifesto is God's encouragement of 'the ongoing Crusade (self defence)',[30] a message that has been blurred by the 'political correctness' of contemporary society. Church leaders, then, need to embrace a confident European Christianity that believes in self-defence. This view of the church spills into the political realm in a glorified vision of Christian muscular masculinity. What's needed is 'a strong and just knight of Christianity' to safeguard Europe, nothing less than a 'Crusader Pope', to defend European Christianity against Islam. What are the consequences of this worldview?

Spencer's Culture Christianity, as adopted by Breivik, has a clear-cut counter-identity and counter-culture in Islam. A jihad is needed to battle against the Islamic jihad: namely, a counter-jihad. According to Spencer, all Muslims are said to accept the necessity of jihad which is understood as 'expansionist, imperialist, totalitarian, and globalist'.[31] Spencer emphasizes the impossibility of dialogue between Christians and Muslims due to their 'irreconcilability', 'and the trend of anti-Christian violence committed by Muslims'.[32] He is clear on what we need in the current situation: we need to fight back. In a revealing statement early on in *Religion of Peace?*, Spencer proclaims that it's not enough to be *against* jihadists: 'We must be contending *for* something'.[33] Culture Christianity can thus function as a marker of identity that draws a strict and stable distinction between friend and foe. If the 'War on Terror' is, as Spencer argues, a struggle against an Islamic jihad that would subjugate the West, then the West faces a choice. We can acquiesce to the demands of Muslims in our countries, adopting provisions of Islamic law little by little until the Islamic social order is implemented. Or we can choose to stand up for Judeo-Christian values, defending them against the ideological challenge of jihad.

Despite speaking in the language of battles, Spencer attempts to stay clear of condoning violence. He states that *Religion of Peace?* is not a call to war 'any more than it was when the Lord Jesus said, "Do not think that I have come to bring peace on earth; I have not come to bring peace, but a sword" (Matt. 10.34)'. It is, however, a call 'to take up a sword', a 'sword of the Spirit, which is the word of God'.[34] Considering the fact that Breivik's manifesto contains a section with quotations from the Bible that seem to condone violence,[35] Spencer's concluding statement about a spiritual sword is noteworthy. Breivik adopts Spencer's views, but takes them several steps further – into violent action. The spiritual sword became a very real weapon on 22 July 2011.

It's worth pointing out here that the racist demonization of non-Christians by Christians isn't new. Theologian J. Kameron Carter argues that the way Western culture has come to be articulated as *Christian* culture is tied up in a racist logic.[36] Carter makes the case that the effort of Christians to differentiate themselves from Jews was a key moment for modern notions of race. First, Jews were racialized as a people of the Orient (or the East), and second, Jews were deemed inferior to Christians of the Occident (or the West). As the Jews became a racialized 'other', Christianity effectively became cast as white. What Carter calls 'the theological problem of whiteness' cuts deep, then, in the history of Christianity. While this problem began with the Jews, the logic of a white Christian culture can be applied to marginalize anyone who is deemed to be an outsider or an other. The point here is not to suggest that far-right figures such as Breivik are consciously drawing on the racist legacy of Christianity. Their worldview can, however, be seen as an outworking of a logic that is not foreign to the history of Christianity.

Altogether then, the Culture Christianity of Breivik's brand of the far right is cultural *and* political. The strong identity that is called for is one that unites people under one banner as Culture Christians. Culture Christianity gathers together faithful and faithless Europeans. But it is crystal clear who is *not* gathered into the fold: Muslims. Interpretations of history determine the Christianity that infuses the identity of the people: a united Christian Europe. For this identity to survive, a future politics must accept Culture Christianity at its core.

The idea of Christianity as inheritance and identity is prevalent when it comes to the role of churches. The primary role of a unified and unifying church should be to sustain cultural unity through common rituals and rites. The theological argument in this claim to Christianity is that religions constitute the hard cores of cultures. Culture Christians are encouraged to defend their culture from contamination at all costs. The crusader knight becomes the exemplar of the contemporary Christian.

Islam

In addition to the Culture Christianity espoused in the theology of Breivik's far right ideology, 'Crusader Christianity' is crucial. A militaristic God can aid in the defence of Europe, just as God aided the people of God in the Bible. Only a Crusader Christianity can do justice to this vision of a militaristic God. Robert Spencer's *A Politically Incorrect Guide to Islam (and the Crusades)* exemplifies how far-right figures put forward the claim that the threat facing 'us' today is the same as that facing Christian Europe during the Middle Ages. Crusader Christianity is Culture Christianity on steroids.

Breivik's Crusader Christianity can be seen as a response to Spencer's call to 'fight back' against the enemy in order to 'defend Judeo-Christian culture'. Breivik's turn to violence is arguably not a strange 'misunderstanding' – if that's what it is – of Spencer's own argumentation. If Islam is essentially violent and essentially irreconcilable with Christianity, then an armed 'defence', as Breivik conceived it, is the consequence. Breivik called his actions on 22 July 2011 'horrible, but necessary'.[37] The theology that underpins the Crusader Christianity can be seen in the biblical verses cited in the manifesto.

One section of Breivik's manifesto is named 'Christian Justification of the Struggle'.[38] It contains a sub-section on the significance of the Bible for the self-defence of Christianity.[39] In this section, it is claimed that Christianity in Europe has been abandoned. According to the manifesto, 'we, the cultural conservatives of Europe,' initiate 'coups against the given multiculturalist European regimes and contribute to repell [sic] Islam from Europe'.[40] The biblical quotations in the manifesto occur within the framework of a warfare against Islam and those seen to aid and abet Islamization. A number of different biblical verses are cited. What unites them is God's apparent justification of violence against the enemy. For instance, Psalm 18.34 is cited to confirm the idea of God's support for battle: 'He teaches my hands to make war'. The manifesto demonstrates a confidence that 'God can anoint you with His supernatural power to defeat any enemy that may come your way'.[41] Exodus 15.3–6 evokes the image of a warrior God and a Lord who can shatter the enemy. Similarly, a verse from Isaiah 42.13 emphasizes the militant nature of God: 'The Lord shall go forth like a mighty man; He shall stir up His zeal like a man of war. He shall cry out, yes, shout aloud; He shall prevail against His enemies'.[42]

It is clear, here, that the reading of scripture hails a militaristic God. Theologically, God is envisioned as a war-lord of a particular people, helping to defend the people against their enemy. There is no love of neighbour, let alone of enemy, in this theology (Lev. 19.18; Luke 6.27; Matt. 5.43–44). Nor is there a call to welcome the stranger (Deut. 10.19; Lev. 19.34). Breivik ignores the parable of the Good Samaritan. Yet the passages that are highlighted in the manifesto *are* in the Bible. They are not made up. As theologian Jone Salomonsen points out, the manifesto concludes similarly to the Christian Bible with an apocalyptic vision of a new heaven and a new earth for the elect.[43] The passages and pericopes of the Bible that the 22 July terrorist draws upon are part of the past and potential of Christianity. They have been activated in the history of Christianity for colonial and cruel purposes.

Theologically, what is key in this Crusader Christianity is its association with the Middle Ages, with the idea of a Christendom conducting a just war against Islamic forces. Islam is deemed the enemy of Christian Europe. The knights of Christianity must fight to protect their people and land. The medieval Christianity of the crusades is hailed as a central reference point for understanding what Christianity is. This view of medieval Christianity doesn't do justice to the range of theological views of the period, but it does tap into particular streams of Christian theology. In this image of the past, the Crusades are seen as a defensive war. Islam is seen as aggressive then and now. Of course, a very partial and prejudiced view of history is involved in this picture of the Crusades in which Christianity innocently defends itself against a brutal Islam. A Crusader Christianity might be able to fight back against Islam to save Europe – territorially and theologically speaking. The manifesto is full of stories of Muslim violence and persecution of Christians. These stories are treated as evidence for the essential violence of Islam and as evidence of the past and present conflicts hidden from view.

The theology of the far right has not simply appeared out of nowhere. As medieval historian Katherine Allen Smith has shown, particular biblical passages were deployed during the Crusades to justify violence. In June 1099, when a fraction of the original First Crusade armies reached Jerusalem, conquering, after a siege of five weeks, the Holy City – a conquest that included the massacring of the majority of its inhabitants – the story of Jesus' 'Cleansing of the Temple' became a popular reference point.[44] The story of Jesus driving the merchants and moneychangers from the Temple in Jerusalem (Matt. 21.12–13; Mark 11.15–18; Luke 19.45–46; John 2.13–16) was a lens through which medieval chroniclers and clergy understood the massacre in Jerusalem. Crusaders played the role of Christ whereas Muslims stood in for the merchants and moneychangers.[45] Breivik makes similar theological moves. Although he claims not to have faith in God, his manifesto draws on the Bible to portray God as the God of Europe who will step in like a mighty warrior in the violent battle against Islam.

Ultimately, a Culture Christianity and a Crusader Christianity are combined in Breivik's worldview to divide Europe into cultural Christians and cultural non-Christians. God is conceived as a militant force on the side of the Christian people of Europe, and thus an aid in the battle. Religion draws the distinction between identity and alterity – regardless of faith. The distinction is violently drawn and violently defended. Islam is held up as the all-time foe of Christian Europe. This is an extreme version of the new racism that runs through the concept of the clash of cultures. The theological assumption is that religions are clearly confined units that map onto particular cultures that are therefore set apart from other cultures. The theological argument is that a Christianity of the Middle Ages must be regained, where the crusader knight becomes the figure par excellence for Christianity. There is nothing straightforward about Breivik's Christianity. He also draws on other religious and non-religious ideas.[46] But these ideas don't make the theology in the manifesto less troubling.

The Muslim other is caught in a trap: nothing she can do can turn her from a foe into a friend. Theology sets the trap where

Christianity is understood in antagonistic and apocalyptic opposition to Islam. The theology at work here not only legitimates inequality, it also justifies killing the other – Muslims and non-Muslims who are seen to support Islam in Europe. This justification can be seen at work in the attack at the Al-Noor Islamic Centre in Bærum, Norway, on 10 August 2019, where a gunman opened fire just after the prayers in the mosque had ended. The perpetrator cited Brenton Tarrant as a 'saint'. Tarrant conducted the Christchurch mosque shootings in New Zealand on 15 March 2019, where 59 people died. Tarrant in turn cited Breivik as an inspiration. Even if it is couched in religious rather than racial language, the new racism is as dangerous and deadly as the old. This danger confronts the Church of Norway.

Confronting the Church

Two days after the attacks of 22 July 2011, Helga Haugland Byfuglien, the Presiding Bishop of the Church of Norway, preached in the Sunday service in the Cathedral in Oslo.[47] Her sermon is indicative of the stance of the Church after the attacks: 'Today we ... and many others all over the country are gathered in our churches. Our country is in grief'.[48] We who live in this country 'belong to a strong but small community'; we feel 'safe and free in our peaceful corner of the world'.[49] But 22 July 2011 put an end to the peaceful safety. The Bishop points to the experience of those who were hit by the attacks, directly or indirectly. Reports, including the death toll, were still coming in. Byfuglien calls people to stay together in compassion and community: '"O stay with me"', she suggests, is a prayer spoken both to God and to God's creatures. God's closeness is communicated through God's creatures.[50] 'In this grief you are not alone.'[51] The Bishop argues that 'we have seen the ability God has laid down in every human being to be a fellow human being these days': the support that was received by the survivors, both psychological and physiological, is a sign of God's gift.⁵² 'People's God-given ability to show kindness' is 'what makes us see glimpses of God in humans'.⁵³ Togetherness, then, is the response to vulnerability. 'We are vulnerable, we humans, but we will not resign, for then other forces prevail.'⁵⁴ By staying and sticking together, 'we will fight together for the values that were attacked.'⁵⁵ It is a fight for diversity. 'In the church space there is place for diversity. It is a place for complaints and cries. It's the place for life as it is, right now.'⁵⁶

The Bishop's sermon is personal, but the personal is countering neither the public nor the political significance of the Church of Norway. The 22 July 2011 attacker (who is not named in any of the statements of the Church) provoked the Church of Norway to think through its position in society as it moved from the establishment to the disestablishment of the Church.⁵⁷ The status of the Church in a pluralizing and polarizing society stirred up considerable controversy. We cannot cover all of these controversies here, but we suggest that the Church tackles the theology of Culture Christianity and of Crusader Christianity through a critical and self-critical theology. The acknowledgement that Christianity can be claimed for attacks against Islam means that the Church has to confront its own claims to Christianity. In its response to terror in the name of Christianity, the Church asks where it 'fits in' in a plurality of religious and non-religious ways of life. While official statements by the Church are few and far between, there are a variety of interventions that are indicative of the Church's response to the far right – a response that proves contested and controversial, both inside and outside the Church.

Confronting Culture Christianity

In his article for the magazine of the Church of Norway, 'The Reputation of the Church after 22 July', Steinar Ims, who works for the Church's International Council,⁵⁸ reflects on the changed and changing role of the Church.[59] After the attacks, Ims argues, both state and society put the Church in a position where it was asked to provide a space for mourning in the public square. At the same time, however, the Church is criticized for being too public and too political. While he agrees that it is correct of the Church to take up the task of mourning, he argues that it is crucial to ask how a church service like the one in Oslo after the attacks can reflect the diversity of society. The victims of the attacks did not necessarily have any affiliation with the Church. Should this be acknowledged in the service? The central concern is the attacker's connection to Christianity. While it is clear that Muslim associations would be asked to condemn terrorism had it been perpetrated in the name of Islam, the Church was not asked to condemn the attacks perpetrated in the name of Christianity. Should it have? 'The terror was directed towards the defenders of a pluralist society, and with a particular aim at Islam. Unfortunately, this is nothing new.'[60] However, given that the prejudice against Islam can be found in the life of the Church past and present, 'what do we do about it?'[61]

Ims characterizes the attacks of 22 July as a calling for the Church. Although it might go against the grain of what people, Christians and non-Christians, want it to be, churches have to become open to others. After the attacks, the square in front of the Cathedral in Oslo became a local and national place for cries and comfort – for all. Believers and non-believers went into the Cathedral. This is what churches are called to be.[62] The consequences are controversial, but clear for Ims: 'If we have now become a large "we" in Norway after the terror, this will mean that next time I as a Christian can quite naturally make use of my local mosque ... as a place for prayer ... when I need it. Maybe it does not even have to take a crisis to do so.'[63] The article, then, points to a conception of churches as open to others, regardless of their religion. This openness goes both ways, from churches to mosques and from mosques to the churches.

Whatever you think about such a conception of the church, the Church of Norway accepted that Christianity has both a positive and a negative impact for relations between religions. In its potential openness, Islam comes into view as a partner for Christianity. Theologian Oddbjørn Leirvik details this partnership between Christians and Muslims in Norway over the years to foster shared practice and principles – principles that are put into practice also in holding others to account for their theological assumptions and actions.[64] He calls this a strong 'value fellowship' which has developed through conversation and collaboration, a value fellowship he contrasts with the more polarizing 'value conflicts' of identity politics.[65]

Contrary to the Culture Christianity of far-right rhetoric, the Christianity that comes to the fore here is a porous Christianity that doesn't assume all in Norway are – or ought to be – subsumed under a Christian banner. A Christianity that is characterized culturally is not enough to decide whether people are or aren't allowed to belong to Norway. The culture of the country has been characterized by Christianity from the past to the present, but today it's plural. This doesn't mean that the Christian cultural heritage of Norway needs to be erased. The Church of Norway as *folkekirke* – which could be roughly rendered as 'church of the people' – points to its own significance through this heritage and history. There is nothing bad about this – unless the idea of 'culture' is defined in an essentialized and exclusivist way. Philosopher Seyla Benhabib critiques the recent tendency to think of cultures in reductionist terms.[66] She points to the frequent but false assumption that cultures can be simply defined and mapped onto particular peoples. There is an over-emphasis on cultural differences and distinctions, stressing the supposed homogeneity internal to cultures. But history and sociology tell us otherwise.

A Christian faith that allows Christians to pray in mosques and Muslims to pray in churches is possible. This may be going further than many Christians feel comfortable with. But in this conception of Christianity, a 'we' is tentative. Who 'we' are is up for debate, rather than shut down in advance and policed according to dictates of religious difference. A 'we' could be made up of Christians and Muslims, not in order to subsume Muslims into an all-embracing Christian 'we', but to form communities of solidarity.

Confronting Crusader Christianity

Also in 2011, Mehtab Afsar, the General Secretary of the Islamic Council of Norway, and Berit Hagen Agøy, the General Secretary of the International Council of the Church of Norway, signed a 'Joint Statement' against extremism in the name of religion.[67] The statement starts with a list of terrorist attacks, ending with that of 22 July 2011. 'Extremism' is the category with which these attacks are captured. The authors insist that the effects of such extremism are felt beyond the cases that attract European and American attention. Its effects are felt in day-to-day lives. Extremism can be religious or non-religious, but often religion is used to justify extremism. One example is the way sacred scripture is interpreted so that it supports extremist attitudes and actions. Because of the justification of extremism through religion, 'we' – meaning the leaders of faith communities – 'have a special responsibility' to counteract such justifications.[68] The statement continues with a list of characteristics of extremism. What runs through them is a clear-cut distinction between insider and outsider. In an extremist worldview, the 'outsider' – the other – is devalued, so much so that they need to be destroyed. Contrary to such a view, the joint statement insists that the other can be found in one's own and in the other's religion.

The statement makes clear that extremism is not the same as having a 'strong commitment to one's faith'.[69] Commitment, as long as it comes with respect for the dignity of others, is not the issue. On the contrary, faith instructs the 'common call' to resist extremism communicated in the statement: 'extremists put themselves in the place of God' which means that they come 'in conflict with the teachings of our religions'.[70] The leaders are concerned about tendencies to extremism 'in our own ranks'.[71] They encourage all faith communities to counteract the different forms of extremism, communally and personally. We must protect each other, ask for more nuanced portrayals of religion in the media, and strengthen the fight against extremism nationally and internationally. What is remarkable about the 'Joint Statement' is that it's a *Joint* Statement': Islam works with Christianity and Christianity works with Islam. Islam is a partner rather than a pariah. The statement puts into practice what it is promoting.

Theologically, history is not taken as the determining factor in future relations between the two faiths. Even if we adopt the view of the Crusades promoted by figures on the far right, this history does not have to be continued. We can change it. Different faith traditions can work together. This doesn't entail an erasure of difference. But it does require a theology in which religions are not regarded as static and stable entities that inevitably clash against each other. Contrary to far-right rhetoric, this is a porous Christianity that doesn't assume that there is a conflict in which Islam fights Christianity and Christianity fights Islam.

Church in Times of Terror

What characterizes the Church's confrontation with far-right Culture Christianity and far-right Crusader Christianity is the significance of self-criticism. In response to terror in the name of Christianity, the Church embarks on a soul-searching mission. Critically charting its past and its present, the Church looks for its own complicity – whether conscious or unconscious – with the worldview that led to the attacks of 22 July 2011. The soul-searching mission cannot be accomplished by the Church alone. It cuts to the core of the Church because it consists of collaboration by Christians with Muslims and Muslims with Christians. The resources on antisemitism, antiziganism (hostility towards Romani people) and Islamophobia that were published by the Church in Norway in 2013 point to the impact of such collaboration.[72]

The title *Homo-hore-jøde-terrorist-svarting* is too rude to translate. It combines racial and religious epithets into one long string of insults. (A dictionary will help those who are now irrepressibly curious.) Steinar Ims and Iselin Jørgensen from the Church's Centre for Dialogue are responsible for the collection of these resources. The prompt to create such a set of resources came out of the dialogue between religions.[73] The resources point to the impact of prejudice in the Church past and present: antisemitism, antiziganism and Islamophobia, although conceptually different, come with a dangerous and destructive force: defining and diminishing others.[74] To counter the force, young people in the Church – those going forward for confirmation in particular – need to be equipped: 'At best, they will be able to correct the priest after the service for using the term "the Jews" in contrast to "the Christians" and "Jesus' message"'.[75]

The intention to offer a Christian critique of the new-racist ideologies to the outsiders and to the insiders of the Church is taken up in Berit Hagen Agøy's 'Preface'. Without mincing words, she points to the ambiguity of Christianity (Christians call for inclusiveness at the same time as they call for exclusiveness) that has characterized churches. Against this ambiguity, the example of Jesus is crystal clear: Jesus went to others 'regardless of belief or background'.[76] Hence, we 'must teach our young people to be safe in, and proud of, their Christian faith and identity, without violating, caricaturing or misrepresenting the faiths of others. We have a Gospel that does not have to be explained by negating others. We must hold on to the inclusive thread that binds us to Jesus' ground-breaking love for all humans.'[77]

The Resources start with statistics about discrimination in

schools across the country, suggesting that the Church has a responsibility to respond.[78] The status of the mainline or majority Church, a status with which Anglicans, Protestants and Catholics are all grappling, as we shall see, is interpreted both as a challenge to embrace all and as a chance to educate all. Here, the Church of Norway takes a provocative but promising approach. The Church is open to all people, but such openness doesn't mean that it can accept all ideas and ideologies. This is justified through Trinitarian theology: God's creation means that all humans are images of God so that 'traces of the Triune God' can be found in each and every human regardless of race or religion.[79] Both the Son and the Spirit underline that we 'can invite other people into our context, not just to tell them our truth, but to open up the truth that is also found in places where we do not expect to find it.'[80]

Historically, 'Christian identity' has been a consequence of competition between Christians and non-Christians, starting with the first Christians, who defined themselves in contrast to the competing religious and non-religious authorities of their time.[81] Crucially, such competition has different effects if it is directed from the majority to the minority or from the minority to the majority – differences that are significant today when Christian churches are frequently in positions of power: 'When we as a Church today preach and proclaim about our faith, the challenge is to do so in a way that does not misrepresent, caricature or denigrate other religions.'[82] The resources condense their discussion into a clear and catchy conclusion: 'The Gospel is strong enough to stand on its own legs.'[83]

The history of hate that has shaped Christianity – not only since Martin Luther – could be seen as a consequence of a lack of courage and confidence in accepting self-criticism. The gospel does not need to be proclaimed by tearing others down or deeming others wrong. The need to affirm one's own superiority by denigrating others leads to defending God with words and weapons. This defence is at the core of Crusader Christianity. A confident and courageous church would and should have known that God doesn't need our defence. Of course, 'the churches are far from being the only European institutions guilty in this history. But this does not make the church's responsibility any smaller'.[84]

The Resources take up this responsibility. They discuss antisemitism, antiziganism and Islamophobia in depth and detail, describing their impact on Norway past and present. For the issue of Islamophobia, the Resources turn to Martin Luther. They point out how the faith of 'the Mohammedans' was condemned in the *Augsburg Confession* of 1530, pointing to the sieges of Vienna as symbols for a history of Islamophobia that spans more than 1000 years.[85] 'The tradition of presenting the Muslim in theological contexts as ... the tool of evil is as old as the emergence of Islam.'[86] Culture Christianity and Crusader Christianity, then, have precedents in church history. Their ideas and ideologies can be found in our confessions. While there are significant differences from antisemitism and antiziganism, Islamophobia still shares the central characteristics of the new racism. 'We experienced the worst consequence of this with the killings ... in Norway on 22 July 2011.'[87]

Without naming the attacker, the Resources explain how Christianity has contributed to the new-racist ideology that motivated the attack. But they aim for more than explanation. What follows are workshops designed for young people to recognize antisemitism, antiziganism and Islamophobia where they encounter them, reflect on their devastating personal and social consequences, read the Bible in a contextually responsible way, and respond to others with curiosity.[88] Crucially, the Resources point to texts of the Bible that are challenging (for example, Matt. 15.21–28; 25.31–46; John 19.1–22). Hence, rather than presenting young people with texts that comfortably fit the theology the Church is promoting, the intention is to enable and equip them with the theological tools to respond critically to the texts that are tricky. Drawing on contextual biblical scholar Gerald West, a contextual reading is commended, where both the context of the text and the context of the reader of the text are considered in order to 'read the Bible with a commitment to change for the better of everyone'.[89] The Church, then, is not offering clear-cut proposals for complicated problems, but is putting young people in a position to think through the problems themselves.

The Resources were updated in 2015 and again in 2018.[90] A webpage was created to allow for wide usage in the Church. As Hanna Barth Hake of the Church Dialogue Centre points out, as rhetoric in the Norwegian public sphere has become more polarized, the material has only seemed to become more important.[91] Used in church and non-church settings, such as schools, by Christian and non-Christian groups, such as the Norwegian Jewish community, the material has become part of a wider effort to tackle theologies that demonize and discriminate against others.[92]

The self-critical approach to the Bible, to the history of Christianity, and to classic and contemporary theological statements is indicative of the Church's response to the challenge of far-right rhetoric in recent years. The Church of Norway understands its position as a majority church differently from the churches we go on to examine. Responding to the significance of the churches in times of terror, the Church of Norway is both critical and careful: it's not enough for churches to be a home for everybody. Churches need to challenge those who are at home in them. The Resources *Homo-hore-jøde-terrorist-svarting*, then, cut to the chase. Tackling the new racism that has characterized themes and traditions of theology means cutting to the core of who and what constitutes the church. In order to be faithful, we have to confront the theologies of (new) racism in our past and our present.

The Semantic Struggle for Christianity

The Church of Norway's self-critical stance continues to stir up controversy. Published in 2019, a recent issue of *Nytt norsk kirkeblad* – the church magazine, edited by the Faculty of Theology in Oslo – revolves around criticisms of the Church for its response to the far right. In her editorial, Merete Thomassen, who teaches practical theology at Oslo, puts it bluntly: is the Church too lefty?[93] She notes that 'we looked with lights and lanterns to find a theologian well on the right that could hold a lecture. It turned out to be impossible!'[94] But if the Church aims to be there for all people who live in Norway, shouldn't it avoid being either left- or right-wing?

Sylvi Listhaug's pronouncement on the Church of Norway is a prominent and provocative example of criticism of the Church as too 'lefty'.[95] Listhaug has been a controversial figure in Norwegian politics. As a prominent spokesperson for the Progress Party (*Fremskrittspartiet*), Listhaug has published *Der andre tier* ('Where others are silent'), a book that criticizes the Church of Norway of which she is a member. She lambasts the church leadership for playing 'politicians'.[96] Instead of proclaiming the Christian faith, the 'leading bishops and priests' are allowing the Church to rot at the root by turning church spaces into a political arena.[97] The Presiding Bishop of the Church, Byfuglien, spoke during the Christmas of 2015 about taking Jesus' message seriously by standing up for refugees.[98] For this she is seen by Listhaug, who was Norway's Minister of Immigration and Integration from 2015 to 2018, to 'take sides' politically.[99] Taking sides politically is deemed to be exclusive. Islam has been welcomed too warmly by the Church, according to Listhaug.[100]

The leader of the International Council of the Church of Norway, Berit Hagen Agøy, is also hung out to dry as someone who has consistently downplayed the differences between Christianity and Islam.[101] Increased immigration to Norway is higher on the Church agenda than the Trinity, Listhaug argues.[102] The idea that these two issues – immigration and the Trinity – are in competition is in itself a problematic construct. Social issues are presented as inevitably detracting from theological doctrine as well as something separate from 'theology' proper. Listhaug's complaint is that the Church has become a haunt of old lefties.[103] The idea of a 'stealth Islamization' (*snikislamisering*) has long been a rallying cry for her party. Breivik was a member before he turned to the more extreme ends of the far right. Listhaug distanced herself and her party from Breivik. She in no way condones violence. There are, however, striking similarities between the political views espoused by both of them, particularly in their accounts of Islam and of identity and their criticism of the Church.

Of course, we aren't saying that the Progress Party is aiding and abetting terrorism. But what we are saying is that there is a struggle for the meaning of Christianity that can be found both in the extremist and the less extremist claims to Christianity on the far right. This is the semantic struggle for Christianity. It's raging in the Church of Norway. The 'fear of the faith of others', as theologian Sturla J. Stålsett puts it, is a catalyst in this struggle.[104] It unites the far right. Stålsett points to the dangers of what he calls the '*sniknormalisering*' – stealth normalization – of extreme views by prominent Norwegian politicians such as Listhaug.[105] The normalization of extreme views is, as Stålsett suggests, deeply troubling. Such views are packaged as Norwegian, European and Christian values. But the language of values masks the violence of these views in trapping Muslims as irredeemably 'other'.

In her editorial in *Nytt norsk kirkeblad*, Thomassen notes that the critique of the Church as too lefty points to a turn. Historically, the Church of Norway has been accused of being on the right rather than the left.[106] The issue of the magazine makes room for arguments from the left and the right. In a short historical study of the engagement of the Church of Norway in politics, Hallgeir Elstad, a priest and professor of church history at the University of Oslo, points to the rhetoric involved in the criticisms: the critique that the Church meddles in politics is voiced from the right rather than the left. But when the Church takes a conservative stand on issues such as abortion it's not seen as meddling.[107] One has to be careful, then, with drawing conclusions from those criticisms. Listhaug showcases a strategy of the far right: while denouncing a political Christianity, she is putting forward her own political-theological understanding by writing that the Christian values of Norway have to be protected against Islam.[108]

Janne Dale Hauger, who works with the Church's International Council, presents a response to such criticisms, drawing on statements from the Lutheran World Federation.[109] She argues that churches are encouraged by the Federation to 'work for "the public sphere as a fair place for all"'.[110] This means working for equal access to common goods and political decisions about common goods, for meaningful interaction between people and groups of people in society, and for safety for the most vulnerable.[111] While these points might be self-evident in Norway, she argues that the far right across Europe counters all of them. Hence, working for the public sphere as a fair place accessible to all means working against the far right. This work needs to encompass people in leadership and in lay positions: 'But at a time of increasing polarization and populism, it is more important than ever that the Church earnestly calls to empower everyone baptized to take part in ecclesial community engagement, including political engagement.'[112] The status of the majority or mainline Church, she makes clear, is not only the challenge to embrace everybody, but to educate and to empower everybody.

Dale Hauger concludes with a vision for a radical church, rooted in God's grace: 'This radical church bursts our political frame of reference, and cannot be ... placed on a right–left axis in politics. That said, the Church must, of course, be aware of how the societal engagement is perceived, and take seriously those who feel offended or excluded by the church's political engagement.'[113] While the article acknowledges that the work of churches can engage people on the one hand and exclude people on the other hand, it is not accepted that such engagement or exclusion fits into a frame of left versus right. The Church is neither too much on the right nor too much on the left. Politics that polarizes the public sphere to a point where some cannot participate needs to be opposed by churches. However, a church that excludes – even if it only excludes those who exclude – is nonetheless exclusive. Dale Hauger's conclusion points to the significance of marginalization:

> 'God comforts the troubled, and troubles the comfortable', says an old saying. I think I speak for more than myself when I acknowledge that I need a radical church as both comforter and challenger. A church that baptizes us into a local and global community, that reminds us that our lives are inextricably linked. A church which reminds us that we are saved by the grace of God, and which sets us free to fight for a more just public space, a more just world.[114]

Here, the Church of Norway also concludes that it has a double role: criticizing racist and far-right politicians that are exclusive, on the one hand, and criticizing the critics of racist and far-right politicians that are exclusive, on the other hand. However, what runs through most of the statements in the discussion of the status of the Church is a call for justice that includes Christians and non-Christians, including Muslims.

The collaboration with Islam leads into a conceptualization or re-conceptualization of the Church. The idea of the inalienable dignity of humans is part of Christian and non-Christian heritage, as Salomonsen argues, but even if it's part of a Christian heritage, it isn't owned by any one religion. It can be owned by all.[115] If the gospel is strong enough to stand on its own legs, then accounts that contrast the Christian and the non-Christian become unnecessary. And if accounts that contrast the Christian and the non-Christian become unnecessary, collaboration becomes possible. And if collaboration becomes possible, Christians can pray in mosques as much as Muslims can pray in churches. To break down the strong barriers erected by far-right figures, perhaps such collaboration is not only possible, but imperative. Events such as the Qur'an-burning in the South of Norway in 2019 are not only pretexts to discuss issues of free speech, but are clear provocations against a religious minority that sow distrust and fear between people. Collaboration between Christians and Muslims doesn't mean Christians become Muslims or Muslims become Christians. It does mean, however, that religious designations such as 'Christian' or 'Muslim' cease to be understood as oppositional. What Jewish philosopher Ephraim Meir calls 'interreligious solidarity' is more important than ever.[116]

Altogether, then, it is understandable why many have been keen to dissociate Breivik from Christianity. Yet when the claims to Christianity made in his manifesto are analysed, it becomes clear that the violence of 22 July 2011 in Norway must be placed in the larger context of the new far right in Europe. In the theology at play here, Christianity is claimed as Culture Christianity and Crusader Christianity. Religion is a marker of absolute difference in new racism. This difference is dangerous: it justifies the need for antagonistic and apocalyptic confrontations with Islam. For Breivik, present confrontations are the continuation of past confrontations – crusades run through the history of Christianity. This historical allusion thus functions as 'evidence' for the absolute difference between identity and alterity. As we saw with Breivik's biblical references, European people are aligned with God's people, a God of European patriots. Many might find the idea that Breivik's Culture Christianity and Crusader Christianity are interpretations of Christianity unpalatable. But the meaning of Christianity is at stake in the semantic struggle over Christianity that runs through the Church of Norway.

In response to the 22 July 2011 attack, the Church of Norway acknowledged that Breivik claimed Christianity. As we will see in the following two chapters, this is in itself noteworthy. These acknowledgements enabled the Church of Norway to confront the theologies of new racism. But there are still questions that need to be asked:

Can we call far-right terrorists 'Christian'? Why? Why not? How can churches come to terms with the crimes that have been committed in the name of Christianity?
Are there sections or stories in the Bible that you consider racist? What do you do with them? Do you tend to forget them or do you tend to focus on them? Do you read them against the grain?

The semantic struggle for Christianity shows that the Church of Norway cannot be placed squarely either on the left or the right. What is made clear in many of the Church's statements after 22 July, however, is that openness to others – regardless of race and religion – is at the heart of their account of Christianity. Churches have a responsibility to challenge Christians where and when they close themselves off against the other. The Church of Norway isn't trying to tell members and non-members what to think, but to engage and educate people about the Christian faith, its positive as well as its negative past and potential. Forms of engagement and education are not just a top-down endeavour, but open themselves up to bottom-up interventions. There is no one way of doing theology. Moreover, it's not as easy as it might seem on the written page! Critical engagement and constructive education about what Christianity has been and what it can be, might well be marked by discomfort and disagreement. But it's honest about its failures and hopeful about its future.

Rather than state simply that Breivik's Christianity is *not* Christianity, a different Christianity is presented and promoted in the Church of Norway's responses to 22 July. This is a Christianity that does not need to be fixed in a monolithic identity that counters others. It is a Christianity that continues to be provoked by the example of Jesus' love for others – regardless of belief or background. The Church thus seemingly acknowledges what is at stake in far-right claims to Christianity: the very meaning of Christianity.

4

The Populist Right

What started as small and scattered protests in Dresden, the capital of Saxony, soon had spin-offs across Europe: the protests of PEGIDA. The letters stand for *Patriotische Europäer gegen die Islamisierung des Abendlandes*, which could be rendered roughly as 'Patriotic Europeans against the Islamization of Europe'. (The translation is tricky – we will return to it.) Lutz Bachmann, the founder of Pegida, had neither experience nor exposure to professional politics when he set up a page on Facebook through which he would soon gather thousands of followers.[1] The protests peaked in 2015 and 2016 in reaction to the arrival in Germany of what turned out to be about one million refugees, mainly from Syria. But they have become smaller and smaller since.[2] The protesters have moved on – into the parliaments. Pegida welcomes the political party *Alternative für Deutschland* (AfD). The Alternative for Germany was set up as a platform for sceptics of Germany's European policy, but the central concern has increasingly shifted to issues of immigration and identity.[3] The programme seems successful. The AfD is represented in parliaments throughout Germany. Polls see its influence increasing rather than decreasing. The forces of far-right populism are not to be ignored.

In this chapter, we argue that claims to Christianity allow the populist far right to draw the distinction between those whom they want and those whom they don't want to belong to Germany.[4] In the theology of the populist far right, Christianity is claimed on the side of vulnerable people against vicious powers. Such claims connect the far-right protesters outside the parliaments with the far-right politicians inside the parliaments. The theology taken up by the populist far right is designed to make them look like 'concerned citizens'. In contrast to the Church of Norway, which had to face far-right terrorism in the name of Christianity, the two mainline churches in Germany – Protestantism and Catholicism – encounter a 'friendlier' face of the far right. Yet although calls to violence are few and far between, the populists continue the rhetoric of new racism. Is the populist right harder to challenge than the terrorist right?

From the Margins to the Middle

Populism is a contested concept.[5] In *What Is Populism?*, political theorist Jan-Werner Müller surveys the surge of populist politics today.[6] He suggests that populists pretend to speak for the people – 'populism' is derived from the Latin *populus*, 'people' – by pitting 'the people' against 'the elites' and 'the elites' against 'the people'. But while populism appears democratic, it actually attacks democracy. As Müller argues: 'Populists claim that they, and they alone, represent the people.'[7] And when politics is reduced to issues of identity, it inhibits democratic deliberation about political positions: if you don't belong to 'the people' your political positions are illegitimate, and if you do belong to 'the people' your political positions are legitimate. But in democracies, politics is about deliberation.[8] For the populist far right, interpretations of Islam and identity are crucial to attack democracy.

Islam

Pegida's protests are livestreamed.[9] Whether online or offline, the slogan 'We are the people (*Wir sind das Volk*)' is displayed like a shield. In Germany, it is associated with the Peaceful Revolution of 1989–90 which brought down the Berlin Wall that separated the two German states, East and West.[10] Pegida plays with this citation, portraying its protest as a democratic critique of totalitarianism in which the oppressed 'people' revolt against the oppressive 'politicians'. The protesters put a 'strategy of calculated ambiguity' into play that allows them to mix snippets from the right and the left,[11] proclaiming that their patriotism isn't racist.[12] However, combined with the statements Bachmann posted on social media, a photo of himself dressing up as Adolf Hitler casts doubt on the claim to be against racism.[13]

A few months after the inauguration of the protests in 2014, Bachmann delivers a speech that sets out the purpose and the programme of Pegida.[14] He insists that Pegida isn't against Islam but against 'Islamism (*Islamismus*)' and 'Islamization (*Islamisierung*)'. Bachmann suggests that freedom of religion isn't used to support but to suppress a religion, namely: Christianity. The 'abolition of Christian culture' throughout Europe shows how Christianity is suppressed. Bachmann laments that Christmas Markets cannot be called Christmas Markets anymore, because the name alludes to Christianity. They have to be called 'Winter Markets'. Although the example is nonsense,[15] Bachmann takes it as evidence that there are the Christian people who are suppressed by politicians and the non-Christian non-people who are supported by politicians. Along with elite politicians, Islam is the enemy that threatens the 'Christianness' of German culture.

In a speech from 2016, Bachmann claims that the cultural contrast to Islam is confirmed by the churches. He cites statements by conservative clergy:[16]

> They come in order to occupy Europe. If Europe was incorporated into *dar al-Islam*, we would have to let go of liberty and equality. ... In the Sharia, we can read that the whole world should be subjugated to *dar al-Islam*. ... Muslims have to learn it by heart. ... They have to do what has been written down.

The scenario of subjugation into the *dar al-Islam*, the 'House of Islam', shows Muslims as invaders.[17] Bachmann continues:

> Whoever knows Islam understands well why the church should fear it. ... It is beyond doubt that Islam wants to rule the world. Once the Muslims are the majority – regardless in which country of the earth – they have the religious duty to rule this country.

Christianity, then, is the identity marker that decides whether you are or aren't part of 'the people'. For populists, this decision is *never* neutral: non-people, following un-Christian values, don't belong to Germany, while people, following Christian values, do belong to Germany.

For Bachmann, it's crucial to recognize the 'radical difference' to Islam. He explains this 'radical difference' with reference to the scenes of executions by 'Daesh', repeatedly reported by the media. These scenes have shocked people worldwide, Muslims and non-Muslims. Bachmann capitalizes on their shock. Since the executioners haven't been stopped by 'the so-called moderate Muslims', he suggests, the distinction between moderate and non-moderate Muslims is questionable. For Bachmann, *all* Muslims have the duty to kill 'the *kafir*, the unbeliever, who is: you.' Here Bachmann denies the distinction between 'Islam', 'Islamism' and 'Islamization' that he himself had drawn in the speech from 2014. He announces that Islam is anything but a 'religion of peace'. It's a religion which has invaded Europe with its 'army of Muslims'. Bachmann's speech culminates in the appeal that 'we' need to work for 'our culture' now, 'not when it is too late as in the 1930s.' For Bachmann, Islam is connected to racism and fascism. Germany can be absolved of its history of racism and fascism inasmuch as totalitarian terror is interpreted as an import from Islam. It's *not* home-grown.

A speech Bachmann delivered in 2017 is paradigmatic for the radicalization of Pegida's interpretation of Islam.[18] Starting with the greeting 'Happy Pentecost, Patriots', Bachmann sets up the contrast between the Christian and the non-Christian again. He suggests that Islam strengthens its war against Europe. Everywhere, 'blood is spilled in the name of Islam'. Against those who argue that murders by Muslims have nothing to do with Islam, he insists that the Qur'an dictates that all unbelievers must be annihilated. While he picks up previous speeches in style and substance here, this speech collapses the differentiation between Islam, Islamization and Islamism completely:

> I consciously say 'Muslim Terrorism (*Moslemterrorismus*)'. There are again and again these newly coined words such as 'Islamism (*Islamismus*)'... Friends, at the end of the day, it is Islam as it is taught in the Qur'an. I therefore refuse to use this word as in 'Islamists not welcome'. I say *Islam* is, after all the things that have happened, not welcome.

To applause from the audience, Bachmann insists that 'we will rather perish uprightly than ... bow to Islamization'. Bachmann taps into the counter-jihad conspiracy that characterizes both European and American right-wing rhetoric here: Islam is defined as ideology, so it's not protected by freedom of religion. It's described as inherently and intrinsically violent. There has been terror in the name of Islam in Germany, but Bachmann withholds that *both* Muslims *and* non-Muslims have fear of such terror. Mohammed Khallouk, chairman of the Central Council of Muslims in Germany, contends that the concentration on the 'Muslimness' of migrants as a marker of the terrorist threat neglects

> the fact that the majority of migrants are forced to migrate precisely because of public and political instrumentalizations of intolerant interpretations of Islam in the countries they come from; but nonetheless the prejudices against migrants prevalent throughout the population of Germany have

thrown their shadow over the Muslim minority. Almost all the resentment against refugees which exists among non-Muslims also exists among Muslims who have been living in Germany for decades.[19]

The new-racist stereotyping that traps Muslims in their 'Muslimness' is in the background when Bachmann presents Pegida's plans for the future: cooperation with the AfD in order to gain seats in a number of parliaments. 'We succeeded in making the AfD the strongest force here in Saxony', he says in a speech in 2018,[20] 'the potentates shudder with fear of us'. Bachmann thus showcases a significant psychological and social-psychological function of stereotyping:[21] the strengthening of self-confidence through the rigorous distinction between identity (evaluated as positive) and alterity (evaluated as negative).[22]

The AfD also taps into the strategies of new-racist stereotyping. Like Pegida, the AfD claims to be for the people by promoting 'the sovereignty of the people' against internal and external attacks[23] – also with programmatic references to the Peaceful Revolution of 1989–90. After a number of leadership changes (including one in which Bernd Lucke, the founding father of the party, left because of the extreme positions taken by the leadership[24]), Islam is now central to the populist political programme. Although the rhetoric is much less radical, the AfD's 'Programme for Germany (*Programm für Deutschland*)' comes close to Pegida's interpretation of Islam. Islam is interpreted as a 'doctrine of salvation (*Heilslehre*)'.[25] It comes up negatively rather than positively throughout the programme, and much more often than Christianity. Islam is in conflict with the democratic order of Germany.[26] It's a 'carrier of cultural traditions ... that cannot be integrated' into the country.[27] It's waging a 'war of culture (*Kulturkrieg*).'[28] Only the political practice and the political programme of the AfD are adequately addressing the 'confrontation by Islam'.[29]

While the protesters outside the parliaments are more radical in their interpretation of Islam than the politicians inside the parliaments, both construct stereotypes through the definition of the minority by the majority. The minority is reduced to one trait: 'Muslimness'.[30] Although the populist far right targets both Muslims and non-Muslims – the critique of Islam(ization) goes hand in hand with critiques of the 'Africanization' or the 'Arabization' of Europe[31] – the concentration on Muslimness is crucial because the appeal to religion camouflages the appeal to race. The populists can claim that Christianity has to be saved. But what is Christianity?

Identity

Christianity was central for the Peaceful Revolution of 1989–90: the 'Monday prayers' went hand in hand with the 'Monday protests' which set in motion the revolution that led to the fall of the Berlin Wall.[32] By citing the slogan 'We are the people', Pegida claims continuity with the Peaceful Revolution. Yet the churches counter this claim to continuity. When Pegida's protests passed the Cathedral in Dresden, the lights were turned off by the congregation in order to demonstrate their dissent. Representatives of both Catholicism and Protestantism released statements that called Pegida *'unchristlich* (un-Christian)', although there have been members of the churches among the protesters. Pegida, however, isn't deterred by this criticism from the churches.

Snapshots of a cross carried around in the protests – large, lit up and painted in the colours of the German flag – have been shared online and offline as a symbol for Pegida's claim to Christianity. The 'A' in Pegida stands for *Abendland*. As mentioned above, the term is tricky to translate, but the contrast between 'Abendland' and 'Morgenland' ('the land of the evening' and 'the land of the morning') captures the conception of a clash between 'occident' and 'orient'. The contrast is conceptualized *through* religion. 'Abendland' is identified with what's Christian and 'Morgenland' is identified with what's non-Christian.[33] Historically, the appearance of the contrast between 'Abendland' and 'Morgenland' coincides with the Siege of Vienna by the Ottoman Empire, revealing its context in the struggle against Islam.[34] These antagonistic and apocalyptic allusions run through the usage of the concept from the past to the present.[35] They are also apparent in the election campaigns of the centre-conservative political party, Christian Democratic Union (CDU), in the 1940s and 1950s that might have inspired Pegida's claim to the concept.[36] Although the CDU's slogan, 'Rettet die abendländische Kultur', which could be rendered as 'Save European Culture', enlisted Germany in the Cold War confrontation against the secularism of the Soviet Union, it didn't take much for Pegida to change the enemy from a secularist to a non-secularist one: Islam. Both are assumed to be *against* Christianity.[37] With its claim to the 'Abendland', then, Pegida communicates that it is concerned with the culture of Christianity.[38] Is Pegida's 'Culture Christianity' also a 'Crusader Christianity'?[39] Would Breivik have joined the protests?

While references to the crusades can be found in the orbit of the populist far right in Germany, the protesters accentuate Christianity through the use of symbols like crosses and candles, culminating in the singing of Christian Christmas carols during Advent. The protesters have been mocked for not knowing the words of the carols that they sometimes sing and sometimes shout. (Maybe that's why they sometimes only hum!) Studies of the sociological make-up of Pegida show that the ratio between members and non-members of churches is approximately 30 per cent to 70 per cent, thus mirroring the church affiliation of the population of Saxony – very low.[40] Because of the lack of knowledge among the protesters, some Christians confidently claim that Pegida has nothing to do with Christianity, thus ridding themselves of the challenge that the protesters present. But instead of mocking the protesters, one could pause over the fact that populist protesters lay claim to the theological traditions of Christianity *even though* they are not familiar with them. Already in the speech from 2014, Bachmann argues: 'Although I am not in a church, I feel impaired ... in the practice of my religion.' He claims Christianity against the churches.

By claiming a Christianity that is suppressed, Pegida is tapping into a theology in which Christianity is on the side of vulnerable people and non-Christianity on the side of vicious powers. Presenting the current situation as a conspiracy of Muslims and non-Muslims who aim to 'Islamize' Europe, the populist far right casts itself in the guise of victims – victims in a struggle against a stealth invasion. The victimhood connects the present critique of the political elites with the past critique of the political elites in 1989–90. The account of Christians as victims of persecution is a powerful way of drawing on theological traditions. There are, then, hints of a Crusader Christianity in Pegida's claims, but the idea of Culture Christians as suffering victims in need of support is much more pronounced.

In the AfD's 'Programme for Germany', Christianity fulfils a similar function. Christianity is identified and interpreted as a core component of the culture of Germany past and present. The programme refers to 'Leitkultur', the 'leading culture' that has to rule and run through the whole country.[41] Such a *Leitkultur* is interpreted as a weapon in the clash of cultures, the 'Kulturkampf' against Islam.[42] But in the AfD, culture isn't considered to be in contrast to faith. On the contrary, Christian faith can support Culture Christianity.[43]

Christian faith is hailed by the 'Christians in the AfD (*Christen in der AfD*)', a group of AfD politicians who want to bring together all the Christians in the party.[44] In their 'Declaration of Principle (*Grundsatzerklärung*)', the Christians in the AfD assert that the confession of the Christian faith is central to their politics.[45] While the democratic state is supposed to be neutral with regard to religious and non-religious worldviews, democracy lives from people who bring their worldviews into politics.[46] This is what the Christians in the AfD want to do with their Christian worldview. In order to become a member, you have to stand by the 'Declaration of Principle' which includes the Apostles' Creed.

Among the political points that the 'Declaration' presents as Christian – they reach from immigration policy to Israel policy – family policy stands out. In accordance with the AfD, Pegida has criticized the 'genderization (*Genderisierung*)' by which they mean, as professor of German language and literature Beverly M. Weber puts it, the 'perceived lack of adequate difference between men and women, thus rendering women unable to "be feminine" and men unable to "be masculine"'.[47] While the protesters appear to fight sexism, both the substance and the style of the protest invigorates sexist stereotypes.[48] Pegida's critique of 'gender mainstreaming' shows the inherent irony.[49] The AfD also calls for equality between women and men,[50] but nonetheless favours the ideal of the stay-at-home-mum.[51]

The fight against sexism is approached as a weapon in the arsenal that the populist far right marshals against Islam. Bachmann knows well how to wield this weapon: 'Friends, the terror has reached Germany', he starts a speech in 2016.[52] The Chancellor 'has blood on her hands' because she is responsible for the crimes committed by Muslim migrants throughout Germany. Bachmann particularly points to the sex crimes committed since the 'event of Cologne'. On New Year's Eve 2015, hundreds of women were attacked in Cologne, mainly by migrants.[53] These attacks changed the media coverage of migration across the country. As journalist Thomas Meany recounts, the 'New Year's Eve assaults ... have given Cologne a new symbolism. The German far right has got what it wanted: ... a more resonant excuse for calling for the closing of the borders. ... The German press has mostly obliged them in its coverage of the Cologne attacks.'[54] Bachmann brands all migrants as 'rapefugees' rather than 'refugees',[55] before he identifies Pegida with the vulnerable victims: 'A word to all the victims (*Opfer*): You are not guilty. The rapists are guilty.'

Again, he creates a logic in which the people are the oppressed while the non-people are the oppressors. The contrast between people and non-people, he explains, is caused by differences in culture that are rooted in religion. According to Bachmann, Muslims are 'deeply rooted' misogynists.

Undoubtedly, there are Muslims who are misogynistic. But what the populist weaponization of equality between women and men against Muslims ignores is that both Muslim women and Muslim men also struggle against it.[56] What about accounts of Khadija bint Khuwaylid, 'the beloved wife of Prophet Mohammed', as 'the first feminist'?[57] Presenting Islam as inherently and inevitably misogynistic not only misses or even masks the misogyny that has run through Christianity past and present, but also plays into the hands of those who insist on misogynistic interpretations of Islamic traditions and texts like the Qur'an.[58]

Interestingly, the notion of equality runs through the AfD's interpretation of the Bible. The 'Declaration of Principle' by the Christians in the AfD refers to the inalienable dignity of human beings, rooted in the image of God.[59] As a consequence, it asserts: 'The equal value of all human beings in front of God also means a fundamental equality of rights and responsibilities in front of the sovereign state that represents God's authority'.[60] Alluding to Romans 13, it would seem that the AfD's theology would preclude any possibility of inequality between Christians and non-Christians. But the opposite is the case. In her contribution to *Confessions of Christians in the AfD*, Beatrix von Storch, one of the leaders of the AfD, takes up the parable of the Good Samaritan in the context of immigration: 'When the Samaritan found the victim of the accident on the roadside, he provided care and organized on-site support in a hostel. But he did not take him home to Samaria, and he did not allow him to bring his family with him either.'[61] Hence, Christians aren't called to accept or accommodate refugees regardless of their background or beliefs. Even if refugees are equal as human beings under God, they are not equal in German culture and country. Refugees need to be sent back. Love of neighbour in the theology of the AfD points to neighbourhood as nearness – not to a love for those who come from far away.[62] The theology that underlies the interpretation of the Good Samaritan, then, draws distinctions – racial and religious – between neighbours. For the AfD, the neighbour is anything but other.

Like Pegida, the AfD plays into the idea of Christians as a persecuted minority that needs to stand up against the threat of an Islam that is welcomed by the elites inside and outside churches. The publication, *Why Christians Vote for the AfD*, a new edition of the *Confessions* mentioned above, collects personal accounts of AfD participants and politicians.[63] Drawing on the call of 1 Peter 3.15 to 'always be ready to make your defence to anyone who demands from you an accounting for the hope that is in you', the publication is meant to respond to what the Christians in the AfD see as a 'stigmatization' of their political positions by the churches.[64] The AfD criticizes churches for what they see as their disavowal of Christianity. They are 'Amtskirchen', hierarchical institutions that have lost touch with individuals – which is to say, the people. As Bachmann puts it in one of his speeches, pertaining to the story of Judas in the Bible (Matt. 26.15; see also Luke 22; John 13) in contrast to the 'fat princes of the church who ... have sold their faith ... for ... a few pieces of silver', Pegida protects Christianity.[65] He plays out familiar Christian debates about what happens to Christianity when it gains power – when, in Bachmann's words, it becomes the 'fat princes of the church'. Christianity, in this theology, needs to be protected against elitist enemies on the inside and extremist enemies on the outside.

Altogether, then, the populist far right claims Christianity. Its theology isn't necessarily about faith. There are some who profess faith in Jesus Christ, but this faith is seen as confirming rather than criticizing Culture Christianity. For the populists, the faithful and the faithless can join in the struggle to defend the culture of Europe. They defend Christendom.

Culture Christianity draws the distinction between those who do and those who don't belong to Germany. This theology is at the core of the populist far right in Germany. The criticism of elites pertains to both ecclesial and non-ecclesial leaders. Elites are portrayed as traitors to Europe. They have fallen from the faith. Religion is reduced to a new-racist trap: in the case of Christianity, the inescapable cultural-religious identity is positive, thus characterizing 'the people'; in the case of non-Christianity, the inescapable cultural-religious identity is negative, thus characterizing 'the non-people'. The populist far right situates and strengthens its position by interpreting itself as the 'underdog'. Thus, the populists can tap into long-standing theological traditions. As a consequence, the populists can argue that 'nobody should be able to say we have nothing Christian in our programme.'[66] But this is exactly what the churches are saying.

Defending Democracy

Both mainline churches in Germany have tackled the rise of the far right. Their support of what came to be called 'Welcome Culture' – the welcoming of about one million refugees in 2015 and 2016 – put them at the centre of the controversies stirred up by the populist far right.[67] Outright condemnation of populism, however, has posed a challenge to the churches. There are Christians among the sympathizers and the supporters of the populist far right – church-going and not so church-going. So how have the churches responded?

Defending the Democratic Corridor

Published by the Evangelische Kirche in Deutschland (EKD), the organization in which Protestant congregations and churches in Germany come together, the statement *Consensus and Con-*

flict: Politics Needs Contestation is a response to populism.[68] The EKD's Chamber of Public Responsibility – consisting of experts in ethics and politics, directed by a professor of theological ethics, Reiner Anselm – is responsible for the statement. Is the EKD calling for contestation, as the title announces?

Consensus and Conflict starts with the significance of faith for democracy.[69] Today, churches interpret the freedoms guaranteed by the *Grundgesetz*, the constitution of Germany, as equivalent to the freedom of Jesus Christ. *Consensus and Conflict* alludes to Martin Luther's theological tract on 'The Freedom of a Christian'.[70] But it took the Church a long time to articulate such an equivalence – until 1985 when the EKD finally made the turn towards democracy.[71] Since then, 'the churches stand for democracy as the way of life of plurality'.[72] Given that the processes of pluralization are on-going, democracy is negotiated in a tension of 'consensus, compromise and conflict'.[73]

Contestation is indeed welcomed by the authors of *Consensus and Conflict*. In order to uncover the promising potential of conflict for democracy, conflicts have to be embedded in a culture that allows them to be carried out productively and positively. Here, the churches come in: 'Such a culture cannot be taken for granted, it has to be created and championed again and again. In this call, Christians recognize their own calling, the calling anchored in the liberating Gospel of Jesus Christ.'[74] The statement encourages Christians not to agree but to disagree. The authors present a vision for democracy, namely

> the vision that controversies …, if carried out with reason, can lead to decisions that ought to be accepted by everyone because of the way in which they were reached. This principle can only be put into practice when all participants question their own position again and again – and let themselves be questioned. The point of such questioning is to make sure that the position is not only promoting one's own interests, but also the common good.[75]

The metaphor of the 'corridor' is used to underscore this principle of questioning and self-questioning.[76] Confronting the polarization of the public square, churches shouldn't take sides but consolidate the 'corridor' in which people from different sides of the polarization can come together.[77] Echoing recent research on the causes and consequences of populism, *Consensus and Conflict* points to the cleavage between those for whom globalization has been profitable and those for whom globalization has been problematic.[78] Even if the controversy between these is less about facts than feelings, it has to be taken seriously.[79] The concerns of citizens have to be respected in order to bring them (back) into the 'corridor' in which conflict, compromise and consensus can be democratically discussed. The metaphor of the corridor is crucial: the role of churches, as envisioned in *Consensus and Conflict*, is *not* to take a political position in the corridor. They aren't supposed to advocate for the left. They aren't supposed to advocate for the right. They aren't supposed to advocate at all. On the contrary, the role of churches is to protect the corridor in which political positions – advocacy for the left or for the right – can be communicated.[80]

Consensus and Conflict stresses the significance of identity. Countering any calls for Culture Christianity as a marker for who can and who can't belong to Germany, the authors argue that Christian values and virtues are played out in the structure rather than the substance of democratic deliberation. Christians are called to be democrats – regardless of their views on immigration and identity. Deliberation is crucial. It shouldn't be shut down too soon through rules that are assumed to be beyond deliberation either by the left or by the right. Both sides have to be heard. 'Of course, controversial debates are allowed.'[81] The polarization of the public sphere, then, is welcomed by the Church because it intensifies the competition between political programmes so crucial to democracy.

Consensus and Conflict is concerned with the fact that fewer and fewer people have turned up at elections. Political parties claiming to represent those who feel under- or unrepresented might turn the tide. *Consensus and Conflict* argues for a procedure, it aims for a political process rather than a political position. However – here the statement is crystal clear – claims to represent 'the people' need to be checked. Populism fails the check. While populists might animate politics, they are critical of the pluralism so crucial to democracy. Referring to what populists claim to be 'the will' of 'the people', 'they simultaneously use and undermine the complex procedures needed to negotiate a compromise'.[82] Here, the polarization kindled by populists is far from helpful.

The statement concludes with a short account of 'churches as spaces of democratic participation'.[83] The Church is a 'mirror of the pluralist society' which means that political positions from the left and from the right are represented.[84] *Conflict and Consensus* acknowledges a cleavage within the Church. In the controversies stirred up by increased immigration, the defenders of immigrants can often be found on the leadership level while the despisers of immigrants can often be found on the lay level. The statement calls the leadership to be more careful with announcements that assume the moral high ground. Albeit implicitly rather than explicitly, the cleavage in the Church is connected to the communication of the gospel.

> The Gospel of Jesus Christ ... proclaims the reconciliation of the human being with God that is given through God's son. Every human being is God's creature, gifted with inalienable dignity. It is precisely in the uniqueness that distinguishes a human being from others that she or he is owed respect. ... The churches ought to be places in which human beings can experience such respect so that they espouse it themselves.[85]

Here is the chance and the contribution of the Church. In its insistence on the inalienable dignity of each and every human being, the gospel

... is eminently political. The first and foremost location for this political practice of the churches is the congregations where very different people come together.... The churches with the breadth and depth of their social embeddedness should and shall be forums where conflicts can be carried out. They are places for democratic participation.[86]

The EKD recognizes the polarization of the public square. The response is not a political position, but a concentration on the corridor in which political positions can be discussed. Congregations are the places where such discussion can take place democratically. The call for democracy inside and outside churches is commendable. Would anyone argue against it? But one issue is striking in the current political context: Islam is conspicuous by its absence.

Islam isn't mentioned in *Conflict and Consensus*, neither directly nor indirectly. What, then, is the EKD's position on Islam? Statements by the EKD that address Islam, such as *Clarity and Good Neighbourhood*, published more than ten years ago, paint a shocking picture.[87] This statement has been criticized for tapping into stale stereotypes about Islam, promoting rather than problematizing Islamophobia.[88] Of course, this statement was written in a context where the impact of 9/11 and 7/7 was very much felt. The 'War on Terror' was raging across the globe. Nonetheless, as far as we can ascertain, the EKD hasn't distanced itself from *Clarity and Good Neighbourhood*. So what does the statement say?

The account of the Qur'an is telling. The authors suggest that there are more surahs that legitimate violence than surahs that limit violence.[89] Whatever you think of quantitative in contrast to qualitative hermeneutics, it's crucial to note that the authors of the statement left the Bible untouched. The lack of a comparison of sacred scripture makes it easy to idealize Christianity.[90] If we're counting, there are many verses in the Bible that pertain to violence. Breivik found some of them. The Bible has been used to justify violence throughout history.

The EKD's silence on the Bible impacts the account of Islam that confirms the significance of Christianity for the culture of Europe. According to the authors of *Clarity and Good Neighborhood*, there is no acceptance of dignity in Islam, because the Qur'an doesn't describe the human being as the image of God.[91] Instead, Islam allocates different degrees of dignity to different human beings: men are more valuable than women, Muslims are more valuable than non-Muslims.[92] The authors declare that Christianity arrived at its account of human dignity through the critical and self-critical engagement with its traditions in a long historical learning process,[93] but what this declaration amounts to is: Christianity has finished its learning process. Islam, however, still needs to learn its lessons.[94] The consequence, spelled out in a chapter titled, 'Muslims in Democracy',[95] is the fundamental difference to Islam. Here, the EKD affirms Culture Christianity and alludes to Crusader Christianity. Whether consciously or unconsciously, it confirms the interpretations of Islam and identity pedalled by the far right.

If *Clarity and Good Neighbourhood* is taken to fill the lack of engagement with Islam in *Consensus and Conflict*, the conclusion is that Islam cannot be included in the democratic corridor that churches aim to keep open. The populist far right would agree.

Defending the Diverse Church

While Catholic and Protestant churches have co-published statements about the state of democracy,[96] the Catholic Bishops' Conference also published *Resisting Populism: Guidelines for Ecclesial Engagements with Populist Tendencies*. Directed by three Bishops, Stefan Heße, Franz-Josef Bode, and Stephan Ackermann, the Guidelines connect the work of a number of commissions in the Church. The Guidelines, including 'best practice' examples from across Germany, are spelled out over almost 100 pages. After a short account of the scope and the strategies of populism, they delve into the issues that are instrumentalized by the populist far right: Islam and identity. What, then, is the advice of the Catholic Church?

At the outset, populism is described and defined. The authors admit that given that there is talk of 'populism from the Left', 'populism from the Right', and even 'populism from the Centre, taking place in the large traditional parties of our country'[97], one could be excused for asking: what's the problem? According to the Catholic Church, the problem with populism is that it refutes the closeness of Jesus Christ to all human beings, particularly the vulnerable.[98] While the presence of populism in churches is acknowledged, the Guidelines' critique of such populism is not a critique of plurality:

> The Church of Jesus Christ has never been a community of uniform, unitary members. ... What has unified them was the clarity of Jesus' calling – the clarity of the good news of the Kingdom of God. This clarity, however, is at stake, when controversies with opposing opinions about politics are carried out at the cost of ... often defenceless groups of people. We have to oppose this.[99]

The Guidelines zoom in on the rise of far-right populism. Like the EKD, the Catholic Church argues that one of the causes of populism is the 'de-politicization of politics'.[100] When politics is reduced to administrative discussions in which opposing political opinions cannot come into view, people lose interest.[101] In order to oppose populism, 'lived democracy' needs to be strengthened.[102] The current challenge, however, is that populism is present across society. The far right is rising by moving from the margins to the middle.[103] The attraction of the far right lies in its simple response to a loss of status among people.[104] Again, the point is that the loss of status is real, regardless of whether it's factual or feared. The populism of the far right addresses the loss through a cultivation of nostalgia, a nostalgia for a Germany that was still 'German'. Christians, however, are called to resist such nostalgias.

Drawing on Pope Francis' Encyclical *Laudato Si'*, the Guidelines insist that Christians have to take care of the communal household, whatever their political opinions.[105] The criterion for churches is the equality of all human beings guaranteed by a democracy rooted in human rights.[106] For a democracy, 'the people' is a *political* concept. Referring to the Greek roots of the concept, it's 'demos' rather than 'ethnos' – and has nothing to do with race.[107] The Guidelines point out that 'people' in the Bible refers to 'the people of God'. The people of God are constituted and called by God which means that they are independent of social, cultural or political identities.[108] The people of God makes up the churches across the globe. The theological theme of the people of God, then, corresponds to the political concept of the people so crucial to democracy: the equality of all human beings is rooted in the inalienable dignity of each and every human being which, in turn, is rooted in them being made in the image of God.[109]

Resisting Populism highlights how populists claim Christianity for their political purpose. The authors argue that Christianity has been hijacked. Given that the populists pit Christianity against the Church, they break people away from the 'universal Church'.[110] Of course, for Catholicism Christianity is often taken to be identical with the one and only Church – namely, the Roman Catholic Church. Because of this identification, it's easy to declare Christians outside the Church hijackers. But the statement does more. The authors argue that 'the churches have to resist every attempt to use Christianity as a means to exclude human beings of a different origin, including the nativist misinterpretation of Christianity'.[111]

Resisting Populism points to the presence of Islam in Germany past and present. The authors clarify that not all who are counted as Muslims in the statistics are actually Muslims: there will be atheists and agnostics among them.[112] Culture is what is at stake here. The devaluation of people because they are culturally characterized by Islam is called 'Islamophobia'.[113] In Islamophobia, culture intersects with ethnicity and religiosity, creating a powerful and pungent mix to ostracize people. The Guidelines point out that such ostracization can spill into violence.[114] Islamophobia isn't called out as racism, but it's called out.

The Guidelines point to the history of the Church in which Christianity often saw itself as fighting Islam even though there were times of peaceful coexistence. Terrorism in the name of Islam is also acknowledged. However, for the Church a central cause of the fear of Islam is the loss of Christian faith. To people who have lost their own faith, the plurality of religions appears threatening.[115] Because they feel threatened, they pit Europe against Islam and Islam against Europe. The Guidelines are clear in their characterization of such a defence of Christianity: 'Without denying that Europe has been characterized by Christianity, it is doubtful whether there ever was a "Christian Europe (*Abendland*)" in the ... homogeneity in which it is presented.'[116] Europe has a 'dynamic' 'multicultural identity'.[117] The Church, then, counters any claim to 'Culture Christianity'. Christianity is about faith. What is needed is a conversation about the characteristics of Europe. Again, the Guidelines acknowledge that the Church has interpreted Islam as a problem rather than a partner for centuries. However, they point to the turn that the Church made in the 1960s. Since then, Jews, Christians and Muslims are seen as praying to the same God.[118]

While the Guidelines acknowledge that the causes of migration are manifold, they point to the significance of forced migration – people are in search for survival.[119] Geopolitically, it's crucial to be conscious of the fact that Europe has contributed to the causes of migration.[120] Given the statistics of the United Nations High Commissioner for Refugees that are referenced in the Guidelines, the authors caution against the use of the concept of the 'refugee crisis'. Globally, there might be such a crisis, but in Europe it's used as a cipher for a multi-layered mix of challenges.[121] The fact that traditional identities and traditional solidarities are breaking down cannot be changed by keeping migrants out, because it's rooted in the socio-economic processes that would occur even 'without a single refugee'.[122] Populists, however, channel the fear of change into the concept of a refugee crisis.[123] Migration is the grist for the populist mill.

The Guidelines agree that tackling the causes of migration that are 'there' rather than 'here' – as the populists are fond of arguing – is necessary. But it mustn't come at the cost of those who are on the flight: '"tackling the causes of migration" becomes an empty formula if it is meant to justify setting up a shield against human beings who are in search of protection.'[124] Against the rhetoric that turns immigration into invasion, the Guidelines point to the significance of human rights for the state. The state has to help those who search for protection – regardless of what other states do or don't do.[125] Germany cannot accommodate all refugees, but it can do more than it does. The Guidelines point to Catholic Social Teaching, the application of the gospel to ethics and politics that was started in the late nineteenth century, that assumes that the right of emigration ought to be paralleled with a right to immigration. There is also Pope Francis' exemplary engagement with migrants. With the Pope, the Guidelines call for a 'Globalization of the love of neighbour'.[126]

The Guidelines point to interpretations of the 'Good Samaritan' that instrumentalize the parable to call for restrictions on immigration. The authors argue that it misses the core of the message. 'A Christianity that would limit the love of neighbour ... to its own brothers and sisters only, would be without ... the encounter with Christ'.[127] It's in the encounter with Christ that migration can be turned into the story of God's liberation, but only if those who have faith respond to the challenge as a calling.[128] Faith in Jesus Christ, then, counters both Crusader Christianity and Culture Christianity.

According to the Guidelines, populists channel the personal, social and national changes that confront Germany into a fear of the migrant. Populists want to create or recreate identity through exclusion rather than inclusion.[129] However, if one takes seriously that identity and alterity are correlated – where the line is drawn between them has consequences for both – then it becomes clear that the Islam that is feared is more produced than present. Populists construct what they claim to fear in order to channel the fear into their political programme.[130] The critique of the populists' ethnopluralism is central: populists use the Bible to advocate for strategies of ethnic segregation. Throughout history, the curse of Ham (also known as the 'Curse of Cain') in Genesis 9.25–27 has been a seminal passage for such strategies.[131] Again, the love of neighbour is limited. But would our identity not be in danger, if we lost our sensibility towards the needs of human beings who suffer and search for shelter? 'There is a lot that indicates that what would be left is not a Christian but ... a Christianist identity.'[132]

The fear of the loss of identity is also apparent in the populists' family politics. The Guidelines acknowledge that the far right appears to advocate for a concept of the family that comes close to that of the Church: mother, father and (at least) one child as the first and fundamental unit of society. But, they add, appearances are deceptive. The emancipation of women is endorsed by the Catholic Church, thus calling for the equality of men and women in partnership.[133] While the Church is also concerned about what the populists call 'genderism', the Guidelines acknowledge that the Church needs to take the field of gender studies more seriously. While the populists want to ban it, the Catholic Church in Germany wants to learn from it.[134] The Catholic Church has published a lot that casts doubt on this response to populism. The recent *Male and Female He Created Them*, a document from the Vatican Council for Education published in 2019, is a telling example.[135] But the Guidelines make a crucial and central point. Even if the conceptualizations of the family come close to each other, the way the Church argues is different. The ideology that interprets ethnicity or nationality as reasons to call for politics that support families – make more *German* babies – has never been endorsed by the Church. For the Church, the family is about dignity rather than demography.[136]

After its discussion of Islam and identity, *Resisting Populism* concludes with concrete suggestions for practical and pastoral work in congregations. The congregations offer the spaces where people with different positions – who wouldn't normally meet – come together.[137] Congregations, then, are themselves a response to the populists who pit 'people' against 'non-people'. In congregations, the dignity of each dialogue partner has to be respected.[138]

Coping with Populism in the Church

Culture Christianity and Crusader Christianity – the one majorly, the other marginally – run through the theology of the populist far right in Germany. Culture Christianity is performed when protesters use Christian symbols and is proclaimed when politicians use Christian statements. Although there are allusions to a Crusader Christianity across the German populist far right, the call for crusades is not as prominent as in Breivik's theology of terror. Instead, Christian culture is characterized as the victim of a conspiracy. Christianity stands with the powerless victims against the powerful villains. The love of neighbour – taken from the creation of all human beings in the image of God – is affirmed, but the populists argue for a difference between this neighbour and that neighbour. In a telling take on the Good Samaritan, the AfD insist that love should be practised only on one's own doorstep for one's own people, which is to say, for Culture Christians. Christianity, then, marks the insiders in contrast to the outsiders: neighbours aren't neighbours.

While the rhetoric is toned down, new racism is still at work in the theology of the populist far right: religion rather than race is used to distinguish between those who are and those who aren't 'the people'. The distinction justifies inequality between them. Europe for Christians. Neither the extra- nor the intra-parliamentary protesters are terrorists. But given that the protesters carried home-made gallows reserved for Chancellor Angela Merkel, it's not too far-fetched to point out that they are flirting with the violent potential of their worldview. Such excess can lead to action.[139] The AfD called for the police to use weapons to prevent migrants from crossing the German borders.[140] Walter Lübcke, a politician who advocated for the acceptance and accommodation of refugees in Germany, was executed by a right-wing extremist in 2019.[141] Less than a year later, ten people were killed in a terror attack on two shisha bars in Hanau, a town in Germany. While the terrorist (who killed himself afterwards) acted alone, the attack has a context and a catalyst, perhaps even a cause, in the mainstreaming of far-right propaganda by populist politicians.[142] Can Catholicism and Protestantism in Germany help to resist?

Churches in Germany have responded to the changes in the German political landscape that the rise of the far-right signals. Comparing Catholicism to Protestantism, as we have done, is tricky. The style, the structure and the substance of statements of these two mainline churches differ. Their strategies differ too: Protestantism calls for the defence of the democratic corridor and Catholicism calls for the defence of the diverse church. The Protestants focus on the state of democracy, formulating a role for churches to create and consolidate conversations between different people and different positions. Churches can thus confirm the corridor in which political positions can be deliberated and discussed. The churches themselves, however, should be careful with taking any political position.

While the Protestants are concerned with the state of democracy today, the Guidelines by the Catholic Church zoom in on the challenge of populism from the right and the far right. Targeting a concrete challenge allows for a much more concrete response. The Catholic Church concentrates on picking apart the claims to Christianity from the far right. It offers a more substantive account, answering with the love of neighbour – whoever the neighbour is, Christian or non-Christian. Crucially, the Catholic Church acknowledges the prejudices towards Islam that Christians have nurtured throughout history. In *Conflict and Consensus* by the EKD, however, Islam is conspicuous by its absence. If this absence is filled with a statement that the Church made about ten years ago, it could be concluded that the lack of engagement with Islam – whether consciously or unconsciously – colludes with the populist far right.

Clearly, challenging positions that are rhetorically less extreme and less explicitly racist is harder than challenging terrorism in the name of Christianity as we saw in the previous chapter. Questions that could and should be asked, then, are:

Can we call far-right populists 'Christian'? Why? Why not?
What is the role of churches in a pluralized and polarized public? Should they make a political claim or should they maintain a political corridor? Or is the political corridor actually a political claim?
Where do you draw the line between acceptable and unacceptable political positions?

However you answer these questions, it seems that for both Catholicism and Protestantism in Germany, churches invite difference and democracy into their ranks. This is precisely what the theology of the populist far right resists in its confident claim to Christianity, the 'Abendland' against the 'Morgenland', the insider against the outsider. But of course, difference and democracy in churches entail the intensification of the semantic struggle for Christianity.

5

The Hard Right

In 2014, Britain First, a xenophobic organization with ties to the British National Party (BNP), invaded mosques across the UK.[1] Muslims were presented with army-issued Bibles. The intruders called it a 'Christian crusade'. Were Christians terrorizing the mosques of the UK? The BNP is the far-right party that has enjoyed the most success in the UK, particularly in local elections.[2] They are commonly characterized as 'fascist' or 'neo-fascist'. When Nick Griffin took up the leadership of the BNP, it went through a modernization process that followed the patterns discernible in the new far right.[3] Their agenda turned Islamophobic.[4] Christianity, meanwhile, has been claimed to be essential to British culture, its inheritance and its identity.[5] For the BNP, 'Culture Christianity' and 'Crusader Christianity' go hand in hand.

Going back a few years, when the BNP attracted a rising number of sympathizers, bishops from a number of churches, spearheaded by the Church of England, issued a statement to denounce racist rhetoric. They urged their congregations not to vote for the BNP.[6] When the BNP membership list was leaked online in 2008, however, it included individuals listed as ministers in the Church of England. The General Synod of the Church of England voted overwhelmingly in favour of banning clergy from being members of the BNP.[7] Archbishops Rowan Williams and John Sentamu advised people against voting for the BNP prior to the European elections in 2009: 'Christians have been deeply disturbed by the conscious adoption by the BNP of the language of our faith ... to foster fear.'[8] The BNP responded to the critiques with a poster featuring a picture of Jesus, citing John 15.20: 'If they have persecuted me, they will also persecute you'.[9] But the opposition from churches may not have been ineffectual. Since 2010, the BNP has had very little success in elections. As political scientist Timothy Peace puts it, the BNP 'has done the most to exploit the issue of religion', but is 'an electoral failure in comparison to its European counterparts'.[10] Although voters of the BNP tailed off after 2010, trends and tendencies of the European new far right also appear in the UK. In this chapter, we focus on politicians and parties on the right that are considered to be moderate or mainstream. Since pride in 'Englishness' is particularly prominent, our focus here is on England and the Church of England.

The far right in Britain is often seen as a story of failure.[11] But with the success of the campaign for the UK to leave the European Union in 2016, much of the rhetoric about identity and Islam so characteristic of the contemporary far right across Europe has reached the centre of British politics. Brexit has been a catalyst for far-right positions and policies. As the Director of the Institute of Race Relations in London, Liz Fekete, puts it: 'A debate that could have been about ... political accountability ... descended into a circus of xenophobia... The fallout was immediately felt on the ground in the form of a huge increase in ... racist incidents'.[12] Fekete coined the concept of the 'hard right' to capture 'the new patterns that emerge when various electoral platforms ... come together'.[13] According to Fekete, 'insider-outsider racism, now proactively pursued by the Conservative Party's Brexit state, aims to win over the "decent working people" to policies that work fundamentally against their interests.'[14]

Building on Fekete's concept of the 'hard right', we tease out how views of Islam and identity are mobilized by two parties, the United Kingdom Independence Party (UKIP) and the Conservative Party. Such views, we argue, make use of exclusivist and essentialist notions of religion that are rife in the new racism of far-right circles. The UK shows that there are hard-right claims that challenge or ought to challenge Christians inside and outside churches, even if invocations of Christianity are hidden. The theology of new racism works in subtle as well as unsubtle ways.

While the Church of England has responded to the extreme ends of the far right, the more mainstream hard right has been left largely untouched. Drawing lines of connection between the margins and the mainstream is not an attempt to conflate extremist with non-extremist right-wing voices. Our point is not to make all political views the same just because they bear resemblance in style or substance. Rather, we want to point out how claims to Islam and identity can move from the periphery to power in insidious ways. These claims are less stark than those made by a party such as the BNP, but they stick. They have real-life consequences that need to be confronted.

The Hard-Right Brexit

The campaign to leave the European Union has united a number of political parties, both in the margins and in the mainstream. The UK Independence Party came to prominence under the leadership of Nigel Farage. Farage has been a prominent and provocative voice in British politics as a politician who has gained headway in pushing populist right-wing narratives in public debates. UKIP had its most successful electoral results in the 2013 UK local elections, in the 2014 EU elections and in the 2015 UK general election. UKIP's raison d'être has been independence from the European Union. As leader of UKIP between 2006 to 2009 and again between 2010 and 2016, Farage was a key figure in the 'Leave campaign' after the then Prime Minister David Cameron called the referendum that asked UK citizens whether they wanted to remain in the EU.[15] As the results of the referendum testify, Farage was not a lonely voice in the wilderness.

A cross-party alliance dubbed 'Vote Leave' was founded

in 2015. One of the more prominent figures to spearhead the movement was the then Mayor of London, Conservative Boris Johnson, now British Prime Minister. One of the mantras of Vote Leave revolved around 'taking back control'. Nigel Farage, then UKIP's leader, endorsed another Leave campaign, dubbed Leave.EU. He later clarified that he supported both Leave campaigns.

Social policy expert Steve Corbett argues that the right-wing populism underpinning much of the discourse on Brexit is drawn from English nationalism.[16] English identity and immigration were major features of the Leave campaign. The white and red of the English flag were used extensively. Corbett argues that the referendum campaign implemented a 'textbook account of populist politics in the UK'.[17] In particular, this can be seen in the imagined past of values and virtues of the English heartland. While many of the arguments to leave the European Union centred on economic gains, there was a concerted focus on the promise of taking back control of UK borders.[18] It's not insignificant that the year prior to the referendum has been characterized as the culmination of Europe's 'refugee crisis', where thousands of refugees entered the European Union, mainly from Syria, a Muslim majority country.[19] While migration from the EU is mentioned by Vote Leave, there are significant hints at Muslim migrants in the imagery displayed in the campaign material. One poster propagates that 'The EU is letting in more and more countries', showing a map of Europe with a large arrow reaching from Turkey into the UK.[20] The only countries named on the map are Syria and Iraq, next-door neighbours to Turkey – all Muslim majority countries. Through Turkey, the poster implies, Muslim migrants make it into the EU. Once they are in the EU, nothing stops them from entering the UK. Under the caption 'Turkey (population 76 million) is joining the EU' another poster shows an UK-EU passport – opened like a door.[21] Footsteps show how Turks gain entry to the UK through the door opened by the EU. The targeting of Muslims is significant.[22]

The tragedy of Labour MP Jo Cox's death during the Brexit campaign pointed to the violent undercurrents of nationalist rhetoric. Campaigning for support of refugees in Syria, Cox was brutally murdered outside her constituency office in Birstall, by a far-right British nationalist, who was reported to have shouted 'put Britain first!' She was stabbed fifteen times before he shot her in the head, chest and hand. As James Meek argues in his account of Brexit, the murder of Cox concerned Farage 'so little that he said in his victory speech the vote had been won "without a single bullet being fired".'[23]

Brexit was neither only about Islam nor only about immigration. Complex economic, social and political conditions underlie the debate about the UK leaving the European Union. Brexit cannot be pinned down to claims to Christianity either. In fact, claims to Christianity aren't central to any of the parties in the Vote Leave campaign. Care is taken by both UKIP and the Conservatives to avoid the crude rhetoric of a party such as the British National Party. Nonetheless, the logic at work in constructions of identity in contrast to Islam is significant in the Brexit debate. For churches like the Church of England, such constructions are challenging.

Islam

For both UKIP and the Conservative Party, Islam is targeted as a security issue. They tap into wider trends regarding Islam as a problem for Europe, while holding the extreme and explicit versions of far-right rhetoric at arm's length. Both can thus avoid accusations of racism while mobilizing on the fears that are whipped up across Europe around the consequences of immigration and Islam.

UKIP bills itself as a party that puts British people first.[24] Similar to the populist appeals to the 'people' found inside and outside the parliaments of Germany, British people should be privileged over non-British people, because democracy is only 'meaningful' when its people share a national identity in the past and the present.[25] Connected to the anti-EU stance that is at the centre of UKIP's political agenda are concerns about immigration. What UKIP calls 'uncontrolled mass-immigration' must end.[26] Islam isn't singled out in relation to their proposals for immigration policy. Instead, the party's views on Islam come to the fore under the policy heading of 'British Culture'. Here we see echoes of the theology we have already discussed. The theological assumption is that different religions map onto different cultures. The theological argument is that these religious cultures neither coincide nor cooperate. They clash. In the section on 'British Culture', Muslims are mentioned in relation to extremism and terrorism. It's claimed that the vast majority of perpetrators of sexual violence are Muslims.[27] No evidence is given to back up this 'fact'.[28] A section on 'Islamic Extremism' notes that 'unprecedented acts of terrorism' have been witnessed around the world. These acts are caused by the 'worst excesses of a literalist interpretation of Islamic doctrine'.[29] Islamic extremism is deemed an on-going problem that will take practical political measures to resolve. From here, the statement moves to 'English Identity and Issues'.

English identity is 'something to be proud of', rather than something that should be airbrushed out of national life.[30] Englishness isn't about blood and biology – anyone can claim English identity regardless of their origins: 'English identity resides in the heart and mind not on the skin.'[31] In this way, UKIP is attempting to avoid accusations of racism. But the scripts and strategies of new racism are apparent between the lines of UKIP's statements. The contrast between (English) identity and Islam, with the one characterized positively and the other characterized negatively, is clear. Including this material under the heading of 'culture' shows the way Islam is understood as an 'other' culture – dangerous when it comes too close to British or English culture. Perhaps race does not determine Englishness, but religion seemingly does. The theological trap of new racism, then, has been set up. It hasn't sprung shut yet.

Outright Islamophobia is avoided. UKIP hides its anti-Islam stance in its proposals for migration policies. In these policy proposals, the legitimation of inequality – a central function of new racism – plays out. As Fekete argues, 'stitched into immigration law, in ways that are largely invisible, is "aliens law", which invokes a "hostile environment" forcing undocumented (bad) migrants to live at the margins of society completely without rights.'[32] Fekete makes clear that it doesn't take UKIP to put such policies into practice. In fact, one reason for the fall in popular support for UKIP in the 2017 elections was the Conservative Party pushing a firm stance on immigration, thereby offering a more credible platform for one of UKIP's core issues.[33] The Conservative Party were thus able to secure much of UKIP's previous support base.[34]

While Theresa May had campaigned to remain in the EU, she quickly sought to act on the results of the referendum, adopting the mantra 'Brexit means Brexit', as Conservative Prime Minister from 2016 to 2019. As the Leave campaign focused on defending Britain's borders, May was an excellent fit as national leader. Her draconian immigration policies as Home Secretary from 2010 to 2016 were well known. In an interview with the *Telegraph* in 2012, May commented on the party's aim to bring immigration numbers down by 'tens of thousands', adding that she wanted to create a 'really hostile environment' for illegal migrants in the UK.[35] Later, the Home Office sent out 'vans across London with an advertising board, illustrated with an image of handcuffs, stating "In the UK illegally? Go home or face arrest"'.[36] 'Hostile environment' policies have relentlessly targeted people without UK or EU passports, who have been treated as illegal until proven otherwise. Often the evidence provided has not been accepted.[37] These measures were solidified in the Immigration Acts of 2014 and 2016 which prevented people from accessing basic services such as healthcare.

May's policies ostensibly focus on *illegal* immigrants, but the hostile environment has targeted thousands of legal and illegal immigrants. One scandal in particular has resulted from the 'hostile environment' policy on immigration – the Windrush scandal – where people, many born in Britain, mostly from a Caribbean background, were deported or threatened with deportation. In *Hostile Environment: How Immigrants Became Scapegoats*, Maya Goodfellow argues that anti-immigration sentiment is one of the most serious problems the UK faces.[38] Goodfellow puts it starkly: 'at its core, the nation's history on immigration legislation is a history of racism'.[39] May – although not alone – was able to capitalize on a long-established register of racializing immigrants.[40]

Although May didn't target Muslims explicitly or exclusively in her immigration policies, problems with views on race in the Conservative Party have come to the fore on several occasions, particularly orbiting around current Prime Minister Boris Johnson. One of Johnson's advisers, Andrew Sabisky, openly declared racist views – he had done so for years, particularly online. Sabisky eventually resigned, but Johnson has not explicitly distanced himself from him or his views.[41] When it comes to Islam, most well-known is perhaps Johnson's comparison of women wearing the burqa to 'letter boxes'.[42] What sounds like the laid-back joke of an eccentric upper class Oxford-educated politician, could and should be characterized as a calculated strategy: tapping into the far-right othering of Muslims, while being able to pass it off as a joke. When he added that these women are also like 'bank robbers', he brought in allusions to Islam as a security threat. The tone might seem light-hearted, but the context of Islamophobia across Europe belies any such innocence. Far-right parties have mobilized on people's fears of unemployment, crime and disintegration as well as decline, scapegoating Muslim migrants in particular.[43] The monitoring organization, Tell MAMA (MAMA stands for Measuring Anti-Muslim Attacks) reported a surge of anti-Muslim incidents in the week after Johnson's 'jokes'.[44] The incidents increased by 375 per cent.[45] According to the *Guardian*, almost half of the street-based incidents reported to

THE CLAIM TO CHRISTIANITY

Tell MAMA referenced Johnson.[46] Johnson's comments aren't new. Writing about the right of a British Muslim girl to wear a jilbab at school in 2006, Johnson stated that the whole case was about 'how far militant Islam could go' in winning the cultural battle over Britain.[47] Lamenting the 'disasters of multiculturalism', 'too many Muslims' disloyal to the British state are the problem for Johnson.

Although the Conservatives are not alone in this,[48] a number of Conservative Party members were suspended from the party for endorsing Islamophobic content online in 2019.[49] While Prime Minister, May avoided accusations of Islamophobia by speaking of the 'perversion of Islam' rather than Islam.[50] David Cameron and Tony Blair had used the phrase before her. Although not all are blamed for terrorism, Muslims are still seen as suspicious. As James Crossley points out in his analysis of the role of religion in British politics, it is difficult to imagine 'Parliament discussing, in a sustained way, notions of "Christian violence", or even a 'distortion' of "true Christianity"'.[51]

The presentation of Islam as dangerous is pervasive. Sometimes Islam and sometimes 'Islamism' is linked to extremism and terrorism. But across the board, fear is stoked around the Muslim who's not quite at home in the UK – in other words, who could at any moment become a traitor and a threat. It's perhaps to be expected that 9/11 and 7/7 have marked the collective consciousness, particularly the 7 July 2005 bombings, where terrorists self-identifying as Muslim conducted a series of suicide attacks across London. People are fearful of terror attacks that have caused tragic loss of life. But to represent Muslims repeatedly as dangerous is a political decision. It's a decision to frame the attacks exclusively in relation to a religious minority in the UK. It's a decision to look away from other factors. And it's a decision to invoke the figure of the Muslim as a dangerous outsider on the inside. The consequence of this decision is that Muslims can be treated differently from non-Muslims.

Identity

In the current party programme of UKIP, there are no references to Christianity as the unifying aspect of the British people. Yet in preparation for the 2015 general elections, UKIP – then led by Farage – published a 'Christian Manifesto' with the title 'Valuing our Christian Heritage'.[52] UKIP gained an unprecedented 12.6 per cent of the votes in these elections, placing them in third place. It's striking that the claim to Christianity UKIP make in this manifesto resonates with far-right claims to Christianity across Europe.

Echoing the language of the wider far right in Europe, Farage calls for a 'much more muscular defence of our Christian heritage'. The constitution of the UK is called 'our Christian Constitution'. Christianity characterizes identity. UKIP's 'Christian Manifesto' states that other faiths should be respected, but this statement is qualified by the claim that the UK should be seen as a fundamentally Christian nation. UKIP's theology, then, is one of Christianity as a marker of cultural inheritance and identity, both of which are connected to nationhood. Farage presents UKIP as the only political party in Britain that 'still cherishes our Judaeo-Christian heritage'. Islam isn't mentioned, but Britain's Judaeo-Christian heritage is said to underpin 'our culture'. The interchangeability of 'Christian' and 'Judaeo-Christian' is striking. If Christianity or Judaeo-Christianity is central to the Constitution, the culture and the character of the country, what is it that's unconstitutional, uncultured and uncharacteristic? The answer is, of course: the Muslim migrant. There's no need for the manifesto to name Islam. The claim to Christianity as Judaeo-Christianity does the trick. The resonances to wider trends in Europe are loud and clear.

UKIP goes further in claiming Christianity politically and practically by stating that 'Christian values' will inform policy decisions. Appeals are made to the 'traditional family'. While UKIP is careful to avoid demonizing Islam, there are obvious parallels with the fearmongering rhetoric of the far right in

UKIP's rhetoric about a 'defence' of Britain's Christian identity, in the association of Muslims with sexual predators and political extremists. Identifying Britishness with ethnicity is avoided, but a link of Britishness with Christianity is established. Christianity isn't claimed consistently throughout UKIP's political agenda, but emerges particularly in 2015 with their 'Christian Manifesto'. A clash of cultures is not announced, but forms a subtle subtext to the claims to a Christian Britain. The theology of UKIP is aligned with 'Culture Christianity'. It culminates in the call for a 'more muscular Christianity' that provides a strong and stable national identity to safeguard the people. Here we see a hint of a Crusader Christianity. Theologically, Christianity is the possession of a particular people. It's a possession and it's precarious: it must be protected from 'others'. UKIP's claim to Christianity bears resemblance to Crusader Christianity but avoids the more explicit calls for battle. So far, UKIP is only flexing its Christian muscles.

What about the Conservatives? As mentioned above, the Conservative Party were keen to attract voters from UKIP. But because of the turn to the right, it was crucial not to be connected to the *far* right. Suspicions of such connections were alleviated by critiquing the English Defence League. As an extreme fascist or neo-fascist organization at the fringes of the political spectrum, the English Defence League could be critiqued without any condemnation of the more moderate far-right tropes in circulation. During her premiership, May arguably played into notions of Britain as Christian, particularly in speaking of her background as a vicar's daughter. Christianity has shaped her views and visions, although she avoided much detail or discussion of her faith. While pushing for the UK's exit from the EU, May spoke of herself as a member of the Church of England, causing an association of God with Brexit to emerge.[53] Newspapers had a field day with May's statements. *The Sun* ran the headline, 'Guide me, O thou great Theresa: Theresa May says her faith in God will guide our path out of Europe as she admits Brexit is keeping her awake.'[54]

As Crossley argues, May tapped into a common tradition embraced by leading politicians, namely, that Christianity is a key part of British heritage. He adds, however, that 'May's spin on it was clearly one that might broadly be associated with the Conservative Right, right-wing tabloids, or, indeed, UKIP'.[55] The idea of Britain as fundamentally Christian isn't explicitly embraced by May. But she gestures towards 'our tradition' in an arguably more pronounced way than her predecessor. During her 2017 Easter speech, May spoke of 'those values that we share – values that I learnt in my own childhood, growing up in a vicarage'.[56] The values she lists are: compassion, community, citizenship. May went on to say that these are 'values we all hold in common, and values that are visibly lived out every day by Christians, as well as by people of other faiths or none'. As Crossley notes, while May borrows one of previous Prime Minister David Cameron's favourite phrases, 'all faiths and none', she alters the phrase from 'all faiths and none' to '*other* faiths or none'.[57] Minority religions in the UK, such as Islam, are not mentioned by name here but are simply 'other' as if to emphasize their foreignness while giving the appearance of including them in the fold of shared values. In her 2017 Christmas message, May speaks of 'all faiths and none' and the 'shared values' of different faiths.[58] But she also hints at Culture Christianity in calling for 'pride in our Christian heritage and the confidence it gives us to ensure that in Britain you can practise your faith free from question or fear'.[59] Although May could be defended for simply speaking of her own personal background, these subtleties are not insignificant. Considering the fact that May can't have been unaware of the tensions spurred on by far-right figures that have become so prevalent in pitting Islam against English and European identity, her speeches could have been a venue to problematize some of these constructs of Christian values.

Muscular Christianity is not embraced by the Conservatives. Cultural Christianity is alluded to, but subtly and sparingly. Where there is a theology, it's tacit. But there is perhaps no need for a more overt claim to Christianity, since parties such as UKIP have already foregrounded a position on Islam and identity that is adopted in more subtle forms by the Conservatives. Perhaps echoes are all that are needed in a political climate where the hard right have moved from the periphery to power. Islam, or interpretations of Islam, are seen as a security threat. Christianity has arguably become a default identity symbolizing a more 'naturally' British and 'naturally' peaceful tradition.

In the context of the hard-right Brexit, then, we find a more benign version of the depictions of Islam in contrast to identity. Muslim migrants are presented as not, or not quite, fitting into UK society. Muslims are seen as a problem – if not at present then potentially. Culture Christianity underlies this perception of Islam as 'other'. UKIP's Christian Manifesto embraced a muscular Christianity that could defend the Christian or the Judaeo-Christian values of the UK against Islam. For the Conservatives, claims to Christianity are neither straightforward nor stark. A softer version of Culture Christianity is presented, often implicitly rather than explicitly. Nonetheless, both parties have successfully mobilized far-right themes and tendencies while critiquing more extreme incarnations of these views. But as Fekete points out: 'To argue that the extreme right is the main carrier of racism is to miss the point. Nativism has been woven into government policy.'[60] What has the Church of England to say to the nativism that privileges the 'natives' 'born and bred' in the UK?

Building Christian Britain

Like the Conservatives, the Church has focused its critique on the extreme ends of the far right. As political scientists Andrea Mammone and Timothy Peace attest, it is clear that churches in the UK across all denominations have condemned extreme parties such as the British National Party.[61] What about the more insidious calls to protect the rights of 'natives' over 'non-natives' in the name of an exclusive or exclusivist cultural identity to be found in the hard right?

Our Neighbours

Addressing members of the Church of England, the Bishops' Letter, *Who is my neighbour? A Letter from the House of Bishops to the People and Parishes of the Church of England for the General Election 2015*, invites all to 'join in the conversation' about politics in the UK.[62] The Letter of more than 50 pages points to the significance of faith for political activity before it moves into the polarized political climate in the UK. The Letter isn't interested in the rise of the far right. However, the Bishops' interest in the political situation, particularly the polarization of the public square, means that we can get insights into the Church's response to the far right. So what do the Bishops want?

The Bishops want a vision: 'a fresh moral vision of the kind of country we want to be.'[63] The question that needs to be asked and answered is 'Who is my neighbour?' Theologically, the Letter points to the significance of the image of God: 'We belong together in a creation which should be cherished' because we are created in 'the image of God'.[64] While 'Anglicans do not have a single view on which political party has the best mix of answers to today's problems', they have the image of God as a criterion with which to check parties.[65] By drawing out and developing this criterion, the Bishops call for 'a new kind of politics' beyond party-political fault lines.[66]

The Bishops acknowledge the fear of '"furious religion"' – religions interpreted or instrumentalized to stir up conflict – but argue that what such fury shows is that faith is so significant for people that it cannot be ignored. On the contrary, 'people of faith within all the historic traditions have much to offer to a vision of a good society'.[67] Christianity is an 'incarnational faith'.[68] According to the Bishops, the incarnation confirms that human beings are created in the image of God so that 'we are called to love our neighbour as ourselves. This is the starting point for all of the church's engagement.'[69] While critics might complain that the commandment to love our neighbours as ourselves is either too loony or too lofty to make politics, the Bishops draw on the practice and the preaching of Jesus in order to come up with a concrete conclusion: Christians critique the 'accumulations of power wherever they take place'.[70] 'The Biblical tradition is not only "biased to the poor", as often noted, but warns constantly against too much power falling into too few hands.'[71] The Bishops add that 'we do not set ourselves up as possessing superior knowledge', but call for critical and self-critical engagement in politics that can hold a balance.[72] According to them, critical and self-critical engagement, however, is lacking.

Countering the 'adversarial politics' that assumes that one's opponent is wholly wrong, conversations are needed – conversations that can be both critical and self-critical.[73] Why is politics failing to strike a balance? For the Bishops, one cause of the failure of politics is that virtues have been forgotten. While virtues cannot be controlled, they can be influenced, indirectly rather than directly.[74] Where is the politician who fosters and facilitates virtues? In order to sustain a virtuous society, 'a sense of "place" helps' because it forms 'people's identity in community'.[75] Here the Church of England comes in. 'Present in every community of England', the Church can counter the 'society of strangers', turning the UK into a 'community of communities'.[76] 'Our hope for a stronger politics of community is driven by the conviction, founded on experience and evidence, that individuals flourish best when they belong with confidence to networks of relationships'.[77] The Church of England can start and sustain such networks.

While the tone and tenor of the Letter accommodates a diversity of political positions, eager as it is to strike a balance between left and right, the Bishops counter parties 'of the extreme right and the extreme left' who have 'sometimes sought to rekindle the language of class – but by trying to tap into class resentments'.[78] Resentments, whether nationally or internationally, are dangerous because they lead to the dehumanization of people, thus opposing the dignity that they have as images of the incarnate God.[79] Both minorities and migrants are mentioned here, but not singled out. The Bishops point to the 'ugly undercurrent of racism' that runs 'in every debate' that understands 'ethnically identifiable communities' as problems rather than promises: 'Crude stereotyping is incompatible with a Christian understanding of human social relationships'.[80] Theologically, then, a claim to Christianity is made that counters far-right rhetoric. However, balance remains crucial. The Bishops aim to:

> challenge the assumption that to question immigration at all must always be racist. Major trends in migration have brought about immense social changes in many parts of the country. Rapid change has often impacted most acutely on communities which are least equipped to handle it – partly because their experience has often been that change is to their detriment.[81]

As a consequence, 'suspicion of people with other ... origins needs to be understood without being endorsed or excused. We need a dialogue about migration which ceases to use people as political cyphers and looks instead at who is being asked to bear the cost of rapid social change'.[82] The Bishops, then, put the balance they promote into practice by criticizing both racism, on the one hand, and the critique of racism, on the other hand. Where racism and critiques of racism capture politics in a conflict between insiders and outsiders, they show 'scant regard for the Christian traditions of neighbourliness'.[83]

The Bishops insist: 'It is a fallacy to believe that a community of communities can be built from a position of assumed neutrality – everybody is rooted somewhere.'[84] The roots to which the

Bishops refer here are the roots in a concrete church.[85] Altogether, the Bishops of the Church of England ask and answer the question 'Who is my neighbour?' in a way that allows theology to inform politics and politics to inform theology. Christianity is claimed as an inclusive religion that can achieve unity.

As one would expect from Christians talking about the question of the neighbour, the parable of the Good Samaritan comes up (Luke 10.25–37). The parable, the Bishops insist, has two points. First and foremost, the foreigner is the one who shows himself to be a neighbour. Neighbourliness, then, cuts across national identity. What the Letter emphasizes, however, is that neighbourliness is 'also about what we are willing to receive from those we fear'.[86] Asking 'Who is my neighbour?', then, means asking both who can I support and by whom can I be supported. The neighbour is: *all of us*. Although xenophobia is not explicitly discussed here, Christianity is claimed to stand against the demonization of foreigners. Theologically, we are connected to the foreigner as someone who may aid us. The foreigner is connected to us as someone whom we may aid. The foreigner, then, isn't to be feared. Here, the trends and tendencies seen in far-right ideology are countered, even if they are not described or defined.

Not Our Neighbours

Islam isn't mentioned at all in *Who is my neighbour?* However, when one thinks through neighbourhoods in the UK, Muslims shouldn't be ignored. What would you respond if you were asked whom you would and whom you wouldn't want as your neighbour, *literally*? Drawing on data from 2016 that compares attitudes towards Muslims in five European countries, the answer for the United Kingdom is clear.[87] Statistically, 'people with many children' are the neighbours that we don't want. Here, people living in the UK stand out by far in European comparison. However, those who are almost as unwanted as people with many children are: Muslims and migrants. Muslims are rejected as neighbours by 21 per cent of the British population. Migrants are rejected as neighbours by 25 per cent of the British population.[88] It is likely that the categories 'Muslim' and 'migrant' intersect in most people's minds: Muslims are often seen as migrants and migrants are often seen as Muslims. While 21 or 25 per cent might not sound like much, in comparison with five European countries only Austrians are more likely to name Muslims and migrants as the people next to whom they don't want to live.[89] Given these statistics, can a Letter from the House of Bishops that calls for neighbourliness ignore Islam? The way Islam is understood has consequences for how a country perceives identity and immigration.

The referendum to leave the EU is one example. According to sociologists Linda Woodhead and Greg Smith, who studied data about the referendum results, Anglicans 'voted by two to one for Brexit'.[90] The members of the Church of England stand out in comparison to other Christian and other non-Christian voters.[91] Crucially, the sociologists point out that 'the top three' reasons why Anglicans value the Church of England have 'nothing to do with God'.[92] Instead, the Church is valued because it's integral to English identity past and present.[93] Woodhead sums these attitudes up as 'English Anglican cultural-ethnic pride'.[94] This ties in with wider studies on the majority support for Brexit, where a resurgent English nationalism is at work.[95] The consequence of the English Anglican cultural-ethnic pride is that Anglicans are anxious about identity and immigration.[96] In *Theologising Brexit*, black British theologian Anthony G. Reddie comes to a crushing conclusion: 'The superiority of Britain is built on a bedrock of Christian-inspired exceptionalism in which God has set apart the British, particularly the English, to occupy a special place in the economy of God's kingdom.'[97] As a consequence, he contends, the 'ambivalence of British Christianity to take a preferential option for the marginalized ... might involve the nature of the collusive relationship that the historic churches, especially the Church of England, has with the operational activity of imperialism and colonialism'.[98]

The rise of religion- and race-related hate crime in the UK after the referendum puts even more power and even more pressure behind Reddie's criticism.[99] Here, the Bishops' acknowledged biblical bias towards the marginalized would seem to point towards support for Muslim migrants. But this connection isn't made in the Bishops' Letter.

Christian Neighbourhoods

After the EU referendum, the Church of England has continued its engagement in politics. In 2018, Archbishop Justin Welby published *Reimagining Britain: Foundations for Hope*.[100] Although the Archbishop points out that the 'views expressed here are my own, not an official position of the Church of England',[101] it's interesting to examine how he sees Islam. Like the Letter from the House of Bishops, *Reimagining Britain* calls us to construct or reconstruct a country characterized by the values and virtues of Christianity. It can be seen as a response to what political scientist Daniel Wincott diagnoses as the 'unsettled times' after the referendum, with disunity marking 'leavers' from 'remainers' as well as disunity within these groups.[102] According to Welby, Christianity has shaped the history of the UK so strongly that it's significant for believers and non-believers also today.[103] Building on the history of the UK, he argues:

> Above all, there is today a lack of common values, due to the breakdown of what was once a shared narrative of virtue in the Christian tradition. The problem has been analysed to death, brilliantly in some cases. ... This book is not a further analysis, but seeks to suggest ways in which policies could be

more closely linked to historic virtues without crushing the diversity ... so attractive in modern life.[104]

Like the Bishops' Letter, Welby similarly points to the question of the neighbour, particularly in the chapter entitled, 'The World Around Us'. He emphasizes the Good Samaritan story as one that shows mercy 'beyond ethnic, national or religious boundaries'.[105] For Welby, the parable is a 'passage about love-in-action' that has 'passed into our culture as a definition of values'.[106] Welby's vision, then, accords with the Bishops' Letter. Here it seems, the theology of the far right is denounced as incompatible with his own claim to Christianity as a religion of neighbourliness that reaches across national, ethnic and religious borders.

But for Welby, as for the Bishops, there is no sign of the Muslim neighbour. Instead, the reflection on the parable of the Good Samaritan is centred in a vision of the British state that is grounded in Christian values. Welby pushes the parable from the person-to-person encounter to the state-to-state encounter. We move from Jericho Road to Westminster. Ultimately, Welby is interested in the moral dilemma of what 'do we do when the problem is not one victim but scores of millions?'[107] In the face of the vastness of suffering in the world, how do we act as the Good Samaritan? In response to this overwhelming problem, Welby's pragmatist Good Samaritan is supported by what he calls an equally important strand of the Bible, namely the wisdom tradition.[108] Radical action, called for by the prophets, is balanced by the voice of wisdom, which is attuned to 'what is realistic as well as what is right'.[109] The Samaritan's deal with the inn-keeper is a good business call. It's a win-win for both parties.[110] Similarly, there are limitations to what we can do as individuals. Welby therefore shifts the question onto the British state rather than the individual British – or Christian – citizen. His question becomes: how can the British state be a Good Samaritan on the international stage?

Welby points to the fact that 'Good Samaritanism', as he

terms it, is already embedded in the British state and the way the state lives out Christian values. One way the British state can be a Good Samaritan on the international stage is in combating the causes of mass migration. Welby invokes the limited way in which the Samaritan helps the injured man: 'The Good Samaritan is the one who does not solve every problem but does the best with what he has'.[111] He can't do everything, and by extension, nor can the UK. It's a matter of taking account of the capacity of the UK to accept and accommodate refugees.[112] *Something* can be done, though – as the Samaritan did – and this is in the interest of the British state. 'Tackling instability abroad is in the interests of the UK because it is protection against uncontrolled movements of people and it potentially opens up foreign markets and cultures to fair and free trade to the benefit of all.'[113] This involves development programmes. Because the British state is thus saving 'lives, tackling global inequalities and leading the way in the creation of a more just world', we have the added benefit of a consequent maintenance of 'British global influence'.[114]

Welby uses the Good Samaritan, then, to showcase the possibility of Christian values played out on the international stage, where a Good Samaritan British state can offer aid – as Jesus' Good Samaritan did – but to be effective must enter into pragmatic business deals with international partners that take account of the Samaritan's interests as well as the moral obligation to help those who suffer. It's not news when Archbishops call for the significance of Christianity for public and political life. But what about Islam?

Throughout *Reimagining Britain*, Islam comes up from time to time. The chapter on 'Family – Caring for the Core' offers the most detailed account. Welby discusses the introduction of Sharia which he interprets as a system of legal propositions and legal practice – so 'more than a system of law' – into the legal system of the UK.[115] Rowan Williams, Welby's predecessor as Archbishop of Canterbury, stirred up considerable controversy with the 'Sharia Speech' in which he dared to make such a suggestion.[116] 'On the face of it,' Welby writes, 'the request is reasonable in a country that is tolerant of different cultures.'[117] But he digs deeper:

> The problem is that reimagining Britain through values applied in action can only work where the narrative of the country is coherent… To put it another way, it is possible to welcome … diversity from within the security of a story about ourselves, an identity that is intuitively recognized, is traceable through our history.[118]

Of course, one can have opposing opinions about Sharia – if even archbishops can, everybody can. Welby praises Sharia as a 'powerful … cultural narrative of its own, deeply embedded in a system of faith …, and thus especially powerful in forming identity', but points out that it 'cannot become part of another narrative.'[119] Welby operates with the idea that different cultural narratives are separated. Reimagining Britain can be done through Islamic values (in contrast to Christian ones) or Christian values (in contrast to Islamic ones), but not through both. The theology here is one in which cultures are clearly circumscribed. Welby concludes that accepting Sharia or accepting Sharia in part 'implies accepting its values around the nature of the human person, attitudes to outsiders, the revelation of God, and a basis for life in law, rather than grace, the formative word of Christian culture.'[120] Here, difference is absolute. We can respect the other but we can't recognize commonalities that go to the core of who we are. The contrast between our cores is clear: Islam stands against Christianity as much as Christianity stands against Islam, because Christianity works with grace as its core concept.

Theologically, it's been exposed how Christians have claimed that theirs is a religion of grace in order to construct other faiths as religions of law. It's a theology that has been criticized and called 'supersessionist' because it rests on the idea that Christianity superseded all other religions. Whether admitted or unadmitted, the idea is that Christianity is better than the others.[121] Since the Protestant Reformation, Paul has been the crown witness of supersessionist theologians. Protestants interpreted Paul in a way that turned Protestantism as a religion of grace against Catholicism as a religion of law.[122] In these interpretations, Catholicism was identified with the Judaism with which Paul grappled in his time. Biblical scholars, however, have shown that these interpretations are – to say the least – incorrect.[123] Judaism has never been only or primarily a religion of law *over* grace. Christianity has never been only or primarily a religion of grace *over* law.[124] Islam doesn't fit these simplistic suggestions either.[125] As Werner G. Jeanrond argues, love is not a Christian possession.[126] But the contrast has been so powerful that it has also been applied to Islam.[127]

Of course, Muslim thinkers and theologians insist that the interpretation of Islam as a religion of the law is polemical. In a number of studies, Mona Siddiqui, professor of Islamic and Interreligious Studies at the University of Edinburgh, has tackled the contrast between 'religion of law' and 'religion of love', asking 'how did Islam come to be seen as a religion of law?'[128] She shows that both Qur'anic and post-Qur'anic texts are indeed interested in law, perhaps more so than the Bible. In both religions, 'God gives himself in his power and potential to transform our lives. Thus, love becomes a central feature of the discussions', assuming convergences as well as divergences in the ways both religions describe God.[129] But Siddiqui clarifies that the contrast between love and law doesn't cut deep enough: 'loving compassion (*raḥma*)' is at the core of the Qur'an's portrayal of God's relation to creation.[130] 'The Qur'an is replete with vocabulary of compassion as the defining essence of God.'[131] 'My mercy (*raḥmati*)', God says, 'extends to everything.'[132] The God that is portrayed in the Qur'an is a God of mercy. Siddiqui explains:

> This overwhelming mercy is a mystery, for it is essentially a plea from God to humankind not to despair of God's mercy.

Mercy, unlike love, is not bilateral – human beings cannot have mercy on God, but God chooses, indeed desires, to be merciful to human beings. ... God ... wants human beings to commit sin so that he can forgive; herein lies a mutual dependency between the divine and the human, a dependency that does not limit God but allows him constant opportunities to show the full magnitude of his love.[133]

There are differences between the portrayal of God in both religions, differences that cut deep. But Siddiqui's interpretation shows that 'grace' cannot be reserved for Christianity.

Welby ignores interpretations and interventions like these. Throughout *Reimagining Britain*, Islam comes up negatively rather than positively. The concluding chapter that points to the potential of faith communities for Britain admits that Islam has a narrative like Christianity which leads it to 'provide profound care for the weakest'.[134] Nonetheless, Islam is contrasted to Christianity.[135] This contrast makes Islam a problem. Welby doesn't include any commentary on the history of Christian–Muslim relations in the UK, a history that includes support of Christians by Muslims.[136] For the Archbishop of Canterbury, then, the reimagining of Britain is one where Islam is welcome *on Christian terms only*. In view of the rhetoric of the far right, Welby's interpretation is either complacent or complicit. His theological vision doesn't lend itself to a critique of the clash of cultures script that informs the hard right in the UK.

Complacency – perhaps also complicity – run through the resources for congregations that the Church of England published to deal with the fallout of the referendum. 'Resources for Prayer Together', a collection of liturgical and non-liturgical texts, can be downloaded from the Church of England website.[137] Although the 'together' in the title might indicate a critique of the outcome of the referendum, there is not much engagement with the views that underpin the referendum debates – such as deeply-felt views on Islam and identity. What runs through the resources, including 'A Prayer for the Nation', is a call for unity: 'God of hope, in these times of change, unite our nation'.[138] The Church of England continues the call for unity that characterized the Letter *Who is my neighbour?* after the vote on Brexit. The resources urge readers to overcome the divisions that have wounded many people through concern for the common good. The readers are asked to pray both for the leaders of the UK and for the leaders of the EU. A selection of snippets from the Bible signifies the call for unity (for example, Deut. 6.1–9; Jer. 29.11–14; Matt. 25. 23–24; Mark 10.42–45; Romans 14.7–12). But can unity be achieved when much of the debate underpinning Brexit was about cutting up national unity into insiders and outsiders? Into those who could or couldn't remain in the UK, those deported or threatened with deportation?

In addition to these resources, 'Some Conversation Starters' are made available to host conversations about Brexit. No matter what you think about it, 'now is the time when we can no longer carry on defining each other by how we voted in the referendum'.[139] Instead, by making 'the local community the focus' we can think through the ramifications of the referendum, taking both sides into the conversation to answer the question: 'How can we work together to build a more just society which is at peace with itself?'[140] Again, Islam is not mentioned. Commendable as it is, the call for unity hides the fact that the rhetoric of the referendum hits migrants and Muslims hard. With the current government of the country creating and consolidating a 'hostile environment' – a policy with real-life ramifications in attitudes and actions – can the Church of England's call for a balanced view be considered anything but silence in the face of the anti-immigrant and anti-Islam rhetoric percolating through British society? Is the theology that can respond to such an environment so tacit that it can't be heard? Considering the theological emphasis on neighbourliness, why not call for solidarity with the Muslim and migrant neighbour? Is such a tack impossible or impractical? Or simply not a priority? What is clear is that the Church of England comes out strongly against racism and xenophobia in its extreme forms. It is less clear how it effectively responds to the pervasive forms such racism and xenophobia take when it comes to views of identity and Islam inside and outside its own ranks.

Complacency or Complicity?

Although there are clear differences in the tone and tenor of marginal and mainstream right-wing parties, there are also striking similarities. Comparing constructions of Islam and identity, it becomes clear that a number of politicians that are considered moderate construct Islam in contrast to the identity of the UK. For a figure such as Nigel Farage, the rhetoric fits the scripts of the new far right, with the new-racist recourse to religion rather than race. For Boris Johnson and Theresa May, the rhetoric is softer. But the ease with which Islam is associated with terrorism is not matched by any critique of claims to Christianity as flirting with racist and new-racist conceptions of the nation. Immigration, Islam and identity are key issues for UKIP and the Conservatives. Islam is linked to terrorism. British identity, meanwhile, is sporadically and subtly linked to Christianity.

While the Church of England has spoken out against the more extreme incarnations of the far right, they have responded obliquely rather than outspokenly to the hard right in the UK through calls for unity in UK politics. Statements from the Church's leadership are keen to address the contemporary polarized political climate that easily slides into fixed categories of identity and alterity. Clearly, the Church is attempting to tread a delicate balance itself, to not exclude any political commitments that its members might have, and to not alienate a population that is fraught with division.

The parable of the Good Samaritan was invoked to call for a theology of Christian virtues and values in practice. For the

Bishops this means an outworking of love towards *everyone* because *all* are made in God's image. If one assumes that the migrant and the Muslim, too, are made in God's image – something that the Letter doesn't say – then the Bishops counter the hard right. In any case, the Bishops' Letter rejects the ethno-national current of hard-right politics by refusing the dichotomy between insiders and outsiders.

The issue that has most riveted the far right, however, namely Islam, is not addressed by the Church. For Archbishop Welby, the Good Samaritan is more a figure for Christian values played out by the British state than a figure for the Christian reaching out to her Muslim neighbour – with or without legal documents to prove her citizenship. For Welby, Muslims can be welcomed, but on Christian terms only. It's not explained why only one cultural narrative ought to characterize a country. Why can't common values and virtues travel from Christianity to Islam and from Islam to Christianity? They are thus, if not clashing, then contrasts. More questions need to be asked:

> Can we call hard-right politicians 'Christian'? Why? Why not?
> Do churches have to make a choice between a Christian culture that excludes Islam and an Islamic culture that excludes Christianity?
> Whom would you want as your neighbour? Whom wouldn't you want as your neighbour? Why?

We encounter a softer version of the contrast between identity and alterity in the UK that can be found in so much far-right rhetoric. Again, the script is recurrent: Christianity and Islam are seen as essentially different, Christianity is 'us'. The semantic struggle for Christianity, then, continues.

6

Challenging Churches: From Complacency to Critique

We're in a small town. A local church congregation is hosting a conversation about immigration. The invitation, published in the newspaper, is clear: all are welcome. More than a hundred people show up in the church. A sheet of paper on each seat lists the rules for the conversation: discrimination is not allowed, statements that diminish people or groups of people will not be accepted. There is one microphone in the church, at the front. After a few words of welcome by both the minister and the mayor of the town, people are invited to come to the front.

Soon a politician starts to speak. Her party is known for its critique of immigration. She is a Christian, she says, but fed up with the churches. For her, the neighbour is the neighbour – not someone who has come here from far away to rest on the resources our neighbourhoods offer. But the churches care about these foreigners. The politician is certain that Christianity is under attack by Islam. 'We all know how people live there. Can the churches want that we live like that, here too? I'm for freedom, the freedom rooted in the values and the virtues of Christianity. I'm for bikinis instead of burqas', she ends. The next speaker is not affiliated with any party. He calls himself a concerned citizen. 'We need to talk about Islam', he insists. He tells two anecdotes – 'something we all know is happening' – of the misogyny and the militancy of Muslims here 'in our Christian country'. 'The Qur'an has no concept of the image of God, so in the Qur'an people aren't equal: Muslims have more dignity than non-Muslims. Men have more dignity than women. Hence, Muslims have to be militant and misogynistic. They have to do what's written in the Qur'an.' Awkward silence follows. The next speaker steps up to the microphone. She is known for her work in a refugee relief organization. A large number of people, including the two first speakers, stand up. They leave before the woman can start to speak. There is something of a kerfuffle. People whisper, some in shock and some in support of the walk-out. In any case, the conversation is over.

Both the mayor and the minister apologize for the end of the event. They promise to organize a follow-up. For the follow-up, they invite speakers: professional politicians from the left, the right, and the centre. They also invite the woman who wasn't heard last time. Yet the woman writes back that she won't come. She sees no point in discussing with those who won't listen. The event still takes place, but few people attend. Disappointed by the woman who declined their invitation to the event, the mayor and the minister ask in the church news afterwards: 'Has Jesus Christ ever said to anybody: "I don't want to talk to you"?'

This scenario plays out challenges and complexities that we have encountered in the cases we have covered in Chapters 3 to 5.[1] Both in the rhetoric of the far right and in the responses to the rhetoric of the far right, statements such as these put the semantic struggle for Christianity on display. In this chapter, we connect these cases by concentrating on the responses and the role of the churches. We argue that the semantic struggle cuts to the core of Christianity – the identity of Christianity, what it is and what it isn't. We advocate for a turn in the interpretation of the identity of Christianity, from a possession (something we can own) to a project (something we can't own). If Christianity is a practical project, it is open to all – Christians and non-Christians. It calls us into contact with each other. Crucially, contact cannot be confined to Christians of differing political leanings. We contend that contact with

Muslims is central to reclaiming Christianity in response to the rise of the far right. Such contact might even equip us to make sense of the small-town scenario we sketched above, with its statements and its silences.

Caught in the Middle?

All of the churches we covered are concerned with one question: who is our neighbour? Theologically, the statements are strikingly similar. Human beings are created in the image of God. The image of God has been confirmed in the practice and preaching of Jesus Christ – for all, regardless of race or religion. Hence, the neighbour is: all of us. In response to the rise of the far right, this interpretation of the image of God puts the churches in a double bind. If all of us are neighbours, churches have to be open to all of us. If churches have to be open to all of us, they have to be open to *both* the political left *and* the political right. But how can churches respond to the rise of the far right? Can they tolerate right-wing politics? Do they risk becoming left-wing if they don't? Can they tolerate left-wing politics? Do they risk becoming right-wing if they don't? Are churches caught in the middle?

The churches we discussed call for a double demarcation – against the extreme left and against the extreme right at the same time. Discrimination from either the left or the right cannot be accepted because it violates the dignity of all human beings who are created in the image of God. But what does discrimination look like in concrete cases? Although the image of God is the central criterion for all the church responses to the rise of the far-right that we covered, Chapters 3 to 5 clarify that the responses vary in concrete cases.

We have identified two overarching strategies in response to the rise of the far right: consolidation and challenge. None of the churches we discussed can be pinned down to only one of these strategies. There's a lot of mixing and matching going on.

Yet clarifying these two strategies allows us to work out what is helpful and what isn't helpful when responding to the far right. To be sure, we're not analysing and assessing the strategies of the consolidating church and the challenging church from the angle of a clear-cut strategy of our own. Rather, our aim is to uncover the building blocks for a response to the far right that can be found in the strategies of the consolidating church and the challenging church. What can churches learn from each other?

The Consolidating Church

Churches have called for either more consensus or more contestation in politics. Comparing these two positions, we can see that they come closer to each other than the slogans of 'consensus' and 'contestation' suggest. Both of these approaches take the churches to be consolidating democracy as a whole. Consolidation is about the capacity of churches to strengthen democracy by bringing people with different and diverse opinions together.

Some churches recommend consensus to bring people together, both inside and outside churches. The Church of England's 'A Prayer for the Nation' calls for unity: 'God of hope, in these times of change, unite our nation.'[2] No matter where you put your cross on the ballot paper in the EU referendum, the Church contends that 'now is the time when we can no longer carry on defining each other by how we voted'.[3] Politically, we need visions that diffuse the conflict in order to unite the country so that a consensus can be formed. The consolidation of democracy is what is sought.

Some churches welcome contestation to bring people together, both inside and outside churches. The rise of far-right populism is considered a consequence of the decline of democracy. In order to revive it, contestation is crucial. 'Of course, controversial debates are allowed', the Protestant Churches in

Germany announce.[4] But the churches themselves aren't called to intervene in the contestation. The churches consolidate the 'democratic corridor' in which conflicts can be confined and carried out.[5] Again, the consolidation of democracy is what is sought.

In the strategy of the consolidating church – a strategy that summarizes both the call for consensus and the call for contestation – churches are *not* called to be political players themselves. Instead, churches help to set the parameters in which political players can play. The statements of the churches that call for consensus and contestation both point to the significance of neutrality: if churches are spaces where people from the left meet people from the right, then these spaces must be as neutral as possible. Because congregations are spaces where people of opposing opinions come together, they are also spaces in which democracy is sustained and saved. The statement from the Church of England argues in a way that all churches we analysed could agree with:

> The fallacy that people can only work together if they agree about every issue is proved wrong day after day. It is precisely this ability to make and break alliances – so that people can work together on issues they share, but may not be on the same side on other issues – which makes intermediate institutions ... so crucial to a flourishing democratic society.[6]

In churches, then, democracy is lived. As a consequence, all the statements agree that the churches should be supported. Both state and society need intermediate institutions like churches for their survival. One statement goes so far as to argue that the loss of faith in Christianity is what makes people feel threatened by the plurality of religious and non-religious life. If only people had a little more faith in Jesus Christ, plurality would be welcomed.[7] All of us would act as neighbours.

In the strategy of the consolidating church, then, churches come close to the state. Since the state ought to be neutral, churches ought to be neutral too. However, the claim of the churches to consolidate a democratic consensus or a democratic contestation is itself a claim to political power. To decide about who can and who can't contribute to the consensus or the contestation – who is and who isn't 'in' the corridor, so to speak – requires a lot of power. Although this presumption is neither acknowledged nor argued for, it has consequences. One consequence is that the churches which assume they are neutral have a blind spot: Islam. If churches can make and maintain the corridor, then *whose* corridor is it?

Muslims aren't mentioned at all in the statements that advocate for the strategy of the consolidating church. While the authors could argue that their statements comment on politics – they weren't asked to write theological tracts on relations between religions – their argument would miss the fact that Islam is already at stake when one writes about immigration and identity in the politics of Europe today. Missing the significance of Islam, the statements run a risk. The commendation of Christianity as a faith that consolidates democracy – a commendation that we would expect from churches – runs the risk of complacency or complicity with the theology of the far right. From the mainstream to the margins, the far right insists that Christianity is the one and only religion that produces democratic culture. Christianity can consolidate the secular state in which religion is kept from meddling with politics and politics is kept from meddling with religion. Christianity, then, is a guarantee against tyranny. Where Christianity is characterized as a consolidation of democracy, however, Muslims are easily evaluated as anti-democratic aliens, intentionally or unintentionally.

The strategy of the consolidating church is ambiguous when it comes to Islam. Are Muslims excluded or included in the democratic consensus? Are Muslims excluded or included in the democratic contestation? Even if they're in, on whose terms are they allowed to contribute? Again, *whose* corridor is it?

The Challenging Church

Conceding the churches' involvement in Islamophobia is a challenge. Some statements acknowledge that Christianity has spurred hatred of Islam for hundreds of years. For the Catholic Church in Germany, this acknowledgement is a significant step towards change. It also allows for a critique of the assumption that Christianity is always already democratic. Instead, Christianity comes into view as a religion that can be at least as dubious and dangerous as Islam. Once the complicity or complacency of Christianity with Islamophobia is acknowledged, the claims of the far-right can be confronted one by one: from Islam to immigration to identity, although the Church loses sight of the significance of family policy here.

The Church of Norway recognizes that the competition that pits Christianity against Islam and Islam against Christianity is embedded in the history of both religions. The Church tackles the consequences of such types of competition as they come out in theological texts and theological traditions, beginning with the Bible. The Church pays attention to the power dynamics at play in such competition: contrasting and competing with Islam is different when churches are in a majority situation from when churches are in a minority situation. A position of power – a position that all of the churches we analysed hold – calls churches to care for the other.[8]

Theologically, the Church of Norway insists, competition isn't necessary. 'The Gospel is strong enough to stand on its own legs.'[9] Here we see a challenge to the Culture Christianity and the Crusader Christianity so crucial to the far right. If the assumption is that Christianity is steeped in essential and eternal conflict with Islam, the crusades can be considered the norm and normative: they show how Christians *should* think of themselves as defenders of the faith. Yet when churches take on the strategy of challenge, they acknowledge particular periods and particular places in which such conflict existed, but they stress that such conflict is *not* necessary for Christianity to be Christianity. On the contrary, these periods and positions can be grounds for repentance. The three monotheistic faiths, including Islam, the Catholic Church in Germany insists, are faithful to the same God.[10]

The churches that acknowledge their responsibility for Islamophobia past and present point out that churches ought *not* to be neutral. Churches are called to stand with the marginalized, which, in the context of the rise of the far right in Europe today, means Muslims. Neutrality comes at the cost of the marginalized. We can call for consensus and contestation in churches, favour agreeing or disagreeing well in order to consolidate a democratic corridor, but all these calls come at the cost of those who are confronted by the rise of the far right: the targets of hate and hate crime. Of course, Muslims aren't the only target of the far right, but given that the theological trap of new racism works by essentializing Muslims as enemies of Christians (and Christians as enemies of Muslims), it's crucial for the churches to stand against the marginalization of Muslims across Europe.

Representatives of the far right claim that they are the ones who are marginalized. But the spikes in anti-Muslim and anti-migrant hate crime across Europe belie such claims.[11] The claim that the far right consists of persecuted Christians who fight the invasion of Islam that is aided and abetted by national and global political elites is ludicrous. Appealing to Christian victimhood through speaking of the persecution of Christians around the globe can be done in order to cement notions of identity, 'us' against the tyrants. The writings of Bat Ye'or are a prime example of this, but by no means the only one. Church of England vicar Bonnie Evans-Hills has pointed to problematic aspects of a recent report by a Church of England bishop on persecuted Christians.[12] There is neither a forbidden past nor a forbidden present of the persecution of Christians in Europe. Both pundits and politicians from the far right are featured in the news each and every day, claiming that the media ignore them.

One has to be careful not to deny marginalization, whether it's factual or feared. Areas that have attracted large numbers of British National Party voters, for instance, are characterized as some of the most deprived areas in the UK.[13] Precariousness is not the possession of one set of people, however, nor does the blame for precarious conditions need to pit one set of people living under precarious conditions against another set of people living under precarious conditions.[14] The far right stokes fear of immigration by suggesting that the support of precarious people who live here stands against the support of precarious people who want to live here. This is a strategy to divide the precarious, pitting them against each other, in order to manipulate discontent. It works two ways: 'concerned citizens' can be easily convinced by the new-racist propaganda of the far right and the new-racist propaganda of the far right can be easily camouflaged by 'concerned citizens'. Hoodwinked by far-right claims to marginalization, churches are calling for the consolidation of democracy through Christianity, while those who are actually marginalized are attacked – also in the name of Christianity.

What is at stake here is the preferential option for the poor. The preferential option for the poor is at the core of theologies of liberation – theologies that seek to liberate both the oppressed and the oppressors from systems of oppression by putting the poor first.[15] Articulated by churches in Latin America in the 1960s and the 1970s, the preferential option for the poor started with those who are literally poor, but it didn't stop there. As Gustavo Gutiérrez, one of the founders of liberation theology, argues, poverty is one strategy to turn a 'person' into a 'non-person' whose dignity is neither acknowledged nor accepted.[16] There are many strategies that turn persons into non-persons – economically, culturally, socially and also racially or religiously. The theological trap of new racism is a strategy that turns persons into non-persons. If they put the preferential option for the poor into practice, churches have to stand against new racism. Christians can learn a lot about theologies of liberation from reading the Qur'an.[17]

New Neighbourhoods

Overall, the preferential option for the poor decides between the strategy of the consolidating church and the strategy of the challenging church. If churches take the preference for the poor seriously, they cannot but challenge their own constituency. The strategy of the consolidating church aims for neutrality in order not to exclude those on the left or those on the right. But the strategy of the challenging church aims to advocate for the poor – the marginalized who are demonized and discriminated against. Do churches lose their capability to bring together left-wingers and right-wingers when they prefer the marginalized?

The contrast between the strategy of the consolidating church and the strategy of the challenging church throws us back into the double bind in which churches find themselves when they respond to the far right. The double bind is indeed a bind. If churches prioritize care for Muslims, they run the risk of being seen as too left-wing for more right-wing Christians. If churches don't prioritize care for Muslims, they run the risk of being seen as too right-wing for more left-wing Christians. Confronted with the claims to Christianity for a construal of the identity of Europe that pits Christianity against Islam and Islam against Christianity, what can they do? Criticizing the far-right claim to Christianity, they are rebuked for renouncing Christianity for the sake of Islam. Not criticizing the far-right claim to Christianity, they are rebuked for renouncing Islam for the sake of Christianity. Clearly, writing statements and strategies for churches is an unenviable task!

Jan-Werner Müller, professor of political theory at Princeton, has studied a variety of statements and strategies in the response to far-right populism.[18] Although he is not concerned with church politics, his studies hold a lesson for churches. Müller argues against the assumption that elections are only expressions of preferences, based on the interests and the identities of the electorate. According to this assumption, populists would be successful because they represented un- or under-represented interests and identities – they would fill a 'representation gap'.[19] Müller contends that the mistake here is to assume that interests and identities are fixed. He argues that representation is actually dynamic rather than static: our identities and interests are formed by the political options on offer as much as the political options on offer are formed by our identities and interests.[20] Representation is not a cul-de-sac. Put more prosaically, people can change their minds. Through participation in the political process, people form their political positions. Politicians can contribute to this formation by offering challenging but convincing proposals. The strategy of the challenging church is in accordance with Müller's advice: when people are challenged, their political opinions are taken to be dynamic rather than static, they can be changed by challenging but convincing proposals. Churches, then, shouldn't try to get out of the double bind in which the rise of the far right has landed them. They should stick with it, stay and sink their teeth in.

To sum up, there are lessons to be learnt from the responses to the far right that we have condensed into the strategy of the consolidating church, on the one hand, and the strategy of the challenging church, on the other hand. Churches need to acknowledge their involvement in Islamophobia past and present. The history of Christianity has been shaped by hatred. Hatred isn't all there is, but it has been there – it still is. Covering it up plays into the hands of far-right figures who want to weaponize Christianity in their war for Europe. In *Reasons to Hope*, theologian Werner G. Jeanrond recounts the story of a 'wounded war memorial' which had a significant impact on him during his childhood.[21] Reflecting on the significance of subversive memories, he insists that 'every act of recollection ought to include the suffering of the others if we genuinely want to face a future' – rather than merely escape from the present to the past.[22] Hence, only if Christians acknowledge their entanglement in the history of hate can they learn how to counter Islamophobia. Churches are called to stand with those who are hated, those who are denigrated and those who are discriminated against, regardless of their race or their religion. We have characterized this call as Christianity's preference for the poor, but this is not the only way to make the case for solidarity with Muslims. Of course, Muslims aren't always 'poor'. Confronted with the rise of the far right, however, many Muslims in Europe suffer from denigration and demonization. To recall, all of the churches we covered are concerned with one question: who is our neighbour? But the question that the parable of the Good Samaritan asks is whose neighbour we should become. It's active rather than passive, it's on us. Christians are called to become neighbours to Muslims.

Calling for Contact

In the 1950s, Gordon W. Allport, Professor of Psychology at Harvard University, came up with the 'contact hypothesis' that has captured the minds of social scientists ever since. In *The Nature of Prejudice*, Allport argued that contact can corrode prejudice. He assumed that prejudice confines the other to one's own conception of her or him.[23] For the rhetoric of the far right, the conceptual confinement of the other is crucial. We described and defined it as the theological trap of new racism. Allport's *The Nature of Prejudice* charts the causes, the characteristics and the consequences of such conceptual confinement on more than 500 pages. Transposing his studies from the past to the present, we argue that contact with Muslims can allow churches to counter the rise of the far right, its racism and its new racism. Whenever and wherever churches encourage and engage in encounters with Muslims, Christianity is reclaimed against the far right. Although Müller contends that one mustn't be naïve about the contact hypothesis, he calls for contact too.[24] Contact is not enough to respond to the rise of the far right, but it is a central component of a challenging and convincing proposal offered by the churches.

In the chapter on 'The Effects of Contact', Allport theorizes and tests the contact hypothesis. Allport takes the race riots in the United States of the 1940s as a point of departure. Across the country, there were riots, but 'people who had become neighbors did not riot against each other'.[25] Why? According to Allport, research had shown that contact between people from different backgrounds can either increase or decrease prejudice.[26] It can't have come as a surprise to him that scholars couldn't agree on the impact of contact. He concluded that some contact might have a positive impact and some contact might have a negative impact, because contact isn't simply contact. There are quantitative and qualitative differences between different kinds of contact. Allport points to these differences with a short but striking scene:

See that man over there?
Yes.
Well, I hate him.
But you don't know him.
That's why I hate him.[27]

Certainly, there's contact between two people from different backgrounds here, but – if anything – the contact confirms rather than corrodes the protagonist's prejudices about 'that man'. Why? Because there is no knowledge transfer: 'that man' doesn't get to know the protagonist and the protagonist doesn't get to know 'that man'. Some might not even consider this contact at all.

Allport distinguishes between types of contact that he describes on a continuum from superficial to serious.[28] He contends that the transfer of knowledge is at the core of contact, but that it has to be personal. If getting to know the other means actual acquaintance, it helps to problematize prejudice. Contact includes affects and actions. Allport again: 'The nub of the matter seems to be that contact must reach below the surface in order to be effective in altering prejudice. Only the type of contact that leads people to *do* things together is likely to result in changed attitudes.'[29] Allport's idea is simple. If people from different backgrounds have contact with each other on a level playing field so that they can discover that they have things in common, they might become less and less prejudiced about each other. Contact can call into question both 'stereotypes' and 'second-hand stereotypes' – prejudice about the other that comes from hearsay.[30] In Allport's science-speak:

> Prejudice ... may be reduced by equal status contact between majority and minority groups in the pursuit of common goals. The effect is greatly enhanced if this contact is sanctioned by institutional supports ..., and provided it is of a sort that leads to the perception of ... common humanity between members of the two groups.[31]

Although it sounds like a fool-proof scientific equation – more contact equals less prejudice and less contact equals more prejudice – it's not. It must be acknowledged that prejudice can be shaped and sustained both with and without contact. As we mentioned above, Christians have attacked both their Christian and their non-Christian neighbours even though they were neighbours. Depending on its context and its characteristics, contact can have positive or negative consequences. It's not a foregone conclusion. Nonetheless, Allport has been taken up by social scientists ever since he came up with the contact hypothesis.[32]

Gert Pickel, professor of sociology of religion at the University of Leipzig in Germany, has explored the contact hypothesis in a number of studies. Together with Cemal Öztürk, Pickel presents measures of Islamophobia, drawing on data from the European Social Survey 2014.[33] According to their presentation, there is more Islamophobia in Eastern Europe than in Western Europe. Unless the sociologists want to assume that there are more prejudiced people among Eastern Europeans than among Western Europeans – which would in itself be a prejudice! – they have to explain where the difference in Islamophobia comes from. The difference, they argue, is that there are fewer Muslims in the East than the West, which means that it's harder to come into contact with Islam. If you don't meet Muslims, you don't have to check your prejudice about them.

There is little evidence here that religion is a precondition for prejudice: if asked whether they would back a Muslim ban, some religious people agree and some religious people disagree.[34] Yet there is a lot of evidence for the significance of contact: 'Less contact with migrants comes along with higher support for a Muslim ban.'[35] The sociologists come up with a catchy conclusion: 'Islamophobia without Muslims'.[36] There can be Islamophobia with Muslims and Islamophobia without Muslims, but, statistically, the more Muslims there are in a country, the less likely it is that Islamophobic prejudices can be shaped and sustained among the population. Again, it's not a forgone conclusion. There are countries in Eastern and in Western Europe that buck the trend.[37] But since there are always exceptions, the sociologists conclude that contact is an 'antivenom to Islamophobic attitudes'.[38] Contact, particularly face-to-face contact, matters.[39]

If you read *The Nature of Prejudice* as a theologian, the issue Allport is interested in is: to whom could and should we become neighbours? In the context of the rise of the far right, then, the issue is: how can Christians become neighbours to Muslims and how can Muslims become neighbours to Christians? Allport considered religion to be crucial for both the production and the problematization of prejudice. He cautioned that 'the role of religion is paradoxical. It makes prejudice and it unmakes prejudice'[40] because it contains 'the warp of brotherhood and the woof of bigotry'.[41] The reason for religion to be connected with prejudice, he argues, is religion itself: religion 'stands for more than faith – it is the pivot of the cultural tradition of a group.'[42] Since religion intersects with identity, 'nothing is easier than to twist one's conception of the teachings of religion to fit one's prejudice.'[43] Culture

Christianity and Crusader Christianity would fit this temptation. Allport concludes: 'What is particularly striking is the ease with which spiritually minded people seem to slip from piety into prejudice.'[44]

In accordance with Allport, Pickel argues that the role of religion is ambiguous. Today, there are Christians who criticize the prejudices in far-right rhetoric (and who perhaps volunteer for refugee relief) and there are Christians who confirm the prejudices in far-right rhetoric (and who perhaps vilify refugee relief). Pickel draws on data from a variety of surveys to show how Christians in Germany are split when it comes to immigration and Islam.[45] The split seems to be stronger inside the churches than outside the churches, which makes sense given that people would want their political position to be taken up by their churches.[46] There is a split within Christianity. Pickel's diagnosis that the split is more severe among Christians than non-Christians supports the idea of the semantic struggle for Christianity. Christians are struggling over the meaning of Christianity.

In view of the comparison of the strategies of the consolidating church and the challenging church, one conclusion is clear: any response to the far right has to go further than create contact between left-wing Christians and right-wing Christians. It has to create contact with Muslims. Again, the issue is: to whom could and should Christians become neighbours? Can Christians become neighbours to Muslims and can Muslims become neighbours to Christians?

The Identity of Christianity

Interviewed on 'Meet the Press' in the 1960s, Martin Luther King Jr commented on the significance of contact, albeit implicitly rather than explicitly: 'I think it is one of the tragedies of our nation, one of the shameful tragedies, that eleven o'clock on Sunday morning is one of the most segregated hours, if not the most segregated hour, in Christian America.'[47] King criticized racial rather than religious segregation here,[48] but his comment can capture why contact with Muslims is so challenging to churches. Christians come together in churches on Sundays, so how could churches encourage contact between Christians and non-Christians? The identity of Christianity seems to inhibit rather than instigate contact with Muslims. We're Christians. Christians aren't Muslims and Muslims aren't Christians. Contact, then, is neither a simple nor a straightforward consequence of Christianity, but calls the identity of Christianity into question. Is it possible to practise Christianity with Muslims? Is it possible to practise Christianity without Muslims? What indeed *is* Christianity?

Christian Identity as Possession

While many Christians would call for the Bible as a benchmark to circumscribe the identity of Christianity, the Bible is actually an excellent example of the difficulty in drawing distinctions between insiders and outsiders. There's not just one Bible. Decisions about the texts that are included in or excluded from the sacred scripture of Christianity were made and remade. What scholars call the process of canonization – the process by which the Bible became the Bible[49] – shows that scripture didn't fall from the sky. Moreover, both in the past and in the present, we find different Bibles according to different traditions and translations – the Bible of Catholicism differs from the Bible of Protestantism. There are also different ways of reading or *not* reading the Bible.

Consider the parable of the Good Samaritan. In our case studies, the theologies of the far right have drawn on the Bible, but not all of them on the Good Samaritan. In a way, we have more than one Bible in the rhetoric of the far right, then: Bibles where the Good Samaritan does and Bibles where the Good Samaritan doesn't make an appearance. When the parable comes up, it produces competing readings. Caricaturing the variety of Good (and not so Good) Samaritans we have come across, we can see the contrasts more clearly. The Alternative for Germany's Good Samaritan is an immigration minister who pays an aid organization a lump sum to manage the injured man but stamps a firm 'decline' on his application for asylum. He will not undertake to support the man's family. There are plenty of Samaritans closer by who need support. Samaria first. Make Samaria Great Again. By contrast, the German Catholic Bishops' Good Samaritan is a self-sacrificing humanitarian aid-worker who cannot set limits on love, because he sees every encounter with suffering as an encounter with Jesus Christ. This Good Samaritan is almost always on the verge of burn-out. There are so many injured people who need help, both inside and outside Samaria. Archbishop Welby's Good Samaritan is a savvy public manager, negotiating deals that will help many injured people. The deals will also aid the Samaritan's homeland: fewer needy victims will come to Samaria. The global influence of Samaria stays strong. The seemingly simple story is perplexing. Will the real Good Samaritan please stand up?

In addition to the parable of the Good Samaritan, the Bible itself fulfils different functions in far-right rhetoric and in the responses to far-right rhetoric. On both sides, the Bible is sometimes seen as a foundation for the culture of Europe. The Bible, then, is essentially and effectively treated as symbolic support for democracy[50] – a treatment that can be combined, as in one of the statements from the German Protestant Churches, with explicit or implicit critiques of the Qur'an, so that the two sacred scriptures are contrasted. Here, the Church of Norway stands out as it presents problematic texts of the Bible (for example, Matt. 15.21–28; 25.31–46; John 19.1–22) for us to learn how to deal with them. We are thus turned to practice: how we do and how we don't read the Bible matters.

What holds for the Bible holds for the identity of Christianity. Both in the past and in the present, we are confronted with competing conceptions of Christianity. What, then, is the identity of Christianity? Our suggestion is that we see the identity of Christianity as a project rather than a possession. We can't own Christianity because it's neither fixed nor finished. It's something we're working on.[51] The parable of the Good Samaritan is a case in point. It has been read in a wide variety of ways – read, received and resisted. But arguably the parable is only complete when it is put into practice: 'Go and do likewise' is how it ends. If the parable was a theatre piece, it would be a piece in which the audience is invited into the play, so that the actions and the reactions of the audience co-constitute the piece – audience turned actors (with all the awkwardness that comes with it). Literally, the play would be out of control – what the philosopher Umberto Eco calls a 'work in movement'.[52] A work in movement is simultaneously complete and incomplete because 'the author offers ... a work *to be completed*'.[53] If we take the Good Samaritan to be indicative of what it means to be Christian, then the identity of Christianity comes into view as a work in movement, a work to be completed, ever again and ever anew. Christian identity as a practical project. But how would a practical project help in responding to the far right?

Christian Identity as Project

If the identity of Christianity cannot be fixed, there is no clear-cut criterion to respond to the far right. In principle, Christianity can come to stand for the extreme right, for the extreme left, or for anything in between. But can it in practice?

Christianity can stand for a lot. The cases we covered in Chapters 3 to 5 show that what is at stake in the rise of the far right is the identity of Christianity. There is a semantic struggle for Christianity. The theologies of the far right shift between Culture Christianity and Crusader Christianity. In response to the far right, churches draw a distinction between two Christianities, sometimes more explicitly and sometimes more implicitly. On the one hand, there is the Christianity of the far right: it's the hijacked Christianity, an inauthentic interpretation. On the other hand, there is the Christianity of the churches' response to the far right: it's the honest Christianity, an authentic interpretation. The image of God, confirmed in the preaching and practice of Jesus Christ, clarifies that each and every human being is gifted with dignity. Christianity, then, stands against discrimination and denigration of human beings, regardless of their race or their religion. What these church responses to the far right ignore, however, is that even the idea of the image of God can be claimed for oppositional political opinions. As the statements from the Church of Norway remind us, Martin Luther was an expert exegete of the creation story in the Bible. He knew that every human being is created in the image of God. But his knowledge didn't keep him from condemning 'the Jews' and 'the Turks' to the devil.[54] Would we want to conclude that Luther 'hijacked' Christianity?

The churches have to admit that it took them a long time to interpret the idea of the image of God in the way they do today. Until very recently, the support for democracy was not a consequence that Christians drew from the idea that all human beings are created in the image of God. In the case of the EKD, it took until 1985 to articulate the connection. While it might allow Christians to pat each other's backs – we've got nothing to do with the rise of the far right, our Christianity has been hijacked – the distinction between hijacked and honest Christianity is too nice and too neat to convince. It operates through essentialism: 'this' is Christian while 'that' is non-Christian, and – by definition – 'this' and 'that' cannot come together. When they draw such a distinction, churches criticize the essence of Christianity communicated by the far right, but confirm the essentialization of Christianity communicated by the far right. They come up with their own essence. Thus, churches run the risk of reinforcing the new-racist logic.

Instead of claiming *this* definition of Christianity in contrast to *that* definition of Christianity, Christianity as a work in movement can be open to the other. It can consider claims to Christianity from the right and claims to Christianity from the left. As mentioned above, Müller suggests that it is a mistake to assume that interests and identities are fixed.[55] Taking the identity of Christianity as a project rather than a possession avoids this mistake. It recognizes that representation is dynamic rather than static. Together, we can decide what Christianity should or shouldn't stand for. We can lay claim to the texts, the traditions and the trajectories of Christianity. Reading the Bible can be central to the Christian project. Anyone who has participated in a Bible study group will know that interpretations of the same text differ among different people. If we look at the way biblical texts have been understood in different periods and different places we see huge diversity. Grappling with the texts of our tradition together is one way of practising Christianity as a project. It is a matter of taking seriously the way scripture is not something that only belongs in church buildings or to an ancient past or an academic present; scripture is lived in diverse ways. Reflecting on what these texts have meant, on what they now mean, and on what they might come to mean, is an on-going process. This is nothing new! The point is to be open about the fact that biblical interpretation cannot be fixed and finished in a search for an unequivocal meaning waiting to be found in the text. Biblical interpretation is a project. Scripture is lived.

To accept and acknowledge that churches are also laying claim to Christianity frees them to offer a challenging but convincing proposal to which everyone is invited. Our proposal to characterize the identity of Christianity as a practical project, then, takes what is commonly considered a shortcoming – that Christianity can be interpreted and instrumentalized for a variety of political purposes, from the left and from the right – to be a strength. It can tackle the problems that became apparent in the comparison of the churches' strategies above.

THE CLAIM TO CHRISTIANITY

First and foremost, when identity is a project rather than a possession, the issue is not whether churches are too much on the left or too much on the right, but what it means to be Christian. Conversations in churches turn towards the identity of Christianity. Where identity is at stake, *all* can have their say. Having a say is more a matter of practice than a matter of principle. Anthony Reddie points out why liberation theology has had little patience for debates about orthodoxy. There 'has been little evidence', he says, that 'supposedly "correct" teaching ... has any substantive relationship with ... non-racist behaviour.'[56] His position is not that we 'should be unconcerned with issues of orthodoxy and heterodoxy. Rather, it is that we should be concerned with what promotes a full life for all'.[57] The practice of Christianity is what is at stake here. What does it look like to be followers of Jesus Christ? The practice of Christianity is open to people on the left, people on the right and people caught in the middle. But if there are people who claim Christianity cynically – 'hijacking' it for their political purposes – chances are they won't be interested in orthopraxis. The involvement in practice takes much more than claiming a Christian value here and a Christian virtue there. With a little luck, the practice of Christianity might become too demanding for cynics. They might even leave it alone.

Further, when Christianity is a project rather than a possession, churches don't have to be and don't have to try to be neutral, but open. Neutrality assumes that one takes a stand in the middle between two positions. In a system of coordinates stretched out between left and right, churches claim to have the same distance from the left and from the right. Openness, however, is not neutrality. There can be no neutral position in the face of the persons who are turned into non-persons, whose dignity is neither acknowledged nor accepted. Unlike neutrality, openness can put the poor first. The Jewish theologian Ephraim Meir speaks of openness as a 'welcoming of others' rooted in the relationality of religion.[58] Drawing on the Senegalese philosopher Souleymane Bachir Diagne, Meir challenges the concentration on identity so central to the clash of cultures.[59] Religions contain the call to decentre rather than centre oneself, to open oneself up to the other.[60] Openness is a matter of creating a 'never-to-be-closed community'.[61] It 'implies striving for equality'.[62]

Finally, when Christianity is a project rather than a possession, the identity of Christianity won't prevent contact between Christians and non-Christians. The definition of Christianity cannot be done only by Christians, because the Christianity of these Christians is at stake in the very definition. When Christians accept that they need a little help from their neighbours, the identity of Christianity is opened up to the other. Churches can call for contact between Christians and non-Christians – including, crucially, Muslims. With Allport, 'the nub of the matter seems to be that contact must reach below the surface in order to be effective in altering prejudice. Only the type of contact that leads people to *do* things together is likely to result in changed attitudes.'[63] The opening of the identity of Christianity is what reaches below the surface – it cuts to the core. It can level the playing field between Christians and non-Christians. The identity of Christianity is not preventing but prompting Christians to become neighbours to Muslims.

The 'idea that the best way to obey God is through care for our fellow human beings is', as Muslim theologian Mahmoud Ayoub argues, 'essential to all three monotheistic faiths.'[64] Hence, Christians don't *own* love of neighbour. (Christians don't own Jesus either.[65]) Ayoub points out that 'the problem lies in our inability to accept each other's faiths on their own terms.'[66] While Muslims have acknowledged 'Islamized Christianity' and Christians have acknowledged 'Christianized Islam', 'both communities have sought to negate, or at least neutralize, the individuality and integrity of the faith of the other in order to find room for it in their own tradition.'[67] Described differently, both communities have confined the other to their respective system of coordinates. The consequence is 'closed religion'.[68] But if we – Christians and non-Christians – believe that 'God's love' extends 'equally to all human beings', we need to open our religions up to the other.[69] Can Christians be open to Muslims without asking them to become Christians? Can Muslims be open to Christians without asking them to become Muslims? According to Ayoub, we are all 'one humanity under God. Theological doctrines may divide us, but faith unites us. In faith, as Muslims and Christians trying to understand the will of God for our lives, we are all challenged by God to be Muslims and Christians in the deepest possible sense.'[70]

Openness is about a porous 'we' that claims Christianity. Imagine eleven o'clock on a Sunday would be neither a racially nor a religiously segregated hour. We're not advocating that we turn all Sunday services into multi-faith events. Christians could and should continue to celebrate as Christians – but as Christians who are neighbours to Muslims. When the identity of Christianity is taken to be a project rather than a possession, there is no reason not to ask for help from Muslims to figure out what Christianity means. We can figure it out together. And while we are figuring it out together, we can problematize our own prejudices.

Putting the Project into Practice

All of this might sound naïve, a pipe dream of theologians comfortably pontificating from their armchairs. (If only we had armchairs in our offices!) What would it look like in practice? One answer might be to recall the small-town scene from above. What went wrong? Our sketch of the scene was inspired by a leaflet from a German team that develops proposals to counter the far right in churches. The leaflet offers some practical pointers that support our proposal.[71]

Although the statement left on every seat pointed out that discrimination wouldn't be allowed, the proponents of the far right were not challenged. Christianity was claimed for right-wing rhetoric. What was meant to be a normal or neutral conversation turned into a conversation that reinforced Islamophobia. In their article for the church news, both the minister and the mayor were correct that churches ought to welcome everybody – Jesus didn't turn anyone away – but they concentrated their critique on the woman who refused to attend their follow-up event. In effect, they called for a welcome of the far right in the church. In its effort to remain neutral, the church turned itself into a platform for right-wing rhetoric. Christianity became complicit because it was complacent.

The neutrality of the church had consequences. Who paid the price for neutrality? The scene contains no representation from marginalized people. The migrants – who were supposed to be the subject of the event – were represented by others: by their despisers who were heard by all and by their defenders who weren't heard by all. The migrants were objects rather than subjects. They had no chance to represent themselves. Assuming that most of them were Muslims, would they have wanted to represent themselves in a church? What could and should the church have done to welcome them? In the end, the contact that the event in the small town created was the contact that, according to Allport, is counterproductive. The right-wingers had no opportunity to talk to the left-wingers. The left-wingers had no opportunity to talk to the right-wingers. Muslims couldn't encounter and couldn't be encountered by anyone else. There was no knowledge transfer, either through analysis or through acquaintance. There was no chance at all to make acquaintance with one's others or opponents, no chance to become a neighbour. There was no opportunity to work together. The fallacy that people can only work together if they agree about every issue was confirmed rather than criticized.

Instead of staging debates for the whole town, the leaflet from the German team recommends that churches take issues such as immigration into the circles that already exist in the congregation. Here, one can assume that there is a level of trust among the participants that allows for knowledge transfer through analysis and acquaintance. The leaflet describes and distinguishes between a variety of public spaces. While it might look as if churches aren't following their public and political responsibility when they take the issue into smaller circles – rather than staging a conversation for the whole town – the opposite is the case. The smaller circle allows those attending to tackle the issue hands-on. It's not about staging a debate between right-wing and left-wing Christians, but it is about grappling with the believing, the behaving and the belonging of Christians. It's about the identity of Christianity.

In these recommendations, Christianity is interpreted as a work in movement. It's assumed that people can change their positions if they are provoked by challenging but convincing proposals. Against neutrality, the idea is to go beyond the parameters of left and right in a way that aims to end the essentializations of identity and alterity. What would speak against inviting Muslims and migrants into these circles? If Christianity is a practical project, it is open to all of us – Christians and non-Christians – calling us into contact with each other. Questions that need to be thought through, then, are:

> What does Christianity's preference for the poor mean in practice? Who can and who can't be called 'poor'? Why?
> How could churches call Christians to meet Muslims? What should Christians and Muslims do together? What should Christians and Muslims not do together?
> What is Christianity for you? Do you agree or do you disagree with other Christians or other non-Christians about it? How?

Christianity is a project and not a possession, because the call to follow Jesus Christ is neither fixed nor finished. If it were, Christianity couldn't be practised. It would be a monument or a mausoleum. Islamophobia rests on such a Christianity that is set in stone. Given that Islamophobia fuels the far right across Europe, opportunities for Christians to be in contact with Muslims and Muslims to be in contact Christians are central to reclaim Christianity in response to the rise of the far right. Churches mustn't be neutral moderators.[72] Churches are spaces where Christianity can be practised in conversation, collaboration and contact with Muslims. Considering the history of conflict between both religions, contact is not a foregone conclusion but a fragile chance. It might be our only chance.

7

Conclusion: Reclaiming Christianity in Response to the Far Right

Is Europe a battleground? Our book started with a battle scenario sketched by the far right in which Islam attacks Christianity and Christianity attacks Islam, with words and weapons. Starting with the scenario of the clash of cultures, we set ourselves three aims – to investigate the rise of the far right, to interpret the rise of the far right, and to invite you to intervene in response to the rise of the far right. Challenging far-right ideas and ideologies is necessary, both inside and outside the parliaments. We targeted all of these aims from the angle of theology, approaching far-right claims to Christianity as theologies, sometimes tacit and sometimes not so tacit. In our understanding, theologies are invocations of themes, tropes and traditions of a religion that are interpreted in view of today's issues. They can be indirect or direct, unconscious or conscious, superficial, substantial or sophisticated. Of course, there are many understandings of what theology should and shouldn't be. If your understanding comes close to ours, our book might have convinced you that the far right *has* a theology. If the far right has a theology, we – Christians and non-Christians – cannot continue to circumvent it. We need to respond to it. We need to respond to it *theologically*. By investigating and interpreting the theology of the far right, our aim was to outline the complexities, the challenges and the chances for such a theological response. No single theology

CONCLUSION

can provide a solution for all cases and all countries. But across Europe a lot is done to tackle the rise of the far right.

Chapters 1 and 2 set the scene by taking stock of the theology of the far right in Europe. We argued that theological assumptions and theological arguments are at the core of the new racism so central to far-right rhetoric. New racism camouflages the category of race with its crude connections to blood and biology. The category of religion does not necessarily replace the category of race, but covers and cloaks it. The construct of the clash of cultures is cobbled together by conceptualizing religions as the hard cores of cultures, caught in an antagonistic and an apocalyptic conflict with each other. The complexities and changes to cultures are denied. Such a denial undermines Christianity's multifaceted significance for the cultures of Europe, past and present.[1] The constructs of 'Islam' versus 'Christianity' and 'Christianity' versus 'Islam' rely on stereotypes: a variety of characteristics are reduced to one simplified concept so as to conclude that 'this' is and 'that' isn't Christianity. The positive Christian identity of 'the West' and the negative non-Christian identity of 'the Rest' – to return to sociologist Stuart Hall's reflections[2] – collapse the difference and the diversity within cultures in order to cement the cultural clash. In the far right, this clash is funnelled into a theological trap: we can't escape our religions. Christians are always already democratic, tolerant and respectful of human rights; Muslims are always already undemocratic, intolerant and disrespectful of human rights – *because* they are Muslims.

Faith in God is not central to the far right's reductionist conceptualization of religion. However, what our short survey of the theology of the far right has brought out is that the interpretation of identity that is at the core of much far-right ideology is itself a matter of faith. The Europe of the far right has to be imagined. It's not just made up, but it does have to be massaged and manipulated into a particular shape. The rhetoric of the far right is built on a theology of believing in belonging. This theology of believing in belonging is not against faith in God. On the contrary, the far right calls for alliances between the faithful and the faithless combatants for Europe's Christian culture. Questions that were raised in this chapter were:

> What makes a culture 'Christian' or 'non-Christian'? Should Europe have a Christian culture?
> How does theology contribute to new racism? How does theology combat new racism?
> Have you encountered new racism?

Having sketched trends and trajectories in the theology of the far right in Europe, we concentrated on three concrete cases.

Chapter 3 covered terrorism in the name of Christianity. The attacks of 22 July 2011 in Norway exemplified how far-right forces fan the flames among their sympathizers. Radicalized online or offline, terrorists such as Anders Behring Breivik put the statements of the far right into practice. Two Christianities, we have argued, are at work in the theology Breivik espoused: a Culture Christianity and a Crusader Christianity. Whether you have faith in God doesn't matter for him. What matters is that you endorse Christianity as a European inheritance and a European identity. Culture Christianity draws the distinction between insider and outsider in Europe. This distinction is tied to an understanding of the Middle Ages, where Europe is seen as standing united under the flag of Christendom. Taking the Crusades as the culmination of the history of Christianity, the present situation is seen as a continuation of the past situation: Islam is an eternal enemy. In Breivik's case, Culture Christianity and Crusader Christianity go hand in hand. We encountered these two Christianities in all the cases we covered throughout our book, even if they were watered down from time to time. The theology of new racism fulfils a function. For Breivik, it legitimizes the terrorist attack on the people whom he characterizes as the elites that have collaborated with Islam in the past and in the potential future. Christianity matters for politics: it's the bulwark against elitist pluralism.

CONCLUSION

The theologies that run through the terrorist attacks don't come out of nowhere. Both Culture Christianity and Crusader Christianity draw on the impact Christianity has had on Europe throughout history. The Church of Norway acknowledged the entanglement of Christianity in racist propaganda and racist politics. This acknowledgement was central in challenging contemporary terrorism in the name of Christianity. In its confrontation with the far right, the Church takes a critical as well as a self-critical approach in order to carve a path out of the new-racist logic. Down to its resources for confirmation classes – classes in which young people are prepared for committing themselves to their churches, classes which shape the future of the church – the Church of Norway couches its response to the rise of the far right in conversations between Judaism, Christianity and Islam. What emerges from our description and discussion of the Church of Norway is the commitment to collaborative rather than competitive inter-faith relations. This commitment is practised in the reflections and resources that are curated by Christians in concert with non-Christians, circulated by the Church. The Church of Norway's commitment has stirred up controversy. Suggestions such as the one that Christians could pray in mosques and that Muslims could pray in churches continue to be controversial. Questions that were raised in this chapter, were:

Can we call far-right terrorists 'Christian'? Why? Why not? How can churches come to terms with the crimes that have been committed in the name of Christianity?
Are there sections or stories in the Bible that you consider racist? What do you do with them? Do you tend to forget them or do you tend to focus on them? Do you read them against the grain?

However you respond to questions like these, the fact that we have to ask and answer them shows that the semantic struggle for Christianity is in full swing.

Chapter 4 covered far-right populism in the name of Christianity. Presenting the case of Germany where populist far-right protesters turned populist far-right politicians, we have argued that the claim to Christianity allows the populist far right to draw a stark distinction between 'the people' and 'the non-people'. Culture Christianity is at work here. Characterizing the current situation as a conspiracy of Muslims and non-Muslims who aim to 'Islamize' Europe by stealth, the populists cast themselves in the guise of victims. The victimhood connects the present critique of the political elites to the past critique of the political elites during the Peaceful Revolution of 1989–90 that brought down the Berlin Wall. This move puts the populists in the position of persecuted Christian protesters revolting against a totalitarian regime. The account of Christians as victims of persecution is a powerful way of drawing on theological traditions.

There are hints of a Crusader Christianity in the populist claims, but the idea of Culture Christians as suffering victims in need of support is much more prominent and pronounced. Again, it's not made up. Theologies responding to Christians' suffering from persecution in the past and in the present are not few and far between. The Bible contains a number of narratives of victimhood that have been used to construct such theologies. Among the populists inside and outside the parliaments, there are Christians who profess faith in Jesus Christ, but their faith is seen as confirming rather than criticizing Culture Christianity. For the populists, the faithful and the faithless can join in their struggle to defend the culture of Europe. Here, too, the theology of new racism fulfils a function. It justifies inequality between those who are culturally Christian and those who are culturally non-Christian – a justification that plays out in calls for diminished policies of immigration and discriminatory policies of integration. Muslims who are always already seen as migrants and migrants who are always already seen as Muslims are the target. There are also calls to take up arms against asylum seekers to protect 'our' borders. Because

CONCLUSION

the justification of these policies is couched in terms of religion rather than race, it allows the populists to present themselves as 'concerned citizens'.

Both mainline churches in Germany – Protestant and Catholic – have responded to the challenge of these 'concerned citizens'. We have chosen statements that showcase two different foci: the one focusing on populism outside churches and the other focusing on populism inside churches. The statement by the Protestants stresses the Church's significance for safeguarding democracy. What the statement calls the 'democratic corridor' – the corridor in which all can come together for deliberation and discussion in order to agree or disagree well – has to be consolidated by churches because churches stand for democracy. The issue we identified here was the absence of any account of Islam. The lack of theological, political or ethical reflection on the role of Islam in democracies runs the risk of confirming the new-racist logic of the clash of cultures that is so crucial to the theologies of the far right. The identification of Christianity with democracy risks sliding down a slippery slope into accounts that see Muslims as, by definition, anti-democratic aliens. Some of the interpretations of Islam that the EKD circulated a while ago corroborate the evidence that it runs the risk of complicity rather than critique of the far right. By contrast, the Catholic Church in Germany confronted populism head-on. Acknowledging the complicity of Christianity with racist ambitions and racist actions throughout history, the authors of the Church's response to populism tackled the far-right claims to Christianity one by one. Like the Church of Norway, the combination of critical and self-critical accounts of Christianity put the Catholic Church in a position to embrace interfaith relations, espousing the idea that the adherents of all monotheistic religions have faith in the same God. Questions that were raised in this chapter were:

Can we call far-right populists 'Christian'? Why? Why not? What is the role of churches in a pluralized and polarized

public? Should they make a political claim or should they maintain a political corridor? Or is the political corridor actually a political claim?
Where do you draw the line between acceptable and unacceptable political positions?

Altogether, Church responses to the populist far right in Germany showcased both the risk and the responsibility that churches have for a democracy that is under pressure from far-right populists. The semantic struggle continues to stir up controversy.

Chapter 5 covered hard-right politics in Great Britain. Drawing on Liz Fekete, who directs the Institute of Race Relations in London, we considered the hard right as a political pattern that is produced by the convergence of various party-political platforms, thus creating the parliamentary (moderate) right in contrast to the extra-parliamentary (less moderate) right. In our discussion of the campaigns for the UK to leave the EU, we teased out how views of Islam and identity were mobilized by prominent figures in the United Kingdom Independence Party and the Conservative Party. Such views, we argued, make use of exclusivist and essentialist notions of religion that are rife in the new racism of far-right circles – regardless of whether the politicians who endorse them counter or confirm more extreme far-right views themselves. Across the party-political spectrum of the Brexit campaign, Islam was identified with doubts and dangers: sometimes the politicians referred to Islam and sometimes the politicians referred to Islamism, but fear was stoked around the Muslim who is not quite at home in the UK – the Muslim as a ticking time bomb. In the hard-right rhetoric of Nigel Farage, Boris Johnson and Theresa May, we found constructions of Islam in contrast to the identity of the UK. UKIP's 'Christian Manifesto' embraced a 'muscular Christianity' that could defend 'the Christian' or 'the Judaeo-Christian' values of the UK against Islam. Here the Culture Christianity of the hard right is palpably present. But even if it is communicated much more carefully – as in May's personal-political claims to Christianity – it fulfils the function of legitimizing inequality: immigrants should be kept out, their rights are unlike 'ours', their responsibilities are unlike 'ours'. This is 'our' home.

In response to political tensions in the UK, the Church of England has addressed the rise of the extreme far right. But while racist extremism in the name of Christianity has been condemned and countered, very little attention has been given to the hard right that mobilizes on the fears of Islam and immigration whipped up in extreme and less extreme circles, turning them into politics and policies. Throughout the pre-referendum and the post-referendum statements that we studied, love of neighbour was espoused by the Church of England. But given that many people in the UK – and not only in the UK – would prefer *not* to have migrants or Muslims as their neighbours, the lack of any account of Islam is striking. The current Archbishop of Canterbury's reflections on Christian Britain could be seen as complacent or even complicit when it comes to far-right views, particularly where he paints a picture of Christianity as a religion of grace in strong and stable contrast with Islam as a religion of law. While we would expect the Archbishop to write about the significance of Christianity for the UK, his claim that only one culture – love-culture versus law-culture, so to speak – can characterize the culture of a country feeds into the narrative of the clash of cultures, whether intentionally or unintentionally. If the gospel is strong enough to stand on its own feet, as the Church of Norway argued, then there is no need for Christians to compete with Muslims. Questions that were raised in this chapter were:

Can we call hard-right politicians 'Christian'? Why? Why not?
Do churches have to make a choice between a Christian culture that excludes Islam and an Islamic culture that excludes Christianity?

Whom would you want as your neighbour? Whom wouldn't you want as your neighbour? Why?

In Chapter 6 we combined our investigation of these three cases, concentrating on the responses of churches to the far right that come in different shapes and different sizes. We condensed these responses into two strategies: the consolidating church and the challenging church. None of the churches we covered map onto these two strategies completely. Yet in order to point out where churches become complicit and where churches counter the far right, it helps to condense the responses into clear and coherent strategies.

In the strategy of the consolidating church, churches are not presented as political players. The churches help to set the parameters in which political players can play. Consequently, the statements of the churches that propose the strategy of the consolidating church suggest that the neutrality of the churches is their strong suit. Congregations are spaces where people of opposing political opinions come together. They are spaces in which democracy is consolidated. However, the strategy of the consolidating church runs a risk. If it includes the identification of Christianity with democracy and democracy with Christianity, it confirms the clash of cultures that traps people in their religious inheritance or their religious identity. It's the risk of new racism.

The statements that tackle the rise of the far right directly rather than indirectly don't fall for the trap of the clash of cultures. These statements showcase the strategy of the challenging church, acknowledging how Christianity has spurred hatred of Islam for hundreds of years. What runs through the statements that favour challenge over consolidation is the idea that churches ought *not* to be neutral. Neutrality comes at the cost of those who are confronted by the rise of the far right. Christianity's preference for the poor – the dismissed, the discarded and the discriminated against – means that churches have to counter such costs. Churches have to stand with the

CONCLUSION

Muslim minorities across Europe. If churches put the preference for the poor into practice, they cannot but challenge their own constituencies and communities. The consolidating church aims for neutrality in order *not* to exclude those on the left or those on the right. The challenging church, however, aims to advocate and act for the poor – *with* the poor. It aims to advocate and act for Muslims – *with* Muslims. Contact, we concluded, is crucial if we are to respond to the far right.

We discussed contact by tackling social psychologist Gordon Allport's contact hypothesis, transposing it from the past to the present. Allport's hypothesis is not the only solution, but it's one way of tackling the questions of neighbourliness that have come up so consistently throughout our book. Our account confirmed that the mechanisms operative in racist prejudice and the mechanisms operative in the countering of racist prejudice are the same for racism and new racism. According to Allport, 'the nub of the matter seems to be that contact must reach below the surface in order to be effective in altering prejudice. Only the type of contact that leads people to *do* things together is likely to result in changed attitudes.'[3] But when it comes to religion, doing things together is tricky. Christianity is not Islam and Islam is not Christianity, so how should the churches produce contact with Muslims? Questions that were raised in this chapter were:

> What does Christianity's preference for the poor mean in practice? Who can and who can't be called 'poor'? Why?
> How could churches call Christians to meet Muslims? What should Christians and Muslims do together? What should Christians and Muslims not do together?
> What is Christianity for you? Do you agree or do you disagree with other Christians or other non-Christians about it? How?

Stressing the significance of contact between religions for challenging the rise of the far right, we suggested that the semantic struggle for Christianity cuts to the core of theology. The identity of Christianity – what is and what isn't Christian – is at stake with the rise of the far right. In order to counter the far right, the identity of Christianity needs to be conceptualized in a new way, in a way that calls for contact. As a consequence, we argued for a turn in the interpretation of identity: from identity as a possession (something we can own) to identity as a project (something we can't own). We acknowledged that this turn avoids a clear-cut conceptualization of who's in and who's out. If such a clear-cut conceptualization could be offered, we would be back with Christianity as a monument or a mausoleum – a Christianity that can cement the clash of cultures.

Instead, the identity of Christianity, we proposed, is a practical project. If Christianity is about following Jesus, it is a matter of figuring out how to 'go and do likewise', to echo Jesus' words at the end of the parable of the Good Samaritan. What such practice looks like is not clear in advance. Could it ever be set in stone? In any case, it's not a matter of each individual figuring it out on their own. The practice of Christianity happens together, it is passed on throughout history, personally and communally.

The turn from possession to project means that far-right figures can claim Christianity too. While some might find it surprising and some might find it shocking that far-right figures can consider themselves to be followers of Jesus Christ, our investigation has shown that they in fact do – sometimes with and sometimes without the churches. Churches telling them they can't won't change anything, because they don't recognize the authority of churches to tell them what they can or can't do. They don't accept that churches have a monopoly on saying what Christianity is or isn't. Christianity can be claimed by everyone.[4] Hence, we suggested that it's more pertinent and more promising to engage in the semantic struggle for Christianity. The upside of engagements in the semantic struggle is that Christians and non-Christians can lay claim to Christianity. Together with Muslims, we can call each other to take responsibility for our religions. In these communal and complementary calls to responsibility, we cannot but make contact with each other – contact that allows us to 'do things together', as Allport argued. Together we can figure out what it means to be Christian, problematizing our own prejudices. We suggest that this call for creative collaboration with Muslims frees churches to offer a challenging but convincing proposal for tackling the rise of the far right. It's challenging for us, because we have to make *changes*. It is convincing for us, because *we* have to make changes. Because Christians belong first and foremost to God – not to a nicely and neatly conceptualized identity of Christianity[5] – we can claim or reclaim Christianity from the clutches of the far right.

Our argument will inevitably meet with criticisms. One criticism is that our turn from identity as a possession to identity as a project means that anything goes. If anybody can decide what Christianity is or isn't, then Christianity can be anything. Our response to this criticism is that we are making decisions about the identity of Christianity all the time. But making these decisions doesn't mean that anything goes. If claiming Christianity is done together, in collaboration rather than competition, then we can call each other to take responsibility for our faith. There are traditions, tropes and texts – the Bible taking pride of place – that we return to again and again when we do theology. But as we have seen, there are many interpretations of these traditions, tropes and texts of Christianity, some with convivial and some with conflictual consequences. Scripture is lived, not a dead document. Churches need to take the plurality of interpretations into account. The collaborative call – the open and open-ended 'we' of Christianity – resists the narrative of a clash of cultures. A monument can be owned. A mausoleum can be owned. But a movement cannot be owned. It's alive. It has to be worked on. Christianity is a work in movement.

It might be argued that the turn from identity as a possession to identity as a project opens Christianity to far-right forces and far-right figures. Are we opening the doors of churches to racism? Our response is that the history of Christianity demonstrates that churches have in fact been open to racist and new-racist rhetoric. We are not interested in discussing whether racism is valid or invalid, whether a biological or a theological logic (or a toxic mix of the two) is used to stereotype the other. Racial differentiations were debunked a long time ago. There can be no neutrality in the confrontation with racism or new racism. But confronting new racism means coming up with convincing and challenging proposals that counter acts of stereotyping. The doors of churches need to be kept wide open because openness enables the contact that combats such stereotyping. But openness is not neutrality.

Our turn from identity as a possession to identity as a project could be criticized for moving the clash of cultures from the outside to the inside of Christianity. In the semantic struggle, this Christianity butts against that Christianity, causing a clash between Christians. Our response to this criticism is that we haven't moved a clash of cultures into the churches. The semantic struggle for Christianity has been there, whether we choose to see it or not. Our suggestion is to own up to it, to see it as a chance. In order to resist the far-right rhetoric of the clash of cultures, it is crucial to put the spotlight on the cracks in Christianity past and present, its internal diversity and its internal differences. These cracks offer us the chance to claim Christianity in a way that counters the strict and stable distinction between insiders and outsiders so crucial to the new racism of the far right.

We suggest that the semantic struggle for Christianity is a promising and pertinent point of departure for a theology that can resist the rise of the far right. Reclaiming Christianity in response to the far right requires Christians to collaborate with non-Christians. It requires becoming and being neighbours to Muslims. Of course, Christians need to recognize and respect the fact that not all Muslims might welcome them with open arms. Yet many Muslims have invited Christians to become and be their neighbours. 'A Common Word between Us and You' is a letter, endorsed by more than a hundred Muslims – spiritual and political representatives from a variety of countries who exercise influence over millions of Muslims[6] – to Christians all over the world.[7] The letter suggests that what Christians call the double commandment of love – love God and love your neighbour (Deut. 6.4–5; Lev. 19.17–18; Matt. 22.35–40; Mark 12.28–34; Luke 10.27) – is part and parcel of 'the very foundational principles of both faiths'.[8] Christians can learn from Muslims and Muslims can learn from Christians here. There is 'common ground' shared by Jews, Christians and Muslims.[9] In the commentaries to 'A Common Word Between Us and You', conflicts are acknowledged, including terrorism in the name of God.[10] As one of the commentators argues: 'With such an explosive mix, … conflicts – even unto genocides – are lurking around the corner.'[11] Yet the construct of the clash of cultures is criticized: Muslims aren't against Christians and Christians aren't against Muslims.[12] On the contrary, all are called to love their neighbours. This invitation to neighbourliness is a promising point of departure to tackle the rise of the far right in practice: where there is a common word there can be a common world.

A lot is done in practice, both inside and outside churches. We have examined the statements made by churches and church representatives. But much of what is done is done in congregations and communities away from the public eye, sometimes with and sometimes without church leadership involvement. While writing and working on this book, we have come across a variety of very good practices.

According to a report from the Church Council of the Church of Norway, there are a number of initiatives run by congregations in which Muslim migrants work with Christians and Christians work with Muslim migrants.[13] One example is 'Hope Evenings' in a diocese in the north of Norway. On one of these evenings, a Muslim asylum seeker rapped about his hopes and dreams for the future. A conversation about the rap followed. The rapper challenged the Norwegians present on their capacity to understand. The experience is described by the church representative as revelatory: 'Incredibly powerful to get to be church amongst Christian and Muslim asylum seekers ... I will probably only understand some of the hopes and dreams they have. But we can be together anyway.'[14] As the report sums up such encounters, it is a matter of being a 'good neighbour'.

In Germany, the chairmen of both mainline churches – Bishop Heinrich Bedford-Strohm, representing German Protestantism, and Archbishop Reinhold Marx, representing German Catholicism – were among the first to welcome the many migrants who arrived in Munich in the summer of 2015, mainly from Muslim majority countries. Their smartphones were buzzing with news of the trains coming in, the two representatives told reporters in retrospect, as they were having lunch together.[15] Spontaneously, they made their way to the station where they welcomed the refugees, shaking hands with the arrivers, talking and thanking those who made the warm welcome possible. The scenes of these handshakes, broadcast around the world, continue to symbolize the welcome of Muslim migrants into Germany.

In the UK, there are many churches that support mosques and many mosques that support churches. A Church of England vicar, Bonnie Evans-Hills, tells one such story of support: 'After hearing there was going to be a protest by the English Defence League outside their mosque ..., a mosque community in York decided to open their doors and offer tea and biscuits. Local clergy came to support. When seven EDL supporters came along to the protest, they shouted outside for a bit, and then, following some friendly conversation, were invited into the mosque for tea ... Their actions inspired a new Facebook group which quickly went viral. The Tea Defence League was born.'[16]

Given these collaborative responses to the rise of the far right, our argument for reclaiming Christianity isn't new at

CONCLUSION

all. We have aimed to offer theological reasons and a theological rationale that help those who are resisting the far right by reclaiming Christianity together with Muslims. Whether and where our suggestions have been helpful (or unhelpful) is of course up to the reader. All we can do in conclusion is to point to practice. When Jesus presents the parable of the Good Samaritan as his interpretation of the double commandment of love, he offers no constraints for the commandment: it's valid when you meet people who share and people who don't share your beliefs and background. The fact that the one who helps does not share the same beliefs and background as the one who needs help suggests that shared beliefs and background might not be the point of the parable. The point is practice: 'Go and do likewise'.

Notes

Chapter 1

1 Harald S. Klungtveit, 12 August 2019, 'PST: – Overasskende mange i Norge som sympatiserer med høyrekstrem terror', *Filter Nyheter*, available at https://filternyheter.no/pst-overraskende-mange-i-norge-som-sympatiserer-med-hoyreekstreme-terrorhandlinger/ (accessed 19.11.2019).

2 Johannes Radke und Toralf Staud, 19 June 2019, 'Die falschen Vorstellungen von rechtsextremem Terror', *Die Zeit*, available at www.zeit.de/gesellschaft/2019-06/rechter-terror-rechtsextremismus-attentat-ermittlungen (accessed 19.11.2019).

3 Vikram Dodd and Jamie Grierson, 19 September 2019, 'Fastest growing UK terrorist threat is from far right, say police', the *Guardian*, available at www.theguardian.com/uk-news/2019/sep/19/fastest-growing-uk-terrorist-threat-is-from-far-right-say-police (accessed 19.11.2019).

4 Antonis A. Ellinas, 2010, *The Media and the Far Right in Western Europe*, Cambridge: Cambridge University Press, p. 5.

5 Andrea Mammone, Emmanuel Godin and Brian Jenkins, 2012, 'Introduction: Mapping the "right of the mainstream right" in contemporary Europe' in Andrea Mammone, Emmanuel Godin and Brian Jenkins (eds), *Mapping the Extreme Right in Contemporary Europe: From Local to Transnational*, London: Routledge, pp. 1–14, p. 3.

6 Jean-Yves Camus and Nicolas Lebourg, 2017, *Far-Right Politics in Europe*, trans. Jane Marie Todd, Cambridge, MA: Belknap Press, p. 45.

7 Ellinas, *The Media and the Far Right in Western Europe*, p. 6.

8 See Sturla J. Stålsett, 2017, *Religion i urolige tider: Globalisering, religiøsitet og sårbarhet*, Oslo: Cappelen Damm.

9 Ellinas, *The Media and the Far Right in Western Europe*, p. 10.

10 Ellinas, *The Media and the Far Right in Western Europe*, p. 11.

11 Mammone, Godin and Jenkins, 'Introduction: Mapping the "right of the mainstream right" in contemporary Europe', p. 5.

12 René Girard has studied this process of 'scapegoating'. See the classic René Girard, 1986, *The Scapegoat*, trans. Yvonne Frecceru, Baltimore: The Johns Hopkins University Press.

13 See Julia Ebner, 2017, *The Rage: The Vicious Circle of Islamist and Far-Right Extremism*, London: Bloomsbury, who explores how far-right terror enables and reinforces Islamic terror and how Islamic terror enables and reinforces far-right terror.

14 Mammone, Godin and Jenkins, 'Introduction: Mapping the "right of the mainstream right" in contemporary Europe', p. 6.

15 Mammone, Godin and Jenkins, 'Introduction: Mapping the "right of the mainstream right" in contemporary Europe', p. 4.

16 Mammone, Godin and Jenkins, 'Introduction: Mapping the "right of the mainstream right" in contemporary Europe', p. 4.

17 Rita Chin, 2017, *The Crisis of Multiculturalism in Europe: A History*, Princeton: Princeton University Press, p. 140.

18 See the contributions to Maleiha Malik (ed.), 2010, *Anti-Muslim Prejudice: Past and Present*, Abingdon: Routledge.

19 See Samuel P. Huntington, 1996, *The Clash of Civilizations and the Remaking of World Order*, New York: Simon and Schuster.

20 Samuel P. Huntington, 1993, 'The Clash of Civilizations' in *The Clash of Civilizations? The Debate*, New York: Foreign Affairs, pp. 22–49, p. 31.

21 See Chiara Bottici and Benoît Challand, 2010, *The Myth of the Clash of Civilizations*, London: Routledge.

22 Rogers Brubaker, 'Between nationalism and civilizationism: the European populist moment in comparative perspective', *Ethnic and Racial Studies*, 40/8 (2017), pp. 1191–226. For a critical account of Brubaker's methodology, see Ulrich Schmiedel, 'The Cracks in the Category of Christianism: A Call for Ambiguity in the Conceptualisation of Christianity' in Cecilia Nahnfeldt and Kaia S. Rønsdal (eds), 2020, *Christian-Cultural Values in Migration Encounters: Troubled Identities in the Nordic Region?*, London: Routledge, forthcoming.

23 For the concept of lived religion, see Robert Orsi, 2005, *Between Heaven and Earth: The Religious Worlds People Make and the Scholars Who Study Them*, Princeton: Princeton University Press. See also the contributions to David D. Hall (ed.), 1997, *Lived Religion in America: Toward a History of Practice*, Princeton: Princeton University Press.

24 Unless specified otherwise we make use of the New Revised Standard Version for all biblical references.

25 Werner G. Jeanrond, 2010, *A Theology of Love*, London: Bloomsbury, p. 34.

26 Werner G. Jeanrond, 2013, 'Love' in Nicholas Adams, George Pattison and Graham Ward (eds), *The Oxford Handbook of Theol-*

ogy and Modern European Thought, Oxford: Oxford University Press, pp. 233–52.

27 Jeanrond, *A Theology of Love*, p. 35.

28 For the chequered career of the parable in politics, see Nick Spencer, 2017, *The Political Samaritan: How Power Hijacked a Parable*, London: Bloomsbury.

29 For a similar approach, see the research on 'ordinary theology'. Jeff Astley, 2002, *Ordinary Theology: Looking, Listening and Learning in Theology*, Farnham: Ashgate; Jeff Astley and Leslie J. Francis (eds), 2013, *Exploring Ordinary Theology: Everyday Christian Believing and the Church*, Farnham: Ashgate.

30 Mahmoud Ayoub, 2007, *A Muslim View of Christianity: Essays on Dialogue*, ed. Irfan A. Omar, Maryknoll: Orbis, p. 14.

31 Liane Bednarz, 2018, *Die Angstprediger: Wie rechte Christen Gesellschaft und Kirchen unterwandern*, München: Droemer, p. 9, who in turn borrows the concept from Thomas Seiterich.

32 Bednarz, *Die Angstprediger*, p. 7.

33 Brian Klug, 2009, *Offence: The Jewish Case*, London: Seagull Books, p. 23. Klug's argument is about claims to Judaism, but we see no reason not to apply it to Christianity.

34 This requirement is confirmed by Jewish theologian Ephraim Meir, 2017, *Becoming Interreligious: Towards a Dialogical Theology from a Jewish Vantage Point*, Münster: Waxmann, pp. 17–18, and by Muslim theologian Mahmoud Ayoub, 2007, *A Muslim View of Christianity: Essays on Dialogue*, ed. Irfan A. Omar, Maryknoll: Orbis, pp. 15–16.

35 Ayoub, *A Muslim View of Christianity*, p. 15. However, for the idea of multiple religious belonging, see the contributions to Catherine Cornille (ed.), 2002, *Many Mansions? Multiple Religious Belonging and Christian Identity*, Maryknoll: Orbis.

36 For the concept of the hard right, see Liz Fekete, 2019, *Europe's Fault Lines: Racism and the Rise of the Right*, London: Verso, pp. 7–9.

37 If not stated otherwise, all translations from primary and secondary literature are our own.

38 See Steve Bruce, 2011, *Secularization: In Defence of an Unfashionable Theory*, Oxford: Oxford University Press.

39 For the discussion, see José Casanova, 1994, *Public Religions in the Modern World*, Chicago: University of Chicago Press; Charles Taylor, 2007, *A Secular Age*, Cambridge, MA: Belknap Press; Hans Joas, 2014, *Faith as an Option: Possible Futures for Christianity*, trans. Alex Skinner, Stanford: Stanford University Press.

40 See Chris Allen, 'Nur "einsame Wölfe"? Rechtsterrorismus als transnationales Phänomen', *Aus Politik und Zeitgeschichte*, 49/50 (2019), pp. 20–6.

Chapter 2

1 Jean-Yves Camus and Nicolas Lebourg, 2017, *Far-Right Politics in Europe*, trans. Jane Marie Todd, Cambridge, MA: Belknap Press, p. 52.

2 See Wendy Brown, 2006, 'Subjects of Tolerance: Why We Are Civilized and They Are the Barbarians' in Hent de Vries and Lawrence E. Sullivan (eds), *Political Theologies: Public Religions in a Post-Secular Age*, New York: Fordham University Press, pp. 298–317.

3 Gabriella Lazaridis, Giovanna Campani and Anne Benveniste, 2016, 'Introduction' in Gabriella Lazaridis, Giovanna Campani and Annie Benveniste (eds), *The Rise of the Far Right in Europe: Populist Shifts and 'Othering'*, New York: Palgrave Macmillan, pp. 1–23, pp. 3–4.

4 Annie Benveniste and Etienne Pingaud, 2016, 'Far-Right Movements in France: The Principal Role of Front National and the Rise of Islamophobia' in Gabriella Lazaridis, Giovanna Campani and Annie Benveniste (eds), *The Rise of the Far Right in Europe: Populist Shifts and 'Othering'*, New York: Palgrave Macmillan, pp. 55–79, p. 55.

5 Olivier Roy, 2016, 'The French National Rally: From Christian Identity to *Laïcité*' in Nadia Marzouki, Duncan McDonnell and Olivier Roy (eds), *Saving the People: How Populists Hijack Religion*, London: Hurst & Co, pp. 79–93, p. 80.

6 Benveniste and Pingaud, 'Far-Right Movements in France', p. 63.

7 Benveniste and Pingaud, 'Far-Right Movements in France', p. 62. For more on the French far right, see James McAuley and Greil Marcus with a response from Mark Lilla, 17 January 2019, 'How to Write about the Right', *The New York Review of Books*, www.nybooks.com/articles/2019/01/17/how-to-write-about-the-right-an-exchange/ (accessed 19.11.2019).

8 Samuel P. Huntington, 1993, 'The Clash of Civilizations' in *The Clash of Civilizations? The Debate*, New York: Foreign Affairs, pp. 22–49, pp. 24–25.

9 Huntington, 'The Clash of Civilizations', pp. 24–25.

10 Huntington, 'The Clash of Civilizations', p. 27.

11 Huntington, 'The Clash of Civilizations', p. 26.

12 Huntington, 'The Clash of Civilizations', p. 26.

13 Huntington, 'The Clash of Civilizations', p. 27.

14 Huntington, 'The Clash of Civilizations', p. 29.

15 Huntington, 'The Clash of Civilizations', p. 31.

16 Stuart Hall, 1992, 'The West and the Rest: Discourse and Power' in Stuart Hall and Bram Gieben (eds), *Formations of Modernity*, Cambridge: Polity Press, pp. 185–227.

17 Huntington, 'The Clash of Civilizations', p. 31.

18 Huntington, 'The Clash of Civilizations', p. 31.

19 Huntington, 'The Clash of Civilizations', p. 31, citing Bernard Lewis, 'The Roots of Muslim Rage', *The Atlantic*, September (1990), pp. 47–54.
20 Arshin Adib-Moghaddam, 2011, *A Metahistory of the Clash of Civilisations: Us and Them Beyond Orientalism*, New York: Columbia University Press, p. 1.
21 See Hugh Goddard, 2020, *A History of Christian-Muslim Relations*, 2nd edn, Edinburgh: Edinburgh University Press.
22 Alfred Dregger, cited in Rita Chin, 2017, *The Crisis of Multiculturalism in Europe: A History*, Princeton: Princeton University Press, p. 159.
23 Chin, *The Crisis of Multiculturalism in Europe*, p. 160.
24 Chin, *The Crisis of Multiculturalism in Europe*, pp. 139–40.
25 Mehdi Semati, 'Islamophobia, Culture and Race in the Age of Empire', *Cultural Studies*, 24/2 (2010), pp. 256–75, p. 266.
26 See Nasar Meer and Tariq Modood, 2010, 'Refutations of Racism in the "Muslim Question"' in Maleiha Malik (ed.), *Anti-Muslim Prejudice: Past and Present*, Abingdon: Routledge, pp. 126–45, where Islamophobia is defined as racism.
27 Nasar Meer discusses intersections of race and religion in relation to Islamophobia in Nasar Meer, 'Racialization and religion: race, culture and difference in the study of antisemitism and Islamophobia', *Ethnic and Racial Studies*, 36/3 (2013), pp. 385–98.
28 J. Kameron Carter, 2009, *Race: A Theological Account*, Oxford: Oxford University Press; Willie James Jennings, 2010, *The Christian Imagination: Theology and the Origins of Race*, New Haven: Yale University Press.
29 Jennings, *The Christian Imagination*, pp. 6 and 8.
30 Jennings, *The Christian Imagination*, p. 9. Jennings goes on to caution against the use of the term 'reconciliation' (p. 10).
31 Thomas Lynch, 'Social Construction and social critique: Haslanger, race, and the study of religion', *Critical Research on Religion*, 5/3 (2017), pp. 284–301, p. 293.
32 Lynch, 'Social Construction and social critique', p. 293.
33 There is much discussion about different forms of racism, such as biological racism as 'modern racism' and cultural racism as 'imperial racism'. See for instance, Michael Hardt and Antonio Negri, 2000, *Empire*, Cambridge, MA: Harvard University Press; Étienne Balibar, 1991, 'Is there a "Neo-Racism"?' in Étienne Balibar and Immanuel Wallerstein (eds), *Race, Nation, Class: Ambiguous Identities*, London, Verso, pp. 17–28.
34 See Naika Foroutan, 2019, *Die postmigrantische Gesellschaft: Ein Versprechen der pluralen Demokratie*, Bielefeld: Transcript, pp. 81–3.
35 Chin, *The Crisis of Multiculturalism in Europe*, pp. 237–86.

36 Liane Bednarz, 2018, *Die Angstprediger: Wie rechte Christen Gesellschaft und Kirchen unterwandern*, München: Droemer, pp. 43–50.

37 Hans-Georg Betz, 2007, 'Against the "Green Totalitarianism": Anti-Islamic Nativism in Contemporary Radical Right-Wing Populism in Western Europe' in Christina Schori Liang (ed.), *Europe for the Europeans: The Foreign and Security Policy of the Populist Radical Right*, Aldershot: Ashgate, pp. 33–54, p. 34.

38 Farid Hafez, 'Shifting borders: Islamophobia as common ground for building pan-European right-wing unity', *Patterns of Prejudice*, 48/5 (2014), pp. 479–99, p. 487.

39 Bednarz, *Die Angstprediger*, pp. 127–54.

40 Ruth Wodak, 2015, *The Politics of Fear: What Right-Wing Populist Discourses Mean*, London: Sage, p. 4.

41 Wodak, *The Politics of Fear*, p. 2.

42 Mehdi Semati, 'Islamophobia, Culture and Race in the Age of Empire', *Cultural Studies*, 24/2 (2010), pp. 256–75, pp. 257 and 269.

43 Gert Pickel, 2018, 'Perceptions of Plurality: The Impact of the Refugee Crisis on the Interpretation of Religious Pluralization in Europe' in Ulrich Schmiedel and Graeme Smith (eds), *Religion in the European Refugee Crisis*, New York: Palgrave Macmillan, pp. 15–37, p. 35.

44 Pickel, 'Perceptions of Plurality', p. 16.

45 Olivier Roy, 2016, 'Beyond Populism: The Conservative Right, the Courts, the Churches and the Concept of a Christian Europe' in Nadia Marzouki, Duncan McDonnell and Olivier Roy (eds), *Saving the People: How Populists Hijack Religion*, London: Hurst & Co, pp. 185–201, p. 187.

46 Roy, 'Beyond Populism', p. 187.

47 Bednarz, *Die Angstprediger*, pp. 154–162.

48 Thomas Grumke, 2012, 'Globalized Anti-Globalists – The Ideological Basis of the Internationalization of Right-Wing Extremism' in Uwe Backes and Patrick Moreau (eds), *The Extreme Right in Europe: Current Trends and Perspectives*, Göttingen: Vandenhoeck & Ruprecht, pp. 323–32, p. 329.

49 For the turn from the emancipation of Jews to the integration of Muslims, see Wolfgang Benz, 2013, *Ansturm auf das Abendland? Zur Wahrnehmung des Islam in der westlichen Gesellschaft*, Wien: Picus, pp. 32–3.

50 Patrik Hermansson, 26 May 2019, 'Matteo Salvini is spearheading an ultra-right alliance to cause havoc across the EU', *The Independent*, available at www.independent.co.uk/voices/matteo-salvini-eu-far-right-rally-marine-le-pen-italy-immigration-extremism-a8930746.html (accessed 19.11.2019).

51 Benveniste and Pingaud, 'Far-Right Movements in France', p. 63.

52 Benz, *Ansturm auf das Abendland?*, p. 42.
53 Benz, *Ansturm auf das Abendland?*, p. 42.
54 Hafez, 'Shifting borders', p. 486.
55 Hafez, 'Shifting borders', p. 486.
56 Wodak, *The Politics of Fear*, p. 120.
57 Wodak, *The Politics of Fear*, p. 120.
58 Hafez, 'Shifting borders', p. 484.
59 See Mattias Martinson, 2015, 'Towards a "Theology" of Christian Monumentality: Post-Christian Reflections on Grace and Nature' in Jonna Bornemark, Mattias Martinson and Jayne Svenungsson (eds), *Monument and Memory*, Berlin: Lit Verlag, pp. 21–42. See also Mattias Martinson, 2017, *Sekularism, populism, xenofobi: En essä om religionsdebatten*, Malmö: Eskaton.
60 Chin, *The Crisis of Multiculturalism in Europe*, p. 181.
61 Chin, *The Crisis of Multiculturalism in Europe*, p. 181.
62 For a nuanced account of the responses to the attack, see Brian Klug, 'In the heat of the moment: Bringing "Je suis Charlie" into focus', *French Cultural Studies*, 27/3 (2016), pp. 223–32.
63 Betz, 'Against the "Green Totalitarianism"', p. 42.
64 Duncan McDonnell, 2016, 'The Lega Nord: The New Saviour of Northern Italy' in Nadia Marzouki, Duncan McDonnell and Olivier Roy (eds), *Saving the People: How Populists Hijack Religion*, London: Hurst & Co, pp. 13–28, p. 23.
65 Antonis A. Ellinas, 2010, *The Media and the Far Right in Western Europe*, Cambridge: Cambridge University Press, p. 225. See also Seyyed-Abdolhamid Mirhosseini and Hossein Rouzbeh (eds), 2017, *Instances of Islamophobia: Demonizing the Muslim Other*, Lanham: Lexington.
66 Benveniste and Pingaud, 'Far-Right Movements in France', p. 56.
67 See for instances the essays collected in Bat Ye'or, 2013, *Understanding Dhimmitude: Twenty-One Lectures and Talks on the Position of Non-Muslims in Islamic Societies*, New York: RVP Press.
68 See Øyvind Strømmen, 2014, *I Hatets Fotspor*, Oslo: Cappelen Damm and Øyvind Strømmen, 2012, *Det Mørke Nettet: Om Høyreekstremisme, kontrajihadisme og terror i Europa*, Cappelen Damm.
69 Sindre Bangstad, 2014, *Anders Breivik and the Rise of Islamophobia*, London: Zed Books, p. 155.
70 See the essay titled 'Christians and Jews: The Forbidden History', in Bat Ye'or, 2013, *Understanding Dhimmitude: Twenty-One Lectures and Talks on the Position of Non-Muslims in Islamic Societies*, New York: RVP Press, pp. 46–55.
71 Ye'or, *Understanding Dhimmitude*, p. 53.
72 Ye'or, *Understanding Dhimmitude*, pp. 126 and 219.
73 Ye'or, *Understanding Dhimmitude*, p. 18.

74 Bangstad, *Anders Breivik and the Rise of Islamophobia*, p. 146.
75 Bangstad, *Anders Breivik and the Rise of Islamophobia*, p. 147.
76 Mattias Ekman, 'Online Islamophobia and the politics of fear: manufacturing the green scare', *Ethnic and Racial Studies*, 38/11 (2015), pp. 1986–2002, p. 1993.
77 Ekman, 'Online Islamophobia', p. 1992.
78 Ekman, 'Online Islamophobia', p. 1994.
79 Ekman, 'Online Islamophobia', p. 1997.
80 Chin, *The Crisis of Multiculturalism in Europe*, p. 281.
81 Ekman, 'Online Islamophobia', p. 1986.
82 Ekman, 'Online Islamophobia', p. 1986.
83 David Art, 2012, 'Memory Politics in Western Europe' in Uwe Backes and Patrick Moreau (eds), *The Extreme Right in Europe: Current Trends and Perspectives*, Göttingen: Vandenhoeck & Ruprecht, pp. 359–81, p. 359.
84 Nicholas L. Paul, 2019, 'Modern Intolerance and the Medieval Crusades' in Andrew Albin, Mary C. Erler, Thomas O'Donnell, Nicholas L. Paul, and Nina Rowe (eds), *Whose Middle Ages? Teachable Moments for an Ill-Used Past*, New York: Fordham University Press, pp. 34–43, p. 35.
85 Kristin Skottki, 2018, 'The Dead, the Revived and the Recreated Pasts: "Structural Amnesia" in Representations of Crusade History"' in Mike Horswell and Jonathan Phillips (eds), *Perceptions of the Crusades from the Nineteenth to the Twenty-First Century*, London: Routledge, pp. 107–32, p. 121.
86 Thomas F. Madden, 'Crusade Myths', *Catholic Dossier*, 1 (2002), available at www.ignatiusinsight.com/features2005/tmadden_crusade myths_feb05.asp (accessed 19.11.2019). See also Thomas F. Madden, 2017, *The Crusades Controversy: Setting the Record Straight*, North Palm Beach: Wellspring.
87 Skottki, 'The Dead, the Revived and the Recreated Pasts', pp. 107–32.
88 See the contributions to Jonathan Riley-Smith (ed.), 1999, *The Oxford History of the Crusades*, Oxford: Oxford University Press.
89 Roy, 'Beyond Populism', p. 193.
90 James Crossley, 2018, *Cults, Martyrs and Good Samaritans*, London: Pluto Press, p. 70.
91 Crossley, *Cults, Martyrs and Good Samaritans*, p. 71.
92 Crossley, *Cults, Martyrs and Good Samaritans*, p. 71.
93 Ben Quinn, 24 August 2016, 'French police make woman remove clothing on Nice beach following burkini ban', the *Guardian*, www.theguardian.com/world/2016/aug/24/french-police-make-woman-remove-burkini-on-nice-beach (accessed 19.11.2019).
94 Mona Eltahawy, 2019, 'Too Loud, Swears Too Much and Goes

Too Far' in Mariam Khan (ed.), *It's Not About the Burqa: Muslim Women on Faith, Feminism, Sexuality and Race*, London: Picador, pp. 3–10, p. 4.

95 Wodak, *The Politics of Fear*, p. 174.

96 Najib George Awad, 'Religio-Phobia: Western Islam, Social Integration and the Resurgence of Religiosity in Europe', *The Muslim World* (2014), pp. 433–47, p. 434.

97 Awad, 'Religio-Phobia', pp. 444–6.

98 See Talal Asad, 2003, *Formations of the Secular: Christianity, Islam, Modernity*, Stanford: Stanford University Press.

99 Roy, 'Beyond Populism', p. 186.

100 Birgit Sauer and Edma Ajanovic, 2016, 'Hegemonic Discourses of Difference and Inequality: Right-Wing Organisations in Austria' in Gabriella Lazaridis, Giovanna Campani and Annie Benveniste (eds), *The Rise of the Far Right in Europe: Populist Shifts and 'Othering'*, New York: Palgrave Macmillan, pp. 81–108, p. 94.

101 Sauer and Ajanovic, 'Hegemonic Discourses of Difference and Inequality', p. 94.

102 Nadia Marzouki and Duncan McDonnell, 2016, 'Populism and Religion' in Nadia Marzouki, Duncan McDonnell and Olivier Roy (eds), *Saving the People: How Populists Hijack Religion*, London: Hurst & Co, pp. 1–11, p. 7.

103 Duncan McDonnell, 2016, 'The Lega Nord: The New Saviour of Northern Italy' in Nadia Marzouki, Duncan McDonnell and Olivier Roy (eds), *Saving the People: How Populists Hijack Religion*, London: Hurst & Co, pp. 13–28, p. 13.

104 Giovanna Campani, 2016, 'Neo-fascism from the Twentieth Century to the Third Millennium: The Case of Italy' in Gabriella Lazaridis, Giovanna Campani and Annie Benveniste (eds), *The Rise of the Far Right in Europe: Populist Shifts and 'Othering'*, New York: Palgrave Macmillan, pp. 25–54, p. 45.

105 McDonnell, 'The Lega Nord:', p. 19.

106 Cited in Olivier Roy, 'The French National Rally: From Christian Identity to Laïcité', p. 91.

107 Roy, 'The French National Rally', p. 91.

108 Roy, 'The French National Rally', p. 91.

109 It is important to note here that not only far-right figures make the case for a coupling of Christian and European values. For instance, in the court cases that culminated in Lautsi v. Italy in 2011, the Italian court held that the crucifix is a symbol of secular, European values. Far-right figures are emphasising issues that are already in more mainstream discussions about religion in Europe.

110 Roy, 'The French National Rally', p. 86.

111 Roy, 'The French National Rally', p. 86.

NOTES TO CHAPTER 2

112 Campani, 'Neo-fascism from the Twentieth Century to the Third Millennium: The Case of Italy', p. 44.

113 Campani, 'Neo-fascism from the Twentieth Century to the Third Millennium: The Case of Italy', p. 44.

114 Campani, 'Neo-fascism from the Twentieth Century to the Third Millennium: The Case of Italy', p. 44.

115 McDonnell, 'The Lega Nord', p. 20.

116 Campani, 'Neo-fascism from the Twentieth Century to the Third Millennium: The Case of Italy', p. 44. For debates about the display of crosses in the public sphere, see Johanna Gustafsson Lundberg, 2018, 'Christianity in a Post-Christian Context: Immigration, Church Identity, and the Role of Religion in Public Debates' in Ulrich Schmiedel and Graeme Smith (eds), *Religion in the European Refugee Crisis*, pp. 123–43, and Ulrich Schmiedel, '"Take Up Your Cross": Public Theology between Populism and Pluralism in the Post-Migrant Context', *International Journal of Public Theology*, 13 (2019), pp. 140–62.

117 See Angela Giuffrida, 7 August 2019, 'Matteo Salvini embarks on beach tour amid election', the *Guardian*, available at www.theguardian.com/world/2019/aug/07/italy-matteo-salvini-embarks-on-beach-tour-amid-election-speculation (accessed 19.11.2019).

118 See Bednarz, *Die Angstprediger*, pp. 66–115.

119 For a nuanced account, see Bonnie Evans-Hills, 2015, 'Speaking the Unspeakable – Is It Possible to be Muslim and Gay?' in Bonnie Evans-Hills and Michael Rusk, *Engaging Islam from a Christian Perspective*, London: Peter Lang, pp. 227–46.

120 Eszter Kováts, 2017, 'The Emergence of Powerful Anti-Gender Movements in Europe and the Crisis of Liberal Democracy' in Michaela Köttig, Renate Bitzan and Andrea Pető (eds), *Gender and Far Right Politics in Europe*, London: Palgrave Macmillan, pp. 175–89, p. 179.

121 Silke Baer, Oliver Kossack and Anika Posselius, 2017, 'Gender Might be the Key. Gender-Reflective Approaches and Guidelines in Prevention of and Intervention in Right-Wing Extremism in Europe' in Michaela Köttig, Renate Bitzan and Andrea Pető (eds), *Gender and Far Right Politics in Europe*, London: Palgrave Macmillan, pp. 351–68, p. 353.

122 Jörg Lauster, 2014, *Die Verzauberung der Welt: Eine Kulturgeschichte des Christentums*, Munich: C. H. Beck.

123 Hall, 'The West and the Rest', p. 215.

124 Hall, 'The West and the Rest', p. 215.

125 Hall, 'The West and the Rest', p. 216.

126 For the classic conceptualisation, see Benedict Anderson, 2006, *Imagined Communities: Reflections on the Origin and Spread of Nationalism*, revised edn, London: Verso.

127 Jayne Svenungsson, 2014, 'Christian Europe: Borders and

NOTES TO CHAPTER 2

Boundaries of a Mythological Conception' in Susanna Lindberg, Sergei Prozorov and Mika Ojakangas (eds), *Transcending Europe: Beyond Universalism and Particularism*, New York: Palgrave Macmillan, pp. 120–34.

128 See Bednarz, *Die Angstprediger*, pp. 13–65.

129 Lundberg, 'Christianity in a Post-Christian Context: Immigration, Church Identity and the Role of Religion in Public Debates', p. 143.

Chapter 3

1 The title alludes to the Siege of Vienna in 1683, when the city was successfully defended against the Ottoman empire.

2 Jorunn Økland, 2012, 'Feminismen, Tradisjonen og Forventning' in Anders Ravik Jupskås (ed.), *Akademiske Perspektiver På 22. Juli*, Bergen: Fagbokforlaget, pp. 115–28, p. 121.

3 Øyvind Strømmen, 2014, *I Hatets Fotspor*, Oslo: Cappelen Damm, p. 51.

4 Strømmen, *I Hatets Fotspor*, pp. 102–3. See also Øyvind Strømmen, 2012, *Det Mørke Nettet: Om Høyreekstremisme, kontrajihadisme og terror i Europa*, Oslo: Cappelen Damm.

5 Jean-Yves Camus and Nicolas Lebourg, 2017, *Far-Right Politics in Europe*, trans. Jane Marie Todd, Cambridge, MA: Belknap Press, p. 112.

6 Camus and Lebourg, *Far-Right Politics in Europe*, p. 113.

7 Sindre Bangstad, 16 September 2019, 'Norway is in denial about the threat of far-right violence', the *Guardian*, available at www.theguardian.com/commentisfree/2019/sep/16/norway-denial-far-right-violence-breivik (accessed 19.11.2019).

8 Camus and Lebourg, *Far-Right Politics in Europe*, p. 114.

9 Throughout this chapter, we are drawing on Hannah Strømmen, 'Christian Terror in Europe? The Bible in Anders Behring Breivik's Manifesto', *The Journal of the Bible and its Reception*, 4/1 (2017), pp. 147–69; Hannah Strømmen, 'Biblical Blood-Lines: From Foundational Corpus to Far Right Bible', *Biblical Interpretation*, 25/4–5 (2017), pp. 555–73.

10 Breivik's Manifesto, '2083 – A European Declaration of Independence', p. 1404. The manifesto is available at publicintelligence.net/anders-behring-breiviks-complete-manifesto-2083-a-european-declaration-of-independence/. The biblical references in the manifesto are taken from different translations. We follow the manifesto's usage.

11 Manifesto, p. 1308.

12 See for instance, 16 March 2016, 'Breivik: Odin er min gud', in

NOTES TO CHAPTER 3

Nettavisen, available at www.nettavisen.no/nyheter/innenriks/breivik--odin-er-min-gud/3423203770.html (accessed 19.11.2019).

13 Franco 'Bifo' Berardi, 2015, *Heroes: Mass Murder and Suicide*, London: Verso, pp. 96–7.

14 Berardi, *Heroes*, p. 97.

15 Manifesto, p. 1308.

16 For a discussion of how ideas about the Bible have informed constructions of Western culture in opposition to Islam, see Yvonne Sherwood, 'Bush's Bible as a Liberal Bible (Strange Though That Might Seem)', *Postscripts*, 2.1 (2006), pp. 47–58. See also Yvonne Sherwood, 2012, *Biblical Blaspheming: Trials of the Sacred for a Secular Age*, Cambridge: Cambridge University Press, particularly pp. 321–9.

17 See Jörg Lauster, 2016, *Die Verzauberung der Welt: Eine Kulturgeschichte des Christentums*, Munich: C.H. Beck.

18 Thomas Hylland Eriksen, 2012, 'Renhetsideologi i en uren tid' in Anders Ravik Jupskås (ed.), *Akademiske Perspektiver På 22. Juli*, Bergen: Fagbokforlaget, pp. 43–8.

19 Eriksen, 'Renhetsideologi i en uren tid', p. 47.

20 Robert Spencer, 2007, *Religion of Peace? Why Christianity Is and Islam Isn't*, Washington D.C: Regnery Publishing, p. 3.

21 Spencer, *Religion of Peace?*, p. 3.

22 Spencer, *Religion of Peace?*, p. 1.

23 Spencer, *Religion of Peace?*, p. 2.

24 Spencer, *Religion of Peace?*, p. 2.

25 Manifesto, p. 1133.

26 Manifesto, p. 1133.

27 Økland, 'Feminismen, Tradisjonen og Forventning', pp. 115–28.

28 Manifesto, p. 1140.

29 Manifesto, p. 1140.

30 Manifesto, p. 1140.

31 Spencer, *Religion of Peace?*, p. 84.

32 Robert Spencer, 2013, *Not Peace but a Sword: the Great Chasm Between Christianity and Islam*, San Diego: Catholic Answers, p. 17.

33 Spencer, *Religion of Peace?*, p. 10.

34 Spencer, *Religion of Peace?*, p. 186. Spencer is drawing on Ephesians 6.17 here.

35 See Strømmen, 'Christian Terror in Europe? The Bible in Anders Behring Breivik's Manifesto'.

36 J. Kameron Carter, 2009, *Race: A Theological Account*, Oxford: Oxford University Press.

37 Geir Lippestad, 2014, *Det Kan Vi Stå For*, Oslo: Aschehaug, pp. 45, 47 and 102.

38 Manifesto, p. 1325.

39 Manifesto, pp. 1328–34.

40 Manifesto, p. 1327.
41 Manifesto, p. 1331.
42 Manifesto, p. 1332.
43 Jone Salomonsen, 2012, 'Kristendom, Paganisme, og Kvinnefiendskap' in Anders Ravik Jupskås (ed.), *Akademiske Perspektiver På 22. Juli*, Bergen: Fagbokforlaget, pp. 73–91, p. 84.
44 Katherine Allen Smith, 2017, 'The Crusader Conquest of Jerusalem and Christ's Cleansing of the Temple' in Elizabeth Lapina and Nicholas Morton (eds), *The Uses of the Bible in Crusader Sources*, Leiden: Brill, pp. 19–41, p. 19.
45 Allen Smith, 'The Crusader Conquest of Jerusalem and Christ's Cleansing of the Temple', p. 20.
46 Salomonsen, 'Kristendom, paganisme og kvinnefiendskap', pp. 74–89.
47 Bishop Helga Haugland Byfuglien, 'Preken i Oslo domkirke 24. juli 2011: Johannes 14.1–3'. We are quoting from the version printed in the Church of Norway annual report, *Bispemøtet*, 2011. The sermon is available at www.fbb.nu/artikkel/helga-haugland-byfugliens-preken-i-anledning-22-juli-2011/ (accessed 19.11.2019).
48 Haugland Byfuglien, 'Preken i Oslo domkirke', p. 70.
49 Haugland Byfuglien, 'Preken i Oslo domkirke', p. 70.
50 Haugland Byfuglien, 'Preken i Oslo domkirke', p. 70.
51 Haugland Byfuglien, 'Preken i Oslo domkirke', p. 70.
52 Haugland Byfuglien, 'Preken i Oslo domkirke', p. 71.
53 Haugland Byfuglien, 'Preken i Oslo domkirke', p. 71.
54 Haugland Byfuglien, 'Preken i Oslo domkirke', p. 70.
55 Haugland Byfuglien, 'Preken i Oslo domkirke', p. 71.
56 Haugland Byfuglien, 'Preken i Oslo domkirke', p. 71.
57 Since 2017, the Church of Norway has been independent. However, the Constitution of Norway defines the Church of Norway as the 'church of the people' (*folkekirke*) that is to be supported by the state. Hence, the status of the Church in Norway is a matter of interpretation. Taking account of a number of historical shifts, it could be argued that the separation from the state took place in 2008, 2012 or 2017, but it could also be argued that the separation is incomplete.
58 What we rendered as 'International Council' is called 'Mellomkirkelig råd for Den norske kirke' in Norwegian. It coordinates the Church of Norway's contacts to churches across the globe.
59 Steinar Ims, 'Kirkens omdømme etter den 22. Juli', *Nytt norsk kirkeblad*, 5 (2011), pp. 3–5.
60 Ims, 'Kirkens omdømme', p. 4.
61 Ims, 'Kirkens omdømme', p. 4.
62 Ims, 'Kirkens omdømme', p. 5.
63 Ims, 'Kirkens omdømme', p. 5.

NOTES TO CHAPTER 3

64 Oddbjørn Leirvik, 2012, 'Religionsdialog og Verdifellesskap' in Anders Ravik Jupskås (ed.), *Akademiske Perspektiver På 22. Juli*, Bergen: Fagbokforlaget, pp. 205–13, p. 209.
65 Leirvik, 'Religionsdialog og Verdifellesskap', pp. 208–10.
66 Seyla Benhabib, 2002, *The Claims of Culture: Equality and Diversity in the Global Era*, Princeton: Princeton University Press, p. 4.
67 Islamsk råd Norge og Mellomkirkelig råd for Den norske kirke, 'Fellesuttalelse mot religiøs ekstremisme', *Nytt norsk kirkeblad*, 8 (2011), pp. 22–4.
68 Islamsk råd Norge og Mellomkirkelig råd for Den norske kirke, 'Fellesuttalelse mot religiøs ekstremisme', p. 22.
69 Islamsk råd Norge og Mellomkirkelig råd for Den norske kirke, 'Fellesuttalelse mot religiøs ekstremisme', p. 23.
70 Islamsk råd Norge og Mellomkirkelig råd for Den norske kirke, 'Fellesuttalelse mot religiøs ekstremisme', p. 23.
71 Islamsk råd Norge og Mellomkirkelig råd for Den norske kirke, 'Fellesuttalelse mot religiøs ekstremisme', p. 23.
72 Kirkelig dialogsenter, 2013, *-sier vi: Ressursmateriell om antisemittisme, islamofobi og antisiganisme til bruk i den norske kirke*, Oslo: Mellomkirkelig råd.
73 Email correspondence with Hanna Barth Hake.
74 Kirkelig dialogsenter, *-sier vi*, p. 2.
75 Kirkelig dialogsenter, *-sier vi*, p. 2.
76 Kirkelig dialogsenter, *-sier vi*, p. 5.
77 Kirkelig dialogsenter, *-sier vi*, p. 5.
78 Kirkelig dialogsenter, *-sier vi*, p. 7.
79 Kirkelig dialogsenter, *-sier vi*, p. 7.
80 Kirkelig dialogsenter, *-sier vi*, p. 9.
81 Kirkelig dialogsenter, *-sier vi*, p. 9.
82 Kirkelig dialogsenter, *-sier vi*, p. 9.
83 Kirkelig dialogsenter, *-sier vi*, p. 9.
84 Kirkelig dialogsenter, *-sier vi*, p. 11.
85 Kirkelig dialogsenter, *-sier vi*, p. 21. See also Philip Melanchthon, 1959, 'Augsburg Confession' in *The Book of Concord: Confessions of the Evangelical Lutheran Church*, trans. Theodore G. Tappert, Philadelphia: Fortress Press, 23–96.
86 Kirkelig dialogsenter, *-sier vi*, p. 21.
87 Kirkelig dialogsenter, *-sier vi*, p. 23.
88 Kirkelig dialogsenter, *-sier vi*, p. 31.
89 Kirkelig dialogsenter, *-sier vi*, p. 33. See also Gerald West, 1991, *Biblical Hermeneutics of Liberation. Modes of Reading the Bible in the South African Context*, Pietermaritzburg: Cluster Publications.
90 See http://siervi.no/ (accessed 19.11.2019).
91 Email correspondence with Hanna Barth Hake.

NOTES TO CHAPTER 3

92 Email correspondence with Steinar Ims.
93 Merete Thomassen, 'Venstrevridd kirke? Om å være folkekirke i et demokrati', *Nytt norsk kirkeblad*, 1 (2019), pp. 1–3.
94 Thomassen, 'Venstrevridd kirke?, p. 2.
95 Thomassen, 'Venstrevridd kirke?, p. 1.
96 Sylvi Listhaug, 2018, *Der Andre Tier*, Oslo: Kagge Forlag, p. 143.
97 Listhaug, *Der Andre Tier*, p. 151.
98 Listhaug, *Der Andre Tier*, p. 151.
99 Listhaug, *Der Andre Tier*, pp. 151–2.
100 Listhaug, *Der Andre Tier*, p. 152.
101 Listhaug, *Der Andre Tier*, p. 152.
102 Listhaug, *Der Andre Tier*, p. 153.
103 Listhaug, *Der Andre Tier*, p. 154.
104 Sturla J. Stålsett, 2018, 'Fearing the Faith of Others? Government, Religion, and Integration in Norway' in Ulrich Schmiedel and Graeme Smith (eds), *Religion in the European Refugee Crisis*, New York: Palgrave Macmillan, pp. 105–20, p. 110.
105 Sturla J. Stålsett, 5 September 2019, 'Ekstreme holdninger pakkes inn som norske verdier', *Dagbladet*, available at www.dagbladet.no/kultur/ekstreme-holdninger-pakkes-inn-som-norske-verdier/71558550?fbclid=IwAR3CJawO3UIsyWfNduTXjPvzv8uyO61ARez ZqnkbsGURHyWiOBiEaKGdSUo (accessed 19.11.2019). The leader of the Progress party, Siv Jensen, and Sylvi Listhaug wrote a response to Stålsett's article.
106 Thomassen, 'Venstrevridd kirke?, p. 2.
107 Hallgeir Elstad, 'Kirke og politikk. Noen historiske perspektiver', *Nytt norsk kirkeblad*, 1 (2019), pp. 37–52, p. 50.
108 Listhaug, *Der Andre Tier*, pp. 143–50.
109 Janne Dale Hauger, 'Radikal kirke, heldigvis?', *Nytt norsk kirkeblad*, 1 (2019), pp. 53–60.
110 Hauger, 'Radikal kirke', p. 55.
111 Hauger, 'Radikal kirke', p. 55.
112 Hauger, 'Radikal kirke', p. 56.
113 Hauger, 'Radikal kirke', p. 59.
114 Hauger, 'Radikal kirke', p. 60.
115 Salomonsen, 'Kristendom, Paganisme, og Kvinnefiendskap', p. 89.
116 Ephraim Meir, 2017, *Becoming Interreligious: Towards a Dialogical Theology from a Jewish Vantage Point*, Münster: Waxmann, p. 13.

Chapter 4

1 See Jörg Michael Dostal, 'The Pegida Movement and German Political Culture: Is Right-Wing Populism Here to Stay?', *The Political Quarterly*, 86/4 (2015), pp. 523–32, p. 523. For Pegida's usage of online and offline media, see Helga Druxes, '"Montag ist wieder Pegida-Tag!": Pegida's Community Building and Discursive Strategies', *German Politics and Society*, 34/4 (2016), pp. 17–33. For a sociological study of the constitution and career of Pegida up to 2015, see Hans Vorländer, Maik Herold and Steven Schäller, 2016, *PEGIDA*, Wiesbaden: Springer VS.

2 There has been considerable controversy about the number of protesters. See the statistics available at https://durchgezaehlt.org/ (accessed 19.11.2019).

3 For a short summary of the history of the AfD, see Marianne Heimbach-Steins, Alexander Filipović, Josef Becker, Marhen Behrensen and Theresa Wasserer, 2017, *Grundpositionen der Partei 'Alternative für Deutschland' und der Katholischen Soziallehre im Vergleich: Eine Sozialethische Expertise*, Münster: Institut für Christliche Sozialwissenschaften, pp. 3–7.

4 Throughout this chapter, we are drawing on Ulrich Schmiedel, 2018, '"We Can Do This!" Tackling the Political Theology of Populism' in Ulrich Schmiedel and Graeme Smith (eds), *Religion in the European Refugee Crisis*, New York: Palgrave Macmillan, pp. 205–24 and Ulrich Schmiedel, 2019, 'Hijacked or Hooked? Religion in Populist Politics in Germany' in Susan Kerr (ed.), *Is God a Populist? Christianity, Populism and the Future of Europe*, Oslo: Frekk Forlag, pp. 96–107.

5 For a short overview of current concepts of populism, see Dirk Jörke and Veith Selk, 2017, *Theorien des Populismus: Zur Einführung*, Hamburg: Junius.

6 Jan-Werner Müller, 2016, *What Is Populism?* Philadelphia: University of Pennsylvania Press.

7 Müller, *What Is Populism?*, p. 3.

8 Müller, *What Is Populism?*, pp. 101–3. See also Jan-Werner Müller, '"Das wahre Volk" gegen alle Anderen: Rechtspopulismus als Identitätspolitik', *Aus Politik und Zeitgeschichte: Zeitschrift der Bundeszentrale für politische Bildung*, 69/9–11 (2019), pp. 18–24.

9 Lutz Bachmann runs a channel on youtube.com which makes clips of the protests, including the speeches, available. Throughout this chapter, we are citing the material that is available on Bachmann's channel on www.youtube.com (accessed 19.11.2019).

10 Saxony was a centre of the Peaceful Revolution. For a comprehensive collection of (autobiographical) accounts of the 1989–90 protests, see Eckhard Jesse (ed.), 2000, *Eine Revolution und ihre Folgen: 14*

Bürgerrechtler ziehen Bilanz, Berlin: Christoph Links Verlag; Eckhard Jesse (ed.), 2006, *Friedliche Revolution und deutsche Einheit: Sächsische Bürgerrechtler ziehen Bilanz*, Berlin: Christoph Links Verlag; and Eckhard Jesse and Thomas Schubert (eds), 2010, *Zwischen Konfrontation und Konzession: Friedliche Revolution und deutsche Einheit in Sachsen*, Berlin: Christoph Links Verlag.

11 Dostal, 'The Pegida Movement', p. 525.

12 See David N. Coury, 'A Clash of Civilizations? Pegida and the Rise of Cultural Nationalism', *German Politics and Society*, 34/4 (2016), pp. 55–67.

13 Helga Druxes and Patricia Anne Simpson, 'Introduction: Pegida as a European Far-Right Populist Movement', *German Politics and Society*, 34/4 (2016), pp. 1–16, p. 3.

14 The speech was delivered on 1 December 2014.

15 See Liane Bednarz, 2018, *Die Angstprediger: Wie rechte Christen Gesellschaft und Kirchen untewandern*, Munich: Droemer, pp. 142–4.

16 The speech was delivered on 1 August 2016. We are not reproducing the names of the clergy, because we were unable to verify the two citations. However, the fact that anti-Islamic attitudes have allowed for an alliance of xenophobes inside and outside the churches is no secret. See Sonja Angelika Strube, 2015, 'Problemanzeige: Rechtsextreme Tendenzen in sich christlich verstehenden Medien' in Sonja Angelika Strube (ed.), *Rechtsextremismus als Herausforderung für die Theologie*, Freiburg: Herder, pp. 18–35.

17 The distinction between 'dar al-Harb' and 'dar al-Islam' is a classic topic in Islamic thought. Mohammed Khallouk, 2018, 'Confronting the Current Refugee Crisis: The Importance of Islamic Citizens' Initiatives in Germany' in Ulrich Schmiedel and Graeme Smith (eds), *Religion in the European Refugee Crisis*, pp. 87–103, p. 92, points out that 'already during the Middle Ages, the twelfth-century Islamic scholar Ala'uddin Abu Bakr al-Kasani counted all countries which accepted and allowed for the practice of Islam among the "dar al-Islam."' As a consequence, 'the Federal Republic of Germany, with its constitutionally guaranteed freedom of religion, would be "dar al-Islam."' For a compelling critique of the contrast between a Muslim and a non-Muslim world, see Cemil Aydin, 2017, *The Idea of the Muslim World: A Global Intellectual History*, Cambridge, MA: Harvard University Press.

18 The speech was delivered on 5 June 2017.

19 Khallouk, 'Confronting the Current Refugee Crisis', p. 89.

20 The speech was delivered on 8 January 2018.

21 See Wolfgang Benz, 2013, *Ansturm auf das Abendland? Zur Wahrnehmung des Islam in der westlichen Gesellschaft*, Wien: Picus, p. 20.

22 See Benz, *Ansturm auf das Abendland?*, p. 31.

23 See AfD, 2017, *Programm für Deutschland: Wahlprogramm der Alternative für Deutschland*, Berlin: AfD, p. 7. The program is available at www.afd.de/wahlprogramm (accessed 19.11.2019).

24 According to Lucke, the party is now 'rechtsextrem', right-wing extremist. See the 'Brandbrief' he published in 2019, available at http://bernd-lucke.de/brandbrief-afd/ (accessed 19.11.2019).

25 AfD, *Programm für Deutschland*, p. 7. It is unclear what's meant by 'Heilslehre' here. The AfD avoids calling Islam a religion so as to contend that it cannot be covered by the 'freedom of religion' in the German Grundgesetz. See Heimbach-Steins, Filipović, Becker, Behrensen and Wasserer, *Grundpositionen der Partei 'Alternative für Deutschland'*, pp. 26–9.

26 AfD, *Programm für Deutschland*, p. 34.

27 AfD, *Programm für Deutschland*, p. 47.

28 AfD, *Programm für Deutschland*, p. 34.

29 AfD, *Programm für Deutschland*, p. 9.

30 See Benz, *Ansturm auf das Abendland?*, pp. 16–17.

31 See the account of a publication by one of the leaders of the AfD in Raoul Löbbert, 17 January 2019, 'Der Volksempfänger', *Die Zeit*, available at www.zeit.de/2019/04/bjoern-hoecke-nie-zweimal-in-denselben-fluss-rechtspopulismus/komplettansicht (accessed 19.11.2019).

32 See the recent reflections by Detlef Pollack, 16 July 2019. 'Die verachtete Bevölkerung der DDR', *Frankfurter Allgemeine Zeitung*, available at www.faz.net/aktuell/feuilleton/debatten/regime-und-wider stand-die-verachtete-bevoelkerung-der-ddr-16286155.html (accessed 19.11.2019). For academic accounts, see Trutz Rendtorff (ed.), 1993, *Protestantische Revolution? Kirche und Theologie in der DDR: Ekklesiologische Voraussetzungen, politischer Kontext, theologische und historische Kriterien*. Göttingen: Vandenhoeck & Ruprecht. For the historical context, see Claudia Lepp and Kurt Nowak (eds), 2001, *Evangelische Kirche im geteilten Deutschland (1945–1989/90)*, Göttingen: Vandenhoeck & Ruprecht.

33 For a succinct summary of the history of the terms in German theology, see Reiner Anselm, 'Abendland oder Europa? Anmerkungen aus evangelisch-theologischer Perspektive', *Zeitschrift für Evangelische Ethik*, 57/4 (2013), pp. 272–81.

34 Lukas Meyer, 'Abendland und Apokalypse', *Evangelische Theologie*, 79/6 (2019), pp. 424–36.

35 Meyer, 'Abendland und Apokalypse', pp. 426–33

36 Coury, 'A Clash of Civilizations?', p. 55.

37 Of course, the contrast between 'Abendland' and 'Morgenland' is not necessarily Islamophobic. For a nuanced analysis, see Jayne Svenungsson, 'Christianity in Crisis: Uses and Abuses of Religion in Modern Europe', *Eco-Ethica*, 8 (2020), forthcoming.

NOTES TO CHAPTER 4

38 Coury, 'A Clash of Civilizations?', p. 55.
39 For the blurred boundaries between these accounts of Christianity, see Bednarz, *Die Angstprediger*, pp. 186–205.
40 See Vorländer, Herold, Schäller, *PEGIDA*, pp. 57–8. The data captures the make-up of Pegida before 2015.
41 AfD, *Programm für Deutschland*, p. 47.
42 AfD, *Programm für Deutschland*, p. 47.
43 Bednarz, *Die Angstprediger*, pp. 218–41.
44 Information about the Christians in the AfD is available online at www.chrafd.de. Last accessed 19.11.2019.
45 Christen in der AfD, 'Grundsatzerklärung der Christen in der AfD', in Joachim Kuhs (ed.), 2018, *Warum Christen AfD wählen*, Eßbach: Arnshaugh Verlag, pp. 95–102. The 'Declaration of Principle' is available at www.chrafd.de. Last accessed 19.11.2019.
46 Christen in der AfD, 'Grundsatzerklärung', p. 95.
47 Beverly M. Weber, '"We Must Talk about Cologne": Race, Gender, and Reconfigurations of Europe', *German Politics and Society*, 34/4 (2016), pp. 68–86, p. 74.
48 Coury, 'Clash of Civilizations?', p. 60.
49 Coury, 'Clash of Civilizations?', p. 60.
50 Joachim Kuhs, 2018, 'Vorwort des Herausgebers' in Joachim Kuhs (ed.), *Warum Christen AfD wählen*, Eßbach: Arnshaugh Verlag, pp. 7–10, p. 9.
51 Heimbach-Steins, Filipović, Becker, Behrensen and Wasserer, *Grundpositionen der Partei 'Alternative für Deutschland'*, pp. 13–15.
52 The speech was delivered on 1 August 2016.
53 For the weaponization of the 'event of Cologne', see Gabriele Dietze, 2019, *Sexueller Exzeptionalismus: Überlegenheitsnarrative in Migrationsabwehr und Rechtspopulismus*, Bielefeld: Transcript, pp. 41–58.
54 Thomas Meany, 'Short Cuts', *London Review of Books*, 38 (2016), p. 9.
55 While delivering the speech, Bachmann is wearing a t-shirt showing male figures chasing a female figure with the title 'Rapefugees not welcome'. As a consequence, charges for 'incitement' (*Volksverhetzung*) were pressed against him.
56 See Bonnie Evans-Hills, 2015, 'Listen to Her Roar! Engaging with Muslim Women' in Bonnie Evans-Hills and Miachel Rusk, *Engaging Islam from a Christian Perspective*, London: Peter Lang, pp. 203–26.
57 See Sufiya Ahmed, 2019, 'The First Feminist', in Mariam Khan (ed.), *It's Not About the Burqa: Muslim Women on Faith, Feminism, Sexuality and Race*, London: Picador, pp. 29–44.
58 See Asma Barlas, 2008, 'Der Koran neu gelesen', in Asma Barlas, Nahide Bozkurt and Rabeya Müller (eds), *Der Koran neu gelesen*,

NOTES TO CHAPTER 4

Berlin: Friedrich-Ebert-Stiftung Politische Akademie, pp. 5–10. See also Asma Barlas, 2019, *Believing Women in Islam: Unreading Patriarchal Interpretations of the Qur'an: Revised Edition*, Austin: University of Texas Press.

59 Christen in der AfD, 'Grundsatzerklärung', p. 95.
60 Christen in der AfD, 'Grundsatzerklärung', p. 95.
61 Beatrix von Storch, 'Grußwort' in *Warum Christen AfD wählen*, pp. 11–13, p. 11.
62 Von Storch, 'Grußwort', p. 11.
63 *Warum Christen AfD wählen* contains the 'Grundsatzerklärung'. It also includes the Apostolic Creed in the appendix.
64 Kuhs, 'Vorwort des Herausgebers', p. 7.
65 Bachmann in a speech delivered on 1 August 2016.
66 Von Storch, 'Grußwort', p. 10.
67 See Ulrich Schmiedel and Graeme Smith, 2018, 'Introduction: Charting a Crisis' and 'Conclusion: The Theological Takeover' in Ulrich Schmiedel and Graeme Smith (eds), *Religion in the European Refugee Crisis*, New York: Palgrave, pp. 1–11 and pp. 297–307.
68 Evangelische Kirche in Deutschland, 2017, *Konsens und Konflikt: Politik braucht Auseinandersetzung. Zehn Impulse der Kammer für Öffentliche Verantwortung der EKD zu aktuellen Herausforderungen der Demokratie in Deutschland*, Hannover: Evangelische Kirche in Deutschland. The statement is available at www.ekd.de (accessed 19.11.2019).
69 Evangelische Kirche in Deutschland, *Konsens und Konflikt*, p. 10.
70 See Martin Luther, 1957, 'The Freedom of a Christian (1520)' in Harold J. Grimm (ed.), *Luther's Works* vol. 31, Philadelphia: Fortress.
71 Evangelische Kirche in Deutschland, 1985, *Evangelische Kirche und freiheitliche Demokratie: Der Staat des Grundgesetzes als Angebot und Aufgabe. Eine Denkschrift der Evangelischen Kirche in Deutschland*, Gütersloh: Gütersloher Verlagshaus. Trutz Rendtorff was responsible for this statement that draws on his explorations in theological ethics, originally published in 1980. See Trutz Rendtorff, 2011, *Ethik*, ed. Reiner Anselm and Stephan Schleissing, Tübingen: Mohr Siebeck. For the English translation, albeit of an earlier edition, see Trutz Rendtorff, 1986/1989, *Ethics*, trans. Keith Grim, 2 vols, Philadelphila: Fortress Press.
72 Evangelische Kirche in Deutschland, *Konsens und Konflikt*, p. 9.
73 Evangelische Kirche in Deutschland, *Konsens und Konflikt*, p. 9.
74 Evangelische Kirche in Deutschland, *Konsens und Konflikt*, p. 10.
75 Evangelische Kirche in Deutschland, *Konsens und Konflikt*, p. 12.
76 Evangelische Kirche in Deutschland, *Konsens und Konflikt*, p. 11.
77 Evangelische Kirche in Deutschland, *Konsens und Konflikt*, p. 11.
78 Evangelische Kirche in Deutschland, *Konsens und Konflikt*, p. 14.

79 Evangelische Kirche in Deutschland, *Konsens und Konflikt*, p. 14.

80 For the metaphor of the corridor, see Reiner Anselm and Christian Albrecht, 2017, *Öffentlicher Protestantismus: Zur aktuellen Debatte um gesellschaftliche Präsenz und politische Aufgaben des evangelischen Christentums*, Zürich: TVZ.

81 Evangelische Kirche in Deutschland, *Konsens und Konflikt*, p. 19.

82 Evangelische Kirche in Deutschland, *Konsens und Konflikt*, p. 24

83 Evangelische Kirche in Deutschland, *Konsens und Konflikt*, p. 26.

84 Evangelische Kirche in Deutschland, *Konsens und Konflikt*, p. 27.

85 Evangelische Kirche in Deutschland, *Konsens und Konflikt*, p. 27.

86 Evangelische Kirche in Deutschland, *Konsens und Konflikt*, p. 28.

87 Kirchenamt der Evangelischen Kirche in Deutschland (ed.), 2006, *Klarheit und gute Nachbarschaft: Christen und Muslime in Deutschland. Eine Handreichung des Rates der EKD*, Hannover: EKD.

88 See the contributions to Jürgen Micksch (ed.), 2007, *Evangelisch aus fundamentalem Grund: Wie sich die EKD gegen den Islam profiliert*, Frankfurt a.M.: Otto Lembeck.

89 Kirchenamt der Evangelischen Kirche in Deutschland (ed), *Klarheit und gute Nachbarschaft*, p. 43.

90 Arnulf von Scheliha, 'Die religionstheologische Hermeneutik der EKD-Handreichung', in *Evangelisch aus fundamentalem Grund*, pp. 65–79.

91 Kirchenamt der Evangelischen Kirche in Deutschland (ed), *Klarheit und gute Nachbarschaft*, p. 20. Here, the statement differs from previous publications of the EKD where the possibility was not precluded.

92 Kirchenamt der Evangelischen Kirche in Deutschland (ed), *Klarheit und gute Nachbarschaft*, pp. 20–1.

93 Kirchenamt der Evangelischen Kirche in Deutschland (ed), *Klarheit und gute Nachbarschaft*, p. 21.

94 See Yasemin Karakaşoğlu, 2007, 'Abgrenzung und Mission statt Toleranz und Dialog' in Jürgen Micksch (ed.), *Evangelisch aus fundamentalem Grund: Wie sich die EKD gegen den Islam profiliert*, Frankfurt a.M.: Otto Lembeck, pp. 238–52.

95 Kirchenamt der Evangelischen Kirche in Deutschland (ed), *Klarheit und gute Nachbarschaft*, p. 22.

96 See Sekretariat der Deutschen Bischofskonferenz and Kirchenamt der Evangelischen Kirche in Deutschland, 2019, *Vertrauen in die Demokratie stärken: Ein Gemeinsames Wort der Deutschen Bischofskonferenz und des Rates der Evangelischen Kirche in Deutschland*, Bonn/Hannover: Deutsche Bischofskonferenz/Evangelische Kirche in Deutschland.

97 Sekretariat der Deutschen Bischofskonferenz, 2019, *Dem Populismus Widerstehen: Arbeitshilfe zum Umgang mit rechtspopulistischen*

NOTES TO CHAPTER 4

Tendenzen im kirchlichen Raum, Bonn: Sekretariat der Deutschen Bischofskonferenz. The Guidelines are available at www.dbk.de (accessed 19.11.2019).

98 Sekretariat der Deutschen Bischofskonferenz, *Dem Populismus Widerstehen*, p. 4.
99 Sekretariat der Deutschen Bischofskonferenz, *Dem Populismus Widerstehen*, p. 8.
100 Sekretariat der Deutschen Bischofskonferenz, *Dem Populismus Widerstehen*, p. 27.
101 See Chantal Mouffe, 2018, *For a Left Populism*, London: Verso.
102 Sekretariat der Deutschen Bischofskonferenz, *Dem Populismus Widerstehen*, p. 27.
103 Sekretariat der Deutschen Bischofskonferenz, *Dem Populismus Widerstehen*, pp. 28–9.
104 Sekretariat der Deutschen Bischofskonferenz, *Dem Populismus Widerstehen*, p. 29.
105 Sekretariat der Deutschen Bischofskonferenz, *Dem Populismus Widerstehen*, p. 31. See also Pope Francis, 2015, *Encyclical Letter Laudato Si' of the Holy Father Francis on Care for Our Common Home*, Vatican City: Liberia Editrice Vaticana, also available at www.laudatosi.com (accessed 19.11.2019).
106 Sekretariat der Deutschen Bischofskonferenz, *Dem Populismus Widerstehen*, p. 17.
107 Sekretariat der Deutschen Bischofskonferenz, *Dem Populismus Widerstehen*, pp. 18–19.
108 Sekretariat der Deutschen Bischofskonferenz, *Dem Populismus Widerstehen*, p. 22.
109 Sekretariat der Deutschen Bischofskonferenz, *Dem Populismus Widerstehen*, p. 17.
110 Sekretariat der Deutschen Bischofskonferenz, *Dem Populismus Widerstehen*, p. 32.
111 Sekretariat der Deutschen Bischofskonferenz, *Dem Populismus Widerstehen*, p. 32.
112 Sekretariat der Deutschen Bischofskonferenz, *Dem Populismus Widerstehen*, p. 46.
113 Sekretariat der Deutschen Bischofskonferenz, *Dem Populismus Widerstehen*, p. 47.
114 Sekretariat der Deutschen Bischofskonferenz, *Dem Populismus Widerstehen*, p. 47.
115 Sekretariat der Deutschen Bischofskonferenz, *Dem Populismus Widerstehen*, p. 48.
116 Sekretariat der Deutschen Bischofskonferenz, *Dem Populismus Widerstehen*, p. 48.

NOTES TO CHAPTER 4

117 Sekretariat der Deutschen Bischofskonferenz, *Dem Populismus Widerstehen*, p. 48.
118 Sekretariat der Deutschen Bischofskonferenz, *Dem Populismus Widerstehen*, p. 50. Here the Guidelines point to two documents from the Second Vatican Council, *Lumen Gentium* and *Nostra aetate*. All of the documents are available at www.vatican.va (accessed 19.11.2019).
119 Sekretariat der Deutschen Bischofskonferenz, *Dem Populismus Widerstehen*, p. 36.
120 Sekretariat der Deutschen Bischofskonferenz, *Dem Populismus Widerstehen*, p. 36.
121 Sekretariat der Deutschen Bischofskonferenz, *Dem Populismus Widerstehen*, p. 38. For the use of the concept of crisis, see also Ulrich Schmiedel and Graeme Smith, 'Introduction: Charting a Crisis', pp. 1–11.
122 Sekretariat der Deutschen Bischofskonferenz, *Dem Populismus Widerstehen*, p. 38.
123 Sekretariat der Deutschen Bischofskonferenz, *Dem Populismus Widerstehen*, p. 39.
124 Sekretariat der Deutschen Bischofskonferenz, *Dem Populismus Widerstehen*, p. 40.
125 Sekretariat der Deutschen Bischofskonferenz, *Dem Populismus Widerstehen*, p. 39.
126 Sekretariat der Deutschen Bischofskonferenz, *Dem Populismus Widerstehen*, p. 40, quoting Pope Francis' 'Message for the World Day of Migrants and Refugees 2015'.
127 Sekretariat der Deutschen Bischofskonferenz, *Dem Populismus Widerstehen*, p. 44.
128 Sekretariat der Deutschen Bischofskonferenz, *Dem Populismus Widerstehen*, p. 44.
129 Sekretariat der Deutschen Bischofskonferenz, *Dem Populismus Widerstehen*, p. 64.
130 Sekretariat der Deutschen Bischofskonferenz, *Dem Populismus Widerstehen*, p. 64.
131 See David Goldenberg, 2005, *The Curse of Ham: Race and Slavery in Early Judaism, Christianity, and Islam*, Princeton: Princeton University Press; David. N. Livingstone, 2008, *Adam's Ancestors: Race, Religion and the Politics of Human Origins*, Baltimore: Johns Hopkins University Press; David M. Whitford, 2009, *The Curse of Ham in the Early Modern Era: The Bible and the Justifications for Slavery*, London: Routledge.
132 Sekretariat der Deutschen Bischofskonferenz, *Dem Populismus Widerstehen*, p. 44. We rendered 'christentümlich' with 'Christianist', but the German neologism 'christentümlich' parallels 'volkstümlich' which rings of traditional, tribal and trivial folklore in German ears.

133 Sekretariat der Deutschen Bischofskonferenz, *Dem Populismus Widerstehen*, p. 52.
134 Sekretariat der Deutschen Bischofskonferenz, *Dem Populismus Widerstehen*, p. 56.
135 *Male and Female He Created Them* is available at www.vatican.va (accessed 19.11.2019). See Susannah Cornwall's '"Male and Female He Created Them" – A Response to the Vatican Report on Gender Education', available at https://shiloh-project.group.shef.ac.uk/male-and-female-he-created-them-a-response-to-the-vatican-report-on-gender-education (accessed 19.11.2019). See also Susannah Cornwall, 2017, *Un/Familiar Theology: Reconceiving Sex, Reproduction and Generativity*, London: Bloomsbury.
136 Sekretariat der Deutschen Bischofskonferenz, *Dem Populismus Widerstehen*, p. 53. See also Heimbach-Steins, Filipović, Becker, Behrensen and Wasserer, *Grundpositionen der Partei 'Alternative für Deutschland'*, pp. 19–23 where the theological critique of the AfD is taken as a point of departure to criticise the Catholic Church for its position on gender and gender studies.
137 Sekretariat der Deutschen Bischofskonferenz, *Dem Populismus Widerstehen*, p. 71.
138 Sekretariat der Deutschen Bischofskonferenz, *Dem Populismus Widerstehen*, p. 71.
139 Druxes, '"Montag ist wieder Pegida-Tag"', p. 28.
140 Heimbach-Steins, Filipović, Becker, Behrensen and Wasserer, *Grundpositionen der Partei 'Alternative für Deutschland'*, p. 5.
141 Heinrich Wefing, 18 June 2019, 'Nichts ist vergangen: Vieles spricht dafür, dass zum ersten Mal seit Weimar ein Politiker von einem Rechtsextremen hingerichtet wurde', *Die Zeit*, available at https://www.zeit.de/2019/26/walter-luebcke-rechtsextremismus-mord-nsu-weimarer-republik (accessed 19 .11.2019).
142 Özlem Topçu, 20 February 2020, 'Rassismus ist überall – das müssen wir endlich anerkennen', *Die Zeit*, available at https://www.zeit.de/gesellschaft/zeitgeschehen/2020-02/hanau-anschlag-rassismus-gewalttat-schuesse-rechtsextremismus (accessed 1 3.2020).

Chapter 5

1 Helen Pidd and Declan Lloyd, 13 May 2014, 'Police investigate far-right "invasions" of Bradford and Glasgow mosques', the *Guardian*, available at www.theguardian.com/world/2014/may/13/police-far-right-invasions-bradford-glasgow-mosques-britain-first (accessed 19.11.2019).

2 See Matthew J. Goodwin, 2012, 'Backlash in the "Hood": Exploring support for the British National Party (BNP) at the local level' in Andrea Mammone, Emmanuel Godin and Brian Jenkins (eds), *Mapping the Extreme Right in Contemporary Europe: From Local to Transnational*, London: Routledge, pp. 17–32.

3 Timothy Peace, 2016, 'Religion and Populism in Britain: An Infertile Breeding Ground?' in Nadia Marzouki, Duncan McDonnell and Olivier Roy (eds), *Saving the People: How Populists Hijack Religion*, London: Hurst & Co, pp. 95–108, p. 103.

4 Andrea Mammone and Timothy Peace, 2012, 'Azione Sociale and the British National Party' in Andrea Mammone, Emmanuel Godin and Brian Jenkins (eds), *Mapping the Extreme Right in Contemporary Europe: From Local to Transnational*, London: Routledge, pp. 288–302, p. 293.

5 Peace, 'Religion and Populism in Britain', p. 104.

6 Peace, 'Religion and Populism in Britain', p. 106.

7 Peace, 'Religion and Populism in Britain', p. 107.

8 See the Joint Statement from the Archbishop of York and Archbishop of Canterbury, available at http://aoc2013.brix.fatbeehive.com/articles.php/1050/joint-statement-from-the-archbishop-of-york-and-archbishop-of-canterbury (accessed 19.11.2019).

9 Peace, 'Religion and Populism in Britain', p. 107.

10 Peace, 'Religion and Populism in Britain', p. 95.

11 Goodwin, 'Backlash in the "Hood"', p. 17.

12 Liz Fekete, 2019, *Europe's Fault Lines: Racism and the Rise of the Right*, London: Verso, p. 119.

13 Fekete, *Europe's Fault Lines*, p. 8.

14 Fekete, *Europe's Fault Lines*, p. 7.

15 Farage went on to form the Brexit Party.

16 Steve Corbett, 'The Social Consequences of Brexit for the UK and Europe: Euroscepticism, Populism, Nationalism, and Societal Division', *International Journal of Social Quality*, 6/1 (2016), pp. 11–31, p. 22.

17 Corbett, 'The Social Consequences of Brexit for the UK and Europe', p. 22.

18 See the material on www.voteleavetakecontrol.org/why_vote_leave.html (accessed 19.11.2019).

19 See the contributions to Ulrich Schmiedel and Graeme Smith (eds), 2018, *Religion in the European Refugee Crisis*, New York: Palgrave Macmillan.

20 The poster is available at www.voteleavetakecontrol.org (accessed 19.11.2019).

21 The poster is available at www.voteleavetakecontrol.org (accessed 19.11.2019).

22 For the significance of religion in the so-called refugee crisis,

see Erin K. Wilson and Luca Mavelli, 2017, 'The Refugee Crisis and Religion: Beyond Conceptual and Physical Boundaries,' in Erin K. Wilson and Luca Mavelli (eds), *The Refugee Crisis and Religion: Secularism, Security and Hospitality in Question*, London: Hurst, pp. 1–22.

23 James Meek, 2019, *Dreams of Leaving and Remaining*, London: Verso, p. 10.

24 UKIP, 'What we stand for', available at www.ukip.org/pdf/What WeStandForJan2019.pdf (accessed 19.11.2019).

25 UKIP 'What we stand for'.

26 UKIP Policies, 'Immigration', available at www.ukip.org/ukip-manifesto-item.php?cat_id=5 (accessed 19.11.2019).

27 UKIP Policies, 'British culture', available at www.ukip.org/ukip-manifesto-item.php?cat_id=20 (accessed 19.11.2019).

28 For the significance of sexist stereotypes in debates about immigration, see Elena Fiddian-Qasmiyeh, 2017, 'The Faith-Gender-Asylum Nexus: An Intersectionalist Analysis of Representations of the "Refugee Crisis"' in Mavelli and Wilson (eds), *The Refugee Crisis and Religion*, pp. 207–22.

29 UKIP Policies, 'British culture'.

30 UKIP Policies, 'British culture'.

31 UKIP Policies, 'British culture'.

32 Fekete, *Europe's Fault Lines*, p. 80. See also Liz Fekete, 2009, *A Suitable Enemy: Racism, Migration and Islamophobia in Europe*, London: Pluto.

33 Monika Brusenbauch Meislová, 'A Single-Issue Party without an Issue? UKIP and British 2017 General Election', *Acta Politologica*, 10/3 (2018), pp. 1–20, p. 9.

34 Brusenbauch Meislová, 'A Single-Issue Party without an Issue?', p. 9.

35 James Kirkup and Robert Winnett, 25 May 2012, 'Theresa May interview: "We're going to give illegal migrants a really hostile reception"', *The Telegraph*, available at www.telegraph.co.uk/news/uknews/immigration/9291483/Theresa-May-interview-Were-going-to-give-illegal-migrants-a-really-hostile-reception.html (accessed 19.11.2019).

36 Fekete, *Europe's Fault Lines*, p. 80.

37 See the personal accounts collected in Maya Goodfellow, 2019, *Hostile Environment: How Immigrants Became Scapegoats*, London: Verso.

38 Goodfellow, *Hostile Environment*, p. 10.

39 Goodfellow, *Hostile Environment*, p. 91.

40 For a discussion of the connection between minorities and Muslims in the history of Europe, see Anour Majid, 2009, *We are all Moors: Ending Centuries of Crusades against Muslims and other Minorities*. Minneapolis: University of Minnesota Press.

NOTES TO CHAPTER 5

41 Peter Walker and Kate Proctor, 18 February 2020, 'No 10 under pressure to say whether it vetted "racist" Andrew Sabisky', the *Guardian*, available at https://www.theguardian.com/politics/2020/feb/18/no-10-under-pressure-andrew-sabisky-hired-cummings-race-intelligence (accessed 1.3.2020).

42 Boris Johnson, 5 August 2018, 'Denmark has got it wrong. Yes the burka is oppressive and ridiculous – but that's still no reason to ban it', *Daily Telegraph*, available at www.telegraph.co.uk/news/2018/08/05/denmark-has-got-wrong-yes-burka-oppressive-ridiculous-still/ (accessed 19.11.2019).

43 Mammone and Peace, 'Azione Sociale and the British National Party', pp. 293, 298.

44 See www.tellmamauk.org (accessed 19.11.2019).

45 For the statistics, see https://tellmamauk.org/press/islamophobic-attacks-in-uk-rose-significantly-after-boris-johnsons-controversial-comments-comparing-veiled-muslim-women-to-letterboxes-watchdog-reveals/ (accessed 19.11.2019).

46 Nazia Parveen, 2 September 2019, 'Boris Johnson's burka comments "led to surge in anti-Muslim attacks"', the *Guardian*, available at www.theguardian.com/politics/2019/sep/02/boris-johnsons-burqa-comments-led-to-surge-in-anti-muslim-attacks (accessed 19.11.2019).

47 See the statement on his website: Boris Johnson, 23 March 2006, 'Dress in Educational Establishments', available at www.boris-johnson.com/2006/03/23/dress-in-educational-establishments/#more-256 (accessed 19.11.2019).

48 Labour politicians have also come out with similarly problematic statements. See James Crossley, 2018, *Cults, Martyrs and Good Samaritans: Religion in Contemporary English Discourse*, London: Pluto Press, pp. 92–3.

49 Alex Forsyth, 20 September 2019, 'Islamophobia: Conservative Party members suspended over posts', *BBC News*, available at www.bbc.co.uk/news/uk-politics-49763550 (accessed 19.11.2019).

50 Crossley, *Cults, Martyrs and Good Samaritans*, p. 92.

51 Crossley, *Cults, Martyrs and Good Samaritans*, p. 96.

52 In what follows we quote from the manifesto, which can be found at: www.support4thefamily.org/UKIPChristian_Manifesto-1.pdf (accessed 19.11.2019).

53 Crossley, *Cults, Martyrs and Good Samaritans*, p. 32.

54 Harry Cole, 27 November 2016, 'Guide me, O thou great Theresa: Theresa May says her faith in God will guide our path out of Europe as she admits Brexit is keeping her awake', *The Sun*, www.thesun.co.uk/news/2274324/theresa-may-says-her-faith-in-god-will-guide-our-path-out-of-europe-as-she-admits-brexit-is-keeping-her-awake/ (accessed 19.11.2019).

NOTES TO CHAPTER 5

55 Crossley, *Cults, Martyrs and Good Samaritans*, p. 35.
56 In what follows we are quoting from Theresa May's 2017 Easter message, which is available at www.gov.uk/government/news/easter-2017-theresa-mays-message (accessed 19.11.2019).
57 Crossley, *Cults, Martyrs and Good Samaritans*, p. 41. Emphasis added.
58 Theresa May's 2017 Christmas message is available at www.gov.uk/government/news/prime-minister-theresa-mays-christmas-message-2017 (accessed 19.11.2019).
59 Theresa May's 2017 Christmas message.
60 Fekete, *Europe's Faultlines*, p. 116.
61 Mammone and Peace, 'Azione Sociale and the British National Party', p. 295.
62 Church of England, 2015, *Who is my neighbour? A Letter from the House of Bishops to the People and Parishes of the Church of England for the General Election 2015*, London: Church of England, p. 2. The letter is available at www.churchofengland.org/GeneralElection2015 (accessed 19.11.2019).
63 Church of England, *Who is my neighbour?*, p. 3.
64 Church of England, *Who is my neighbour?*, p. 3.
65 Church of England, *Who is my neighbour?*, p. 3.
66 Church of England, *Who is my neighbour?*, p. 4.
67 Church of England, *Who is my neighbour?*, p. 6.
68 Church of England, *Who is my neighbour?*, p. 7.
69 Church of England, *Who is my neighbour?*, p. 8.
70 Church of England, *Who is my neighbour?*, p. 9.
71 Church of England, *Who is my neighbour?*, p. 9.
72 Church of England, *Who is my neighbour?*, p. 10.
73 Church of England, *Who is my neighbour?*, p. 18.
74 Church of England, *Who is my neighbour?*, p. 18.
75 Church of England, *Who is my neighbour?*, p. 22.
76 Church of England, *Who is my neighbour?*, p. 23.
77 Church of England, *Who is my neighbour?*, p. 26.
78 Church of England, *Who is my neighbour?*, p. 33.
79 Church of England, *Who is my neighbour?*, p. 33.
80 Church of England, *Who is my neighbour?*, p. 44.
81 Church of England, *Who is my neighbour?*, p. 44.
82 Church of England, *Who is my neighbour?*, p. 44.
83 Church of England, *Who is my neighbour?*, p. 44.
84 Church of England, *Who is my neighbour?*, p. 39.
85 Church of England, *Who is my neighbour?*, p. 40.
86 Church of England, *Who is my neighbour?*, p. 44.
87 Yasemin El-Menouar, 2017, *Muslims in Europe*, Gütersloh: Bertelsmann Foundation.

88 El-Menouar, *Muslims in Europe*, p. 9.
89 El-Menouar, *Muslims in Europe*, p. 9, compares the UK to Austria, France, Germany and Swizerland. The UK figures contrast with the sense of connectedness with the UK among Muslims. If asked which country they feel connected to, only 8 per cent of the Muslims living in Britain name only their country of origin. By contrast, 20 per cent name only the UK and 69 per cent name their country of origin in addition to the UK. El-Menouar, *Muslims in Europe*, p. 7.
90 Greg Smith and Linda Woodhead, 'Religion and Brexit: Populism and the Church of England', *Religion, State & Society*, 46/3 (2018), pp. 206–23, p. 207. See also the table on p. 208, where the influence of Anglicanism is controlled against demographic characteristics such as gender, class, age and region. In all these categories, Anglicans were more likely to vote Leave than non-Anglicans.
91 Smith and Woodhead, 'Religion and Brexit', p. 213.
92 Smith and Woodhead, 'Religion and Brexit', p. 216. The data they are drawing on here is from 2013.
93 Smith and Woodhead, 'Religion and Brexit', p. 216.
94 Smith and Woodhead, 'Religion and Brexit', p. 216.
95 Steve Corbett, 'The Social Consequences of Brexit for the UK and Europe: Euroscepticism, Populism, Nationalism, and Societal Division', p. 16.
96 Smith and Woodhead, 'Religion and Brexit', p. 216.
97 Anthony G. Reddie, 2019, *Theologising Brexit: A Liberationist and Postcolonial Critique*, London: Routledge, p. 16.
98 Reddie, *Theologising Brexit*, p. 27.
99 For a scholarly account, see Wendy Laverick and Peter Joyce, 2019, *Racial and Religious Hate Crime: The UK from 1945 to Brexit*, New York: Palgrave Macmillan, particularly pp. 295–342.
100 Justin Welby, 2018, *Reimagining Britain: Foundations for Hope*, London: Bloomsbury.
101 Welby, *Reimagining Britain*, p. x.
102 Daniel Wincott, 'Brexit Dilemmas: New opportunities and tough choices in unsettled times', *The British Journal of Politics and International Relations*, 19/4 (2017), pp. 680–95, p. 684.
103 Welby, *Reimagining Britain*, pp. 2–3. Welby refers to 'Western Christianity' here, by which he means 'Christianity originally from Rome'. He distinguishes this Christianity from the Christianity of the Celts and the Christianity of Constantinople.
104 Welby, *Reimagining Britain*, p. 15.
105 Welby, *Reimagining Britain*, p. 187.
106 Welby, *Reimagining Britain*, p. 178.
107 Welby, *Reimagining Britain*, p. 181.
108 Welby, *Reimagining Britain*, p. 181.

109 Welby, *Reimagining Britain*, p. 181.
110 Welby, *Reimagining Britain*, p. 180.
111 Welby, *Reimagining Britain*, p. 189.
112 Welby, *Reimagining Britain*, p. 189.
113 Welby, *Reimagining Britain*, p. 191.
114 Welby, *Reimagining Britain*, p. 188.
115 Welby, *Reimagining Britain*, p. 81.
116 Rowan Williams, 'Civil and Religious Law in England: A Religious Perspective', *Ecclesiastical Law Journal*, 10 (2008), pp. 262–82, particularly pp. 266–7 where he argues that 'if the law of the land takes no account of what might be for certain agents a proper rationale for behaviour – for protest against certain unforeseen professional requirements, for instance, that would compromise religious discipline ... – it fails in a significant way to communicate ..., and so, on at least one kind of legal theory ..., in one of its purposes.'
117 Welby, *Reimagining Britain*, p. 81.
118 Welby, *Reimagining Britain*, p. 81.
119 Welby, *Reimagining Britain*, p. 82.
120 Welby, *Reimagining Britain*, p. 82.
121 Vincent Lloyd, 2011, *The Problem with Grace: Reconfiguring Political Theology*, Stanford: Stanford University Press, p. 29: 'Love opposed to law: that is the quintessential image of supersessionism.'
122 See the classic Krister Stendhal, 'The Apostle Paul and the Introspective Conscience of the West', *Harvard Theological Review*, 56/3 (1963), pp. 199–215.
123 See the classic E. P. Sanders, 1977, *Paul and Palestinian Judaism: A Comparison of Patterns of Religion*, Minneapolis: Fortress, 1977.
124 Jayne Svenungsson, 2016, *Divining History: Prophetism, Messianism and the Development of the Spirit*, trans. Stephen Donovan, New York: Berghahn, traces the supersessionism that runs through the history of theology and philosophy in Europe.
125 See Joshua Ralston, 2020, *Law and the Rule of God: A Christian Engagement with Shari'a*, Cambridge: Cambridge University Press.
126 Werner G. Jeanrond, 2010, *A Theology of Love*, London: Bloomsbury, pp. 105–34. See also Werner G. Jeanrond, 2010, 'Towards an Interreligious Hermeneutics of Love' in Catherine Cornille and Christopher Conway (eds), *Interreligious Hermeneutics*, Eugene: Cascade Books, pp. 44–60.
127 See Joshua Ralston, 'Islam as a Christian Trope: The Place and Function of Islam in Reformed Dogmatic Theology', *The Muslim World*, 107/4 (2017), pp. 754–76.
128 Mona Siddiqui, 2012, *The Good Muslim: Reflections on Classical Islamic Law and Theology*, Cambridge: Cambridge University Press, p. 137.

NOTES TO CHAPTER 5

129 Siddiqui, *The Good Muslim*, p. 153.
130 Siddiqui, *The Good Muslim*, p. 159.
131 Siddiqui, *The Good Muslim*, p. 159.
132 Siddiqui, *The Good Muslim*, pp. 159–60 is citing Q 7:156.
133 Siddiqui, *The Good Muslim*, p. 161.
134 Welby, *Reimagining Britain*, p. 264.
135 Welby, *Reimagining Britain*, p. 281.
136 See Bonnie Evans-Hills and Michael Rusk, 2015, *Engaging Islam from a Christian Perspective*, Berlin: Peter Lang.
137 The Church of England, 2019, *Resources for Prayer Together*, London: Church of England. The resources are available at www.churchofengland.org/together (accessed 19.11.2019).
138 The Church of England, *Resources for Prayer Together*, p. 1.
139 The Church of England, 2019, *Tea and Prayer Together: Some Conversation Starters*, London: Church of England, p. 1. The resources are also available at www.churchofengland.org/together (accessed 19.11.2019).
140 The Church of England, *Tea and Prayer Together*, p. 1.

Chapter 6

1 This scenario is inspired by Bundesarbeitsgemeinschaft Kirche & Rechtsextremismus, 2017, *Impulse für den Umgang mit Rechtspopulismus im kirchlichen Raum*, Berlin: BAG K&R, pp. 24–7, available at www.kirche-demokratie.de (accessed 19.11.2019).

2 The Church of England, 2019, *Resources for Prayer Together*, London: Church of England, p. 1.

3 The Church of England, 2019, *Tea and Prayer Together: Some Conversation Starters*, London: Church of England, p. 1.

4 Evangelische Kirche in Deutschland, 2017, *Konsens und Konflikt: Politik braucht Auseinandersetzung. Zehn Impulse der Kammer für Öffentliche Verantwortung der EKD zu aktuellen Herausforderungen der Demokratie in Deutschland*, Hannover: Evangelische Kirche in Deutschland, p. 19.

5 Evangelische Kirche in Deutschland, *Konsens und Konflikt*, p. 11.

6 Church of England, 2015, *Who is my neighbour? A Letter from the House of Bishops to the People and Parishes of the Church of England for the General Election 2015*, London: Church of England, p. 40.

7 Sekretariat der Deutschen Bischofskonferenz, 2019, *Dem Populismus Widerstehen: Arbeitshilfe zum Umgang mit rechtspopulistischen Tendenzen im kirchlichen Raum*, Bonn: Sekretariat der Deutschen Bischofskonferenz, p. 48.

NOTES TO CHAPTER 6

8 See Jayne Svenungsson, 'Public Faith and the Common Good: A Radical Messianic Proposal', *Political Theology*, 14/6 (2013), pp. 744-57.

9 Kirkelig dialogsenter, 2013, *-sier vi: Ressursmateriell om antisemittisme, islamofobi og antisiganisme til bruk i den norske kirke*, Oslo: Mellomkirkelig råd, p. 9.

10 Sekretariat der Deutschen Bischofskonferenz, *Dem Populismus Widerstehen*, p. 50.

11 Reports about Islamophobia across Europe are available at www.islamophobiaeurope.com (accessed 19.11.2019). Reports that are compiled for a number of countries are published annually.

12 See Bonnie Evans-Hills, 2019, 'A Response to the Bishop of Truro's Independent Review for the Former Foreign Secretary of FCO Support for Persecuted Christians', available as a pdf at: www.uspg.org.uk/docstore/245.pdf (accessed 19.11.2019).

13 Mathew Goodwin, 2012, 'Backlash in the "Hood": Exploring support for the British National Party (BNP) at the local level' in Andrea Mammone, Emmanuel Godin and Brian Jenkins (eds), *Mapping the Extreme Right in Contemporary Europe: From Local to Transnational*, London: Routledge, pp. 17–32, p. 23.

14 See James Meek, 2019, *Dreams of Leaving and Remaining*, London: Verso, for a sensitive account of the different layers and the distinct levels of precariousness in the context of the UK's referendum on leaving the EU.

15 See Gustavo Gutiérrez, 1993, 'Option for the Poor' in Ignácio Ellacuría and Jon Sobrino (eds), *Mysterium Liberationis: Fundamental Concepts of Liberation Theology*, Maryknoll: Orbis, pp. 235–50. The classic is of course Gustavo Gutiérrez, 2006, *A Theology of Liberation: History, Politics, and Salvation*, Maryknoll: Orbis.

16 Gustavo Gutiérrez, 1997, 'Renewing the Option for the Poor' in David Batstone, Eduardo Mendieta and Lois Ann Lorentzen (eds), *Liberation Theologies, Postmodernity, and the Americas*, London: Routledge, pp. 69–82, p. 72. Rudolf von Sinner, 'Brazil: From Liberation Theology to a Theology of Citizenship as Public Theology,' *International Journal of Public Theology*, 1 (2007), pp. 338–63, offers a short overview of the development of the preferential option for the poor. Theologians in Europe could learn a lot from his call for a theology of citizenship.

17 See Shadaab Rahemtulla, 2017, *Qur'an of the Oppressed: Liberation Theology and Gender Justice in Islam*, Oxford: Oxford University Press.

18 Jan-Werner Müller, 2016, *What Is Populism?* Philadelphia: University of Pennsylvania Press. See also Jan-Werner Müller, 'The People

NOTES TO CHAPTER 6

Must Be Extracted from Within the People: Reflections on Populism', *Constellations*, 21/4 (2014), pp. 483–93.

19 Jan-Werner Müller, '"Das wahre Volk" gegen alle anderen: Rechtspopulismus als Identitätspolitik', *Aus Politik und Zeitgeschichte*, 69/9–11 (2019), pp. 18–24, p. 22.

20 Müller, '"Das wahre Volk"', p. 22.

21 Werner G. Jeanrond, 2020, *Reasons to Hope*, London: Bloomsbury: T&T Clark, pp. 95–6.

22 Jeanrod, *Reasons to Hope*, p. 107.

23 Gordon W. Allport, 1954, *The Nature of Prejudice*, Reading, MA: Addison-Wesley, p. 7.

24 Müller, *What Is Populism?*, p. 114.

25 Allport, *The Nature of Prejudice*, p. 261, citing Alfred M. Lee and Norman D. Humphrey, 1943, *Race Riot*, New York: Dryden, p. 130.

26 Allport, *The Nature of Prejudice*, p. 262.

27 Allport, *The Nature of Prejudice*, p. 265.

28 See Allport, *The Nature of Prejudice*, pp. 262–3, for different types of contact.

29 Allport, *The Nature of Prejudice*, p. 276.

30 Gordon W. Allport and Bernard M. Kramer, 'Some Roots of Prejudice', *The Journal of Psychology*, 22 (1946), pp. 9–39, p. 26.

31 Allport, *The Nature of Prejudice*, p. 281.

32 Of course, there have been criticisms of Allport's contact hypothesis. The critics point to the conditions and the causality of contact. Allport already argued that there are conditions that have to be met for contact to criticize rather than confirm prejudice. The causality criticism is more cutting. Statisticians insist on the difference between correlation and causation. What statistics can show is that more contact correlates with less prejudice and that less prejudice correlates with more contact, but can they show that contact *causes* less prejudice? If people with prejudice don't and people without prejudice do like meeting others – could less prejudice be causing contact rather than contact be causing less prejudice? There are studies that point to both directions of causality, but the direction advocated by Allport seems to have a more sustained and stronger effect. See Thomas F. Pettigrew, 'Generalized Intergroup Contact Effects on Prejudice', *Personality and Social Psychology Bulletin*, 23/2 (1997), pp. 173–85.

33 Gert Pickel and Cemal Öztürk, 'Islamophobia Without Muslims? The "Contact Hypothesis" as an Explanation for Anti-Muslim Attitudes – Eastern European Societies in Comparative Perspective', *Journal of Nationalism, Memory & Language Politics*, 12/2 (2018), pp. 162–91.

34 Pickel and Öztürk, 'Islamophobia Without Muslims?', pp. 179–80.

35 Pickel and Öztürk, 'Islamophobia Without Muslims?', p. 182.

NOTES TO CHAPTER 6

36 Pickel and Öztürk, 'Islamophobia Without Muslims?', p. 184.
37 Pickel and Öztürk, 'Islamophobia Without Muslims?', p. 184.
38 Pickel and Öztürk, 'Islamophobia Without Muslims?', p. 184. Gert Pickel and Alexander Yendell, 'Islam als Bedrohung? Beschreibung und Erklärung von Einstellungen zum Islam im Ländervergleich', *Zeitschrift für Vergleichende Politikwissenschaft*, 10 (2016), pp. 273–309, come to similar conclusions, drawing on data from 2010 and 2013.

39 See Katherine Clayton, Jeremy Ferwerda and Yusaki Horiuchi, 'Exposure to Immigration and Admission Preferences: Evidence from France', *Political Behavior* (2019), pp. 1–26.

40 Allport, *The Nature of Prejudice*, p. 444.

41 Gordon W. Allport, 'The Religious Context of Prejudice', *Pastoral Psychology*, 5 (1967), pp. 20–30, p. 20.

42 Allport, *The Nature of Prejudice*, p. 446.

43 Allport, *The Nature of Prejudice*, p. 447.

44 Allport, *The Nature of Prejudice*, p. 448.

45 Gert Pickel, 'Religion als Ressource für Rechtspopulismus? Zwischen Wahlverwantschaften und Fremdzuschreibungen', *Zeitschrift für Religion, Gesellschaft und Politik*, 2 (2018), pp. 277–312, pp. 303–4.

46 Pickel, 'Religion als Ressource für Rechtspopulismus?', p. 308.

47 Martin Luther King, Jr. interviewed on 'Meet the Press', 17 April 1960. The interview is available on Stanford University's The Martin Luther King, Jr. Research and Education Institute at http://okra.stanford.edu/transcription/document_images/Vol05Scans/17Apr1960_InterviewonMeetthePress.pdf (accessed 19.11.2019).

48 Of course, Martin Luther King Jr. criticized both racial and religious segregation. His concepts of community and church were multi-religious. See Lewis V. Baldwin, 2010, *The Voice of Conscience: The Church in the Mind of Martin Luther King, Jr*, Oxford: Oxford University Press, pp. 101–40.

49 For a short survey of the biblical canonization process, see John Barton, 1997, *How the Bible Came to Be*, Louisville: Westminster John Knox Press. See also Konrad Schmid and Jens Schröter, 2019, *Die Entstehung der Bibel: Von den ersten Texten zu den heiligen Schriften*, Munich: C.H. Beck.

50 See Yvonne Sherwood, 2012, *Biblical Blaspheming: Trials of the Sacred for a Secular Age*, Cambridge: Cambridge University Press.

51 See Ulrich Schmiedel, 2017, *Elasticized Ecclesiology: The Concept of Community after Ernst Troeltsch*, New York: Palgrave Macmillan.

52 Umberto Eco, 1989, *The Open Work*, trans. Ana Cancogni, Cambridge, MA: Harvard University Press, p. 12.

53 Eco, *The Open Work*, p. 19.

54 For a short summary, see Gregory Miller, 2014, 'Luther's Views of the Jews and Turks' in Robert Kolb, Irene Dingel and L'ubomír Batka (eds), *The Oxford Handbook of Martin Luther's Theology*, Oxford: Oxford University Press, pp. 427–34.

55 Müller, '"Das wahre Volk"', p. 22.

56 Anthony G. Reddie, 2019, *Theologising Brexit: A Liberationist and Postcolonial Critique*, London: Routledge, p. 77.

57 Reddie, *Theologising Brexit*, p. 137.

58 Ephraim Meir, 2019, *Faith in the Plural*, Tel Aviv: Idra Publishing, p. 10.

59 Meir, *Faith in the Plural*, p. 110, referring to Souleymane Bachir Diagne, 2004, 'Religion and the Challenge of Spirituality in the Twenty-First Century', in Jérome Bindé (ed.), *The Future of Values: 21st-Century Talks*, New York: Berghahn Books, pp. 98–102.

60 Meir, *Faith in the Plural*, pp. 110–11. See also the theological-philosophical account by Bengt Kristensson-Uggla, 'What Makes Us Human? The Lutheran Anthropological Link Between Gustaf Wingren and Paul Ricoeur', *Open Theology*, 4 (2018), pp. 308–15.

61 Meir, *Faith in the Plural*, p. 10. See also Ulrich Schmiedel, 'Opening the Church to the Other: Dietrich Bonhoeffer's Reception of Ernst Troeltsch,' *International Journal for the Study of the Christian Church*, 17/3 (2017), pp. 184–98.

62 Meir, *Faith in the Plural*, p. 21.

63 Allport, *The Nature of Prejudice*, p. 276.

64 Mahmoud Ayoub, 2007, *A Muslim View of Christianity: Essays on Dialogue*, ed. Irfan A. Omar, Maryknoll: Orbis, p. 15.

65 Jesus was a Jew. For the significance of Jesus in Judaism, see Peter Schäfer, 2012, *The Jewish Jesus: How Judaism and Christianity Shaped Each Other*, Princeton: Princeton University Press. For the significance of Jesus in Islam, see Mona Siddiqui, 2013, *Christians, Muslims and Jesus*, New Haven: Yale University Press.

66 Ayoub, *A Muslim View of Christianity*, p. 69.

67 Ayoub, *A Muslim View of Christianity*, p. 69.

68 Ayoub, *A Muslim View of Christianity*, p. 37.

69 Ayoub, *A Muslim View of Christianity*, p. 69.

70 Ayoub, *A Muslim View of Christianity*, pp. 15–16.

71 See again Bundesarbeitsgemeinschaft Kirche & Rechtsextremismus (ed), *Impulse für den Umgang mit Rechtspopulismus im kirchlichen Raum*, pp. 24–7.

72 Bundesarbeitsgemeinschaft Kirche & Rechtsextremismus (ed), *Impulse für den Umgang mit Rechtspopulismus im kirchlichen Raum*, p. 27.

Chapter 7

1 See Jörg Lauster, 2014, *Die Verzauberung der Welt: Eine Kulturgeschichte des Christentums*, Munich: C. H. Beck.

2 Stuart Hall, 1992, 'The West and the Rest: Discourse and Power' in Stuart Hall and Bram Gieben (eds), *Formations of Modernity*, Cambridge: Polity Press, pp. 185–227.

3 Gordon W. Allport, 1954, *The Nature of Prejudice*, Reading, MA: Addison-Wesley, p. 276.

4 See Brian Klug, 2009, *Offense: The Jewish Case*, London: Seagull, pp. 5–27, arguing that anyone who lays claim to the tradition of Judaism contributes to Judaism. Again, we see no reason not to apply his argument to Christianity.

5 See Werner G. Jeanrond, 2010, 'Belonging or Identity? Christian Faith in a Multi-Religious World' in Catherine Cornille (ed.), *Many Mansions? Multiple Religious Belonging and Cultural Identity*, Maryknoll: Orbis, pp. 106–20.

6 Michael Rusk, 2015, 'A Common Word' in Bonnie Evans-Hills and Michael Rusk (eds), *Engaging Islam from a Christian Perspective*, London: Peter Lang, pp. 73–88, pp. 73–4.

7 'A Common Word Between Us and You' in Miroslav Volf, Ghazi bin Muhammad and Melissa Yarrington (eds), 2010, *A Common Word: Muslims and Christians on Loving God and Neighbor*, Grand Rapids: Eerdmans, pp. 28–50.

8 'A Common Word Between Us and You', p. 28.

9 'A Common Word Between Us and You', p. 45.

10 H.R.H. Prince Ghazi bin Muhammad of Jordan, 2010, 'On "A Common Word Between Us and You"' in Miroslav Volf, Ghazi bin Muhammad and Melissa Yarrington (eds), *A Common Word: Muslims and Christians on Loving God and Neighbor*, Grand Rapids: Eerdmans, pp. 3–17, pp. 4–5.

11 Ghazi bin Muhammad, 'On "A Common Word Between Us and You"', p. 7.

12 'A Common Word Between Us and You', pp. 47–8.

13 See the report by Den Norske Kirke, Kirkerådet, 'Menigheten møter flyktninger: Rapport om Den norske kirkes lokale arbeid med flyktninger, asylsøkere og migranter', available at https://kirken.no/globalassets/kirken.no/om-kirken/samfunnsansvar/diakoni/rapport_diakoni.pdf (accessed 19.11.2019).

14 Den Norske Kirke, Kirkerådet, 'Menigheten møter flyktninger', p. 14.

15 See the report 'Bischöfe begrüßen Flüchtlinge in München', 5 September 2015, available at https://archiv.ekd.de/aktuell/edi_2015_09_06_bedford-strohm_marx_fluechtlinge.html (accessed 19.11.2019).

16 Bonnie Evans-Hills, 2015, 'Muslims in Britain: An Overview of Recent Church of England Engagement' in Bonnie Evans-Hills and Michael Rusk, *Engaging Islam from a Christian Perspective*, London: Peter Lang, pp. 5–26, p. 17.

Index of Biblical References

Genesis		Jeremiah		10.27	159
9.25–27	88	29.11–14	116	19.45–46	49
				22	77
Exodus		Matthew			
15.3–6	47	5.43–44	48	John	
		10.34	33, 45	2.13–16	49
Leviticus		15.21–28	58, 136	13	77
19.17–18	159	21.12–13	49	15.20	93
19.18	48	22.35–40	159	19.1–22	58, 13
19.34	48	25.23–24	116		
		25.31–46	58, 136	Romans	
Deuteronomy		26.15	77	13	76
6.1–9	116			14.7–12	116
6.4–5	159	Mark			
10.19	48	10.42–45	116	Ephesians	
		11.15–18	49	6.17	173
Psalms		12.28–34	159		
18.34	47			1 Peter	
		Luke		3.15	77
Isaiah		6.27	48		
42.13	47	10.25–37	7, 108,		

Index of Names and Subjects

Allport, Gordon 12, 130–4, 141, 143, 155, 157, 194
Anglicanism 57, 105, 109, 190
Antisemitism 3, 16, 20, 24, 56, 58
Antiziganism 56, 58
Apocalyptic 5, 38, 48, 50, 64, 73, 147
Ayoub, Mahmoud 9, 11, 141–2

Bachmann, Lutz 66, 68–71, 74–7, 177, 180, 181
Bednarz, Liane 10, 20, 22–3, 34, 37, 180
Believing 36, 144, 147
Belonging 7, 35–6, 144, 147, 164
Breivik, Anders Behring 38–50, 61, 64–5, 73, 82, 89, 148
Brexit 93–6, 98, 102, 104, 109, 116, 152
Burqa 21, 30, 99, 119

Catholicism 28, 32, 57, 67, 72, 83–8, 90–1, 114, 125–6, 135–6, 151, 160, 185
Chin, Rita 4, 18–21, 26, 28
Christendom 44, 48, 77, 148
Church of Norway vii, 40, 43, 50–4, 57, 59–61, 63–7, 125, 136, 138, 149, 151, 153, 159, 174
Church of England 92–6, 102–17, 122–3, 126, 153, 160

Clash of civilizations 4–5, 16–18, 29, 35
Clash of cultures 2–4, 11–12, 15, 19, 29, 35, 49, 74, 102, 115, 141, 146–7, 151, 153–9
Common good 62, 79, 116
Conspiracy 27, 70, 74, 89, 150
Contact hypothesis 130–2, 155, 194
Colonization 20, 28, 48, 110
Counter-jihad 28, 44, 70
Creation 57, 89, 105, 114, 138
Crusade 29–30, 32, 38, 41, 44, 46–9, 55, 64, 73, 89, 92, 125, 148

Dehumanization 107
Democracy 6, 13, 67–8, 71, 74, 78–85, 90–1, 96, 122–7, 136, 138, 147, 151–4
Deus vult 30
Dialogue 44, 56, 89, 107
Dignity 54, 63, 76, 81, 83, 85, 89, 107, 120–1, 127, 138, 140
Discrimination 4, 17, 36, 56, 59, 119, 121, 128, 130, 138, 142, 150, 154
Diversity 42, 51–2, 106, 111, 113, 139, 147, 158
Double Commandment (of love) 7–8, 159, 161

Elite 32, 38, 67–8, 74, 77–8, 126, 148, 150

INDEX OF NAMES AND SUBJECTS

Essentialism 19–21, 29–30, 53, 93, 126, 138, 144, 152
Ethnicity 3, 17, 86, 88–9, 102, 107, 109, 111
Ethnocentrism 3, 22
Ethnopluralism 22, 88
Eurabia 27, 39
Extremism 16, 23, 26, 28, 39, 41–2, 49, 54–5, 61, 71, 77, 90–1, 94, 96–7, 100, 102, 104, 107, 117, 121, 137, 152–3, 179

Family 34, 75–6, 88–9, 101, 112, 136
Faith 8, 10, 23, 30, 33, 36, 41–2, 49, 53–61, 65, 74, 77–9, 86–7, 92, 101–6, 113, 115, 123–6, 133, 141–2, 147–8, 150–1, 157
Farage, Nigel 94–6, 101, 117, 152, 186
Feminism 44, 76

Gender 34, 44, 75, 88, 185, 190
Globalization 2, 80, 87
God 7, 10–11, 20, 30, 36, 41–2, 44–51, 55, 57–8, 62–4, 76, 81, 84–7, 89, 102, 107, 109, 113–16, 122, 126, 141–2, 147–8, 151, 157, 159 (*see also* image of God)
Good Samaritan 7, 12, 48, 76–7, 87, 89, 108, 111–12, 117–18, 130, 135–7, 156, 161
Gospel 56–7, 63, 79, 81, 87, 125, 153
Grace 62–3, 113–15, 153

Hall, Stuart 17, 35, 147
Hate 14, 57, 126, 129, 130–1
Hate crime 110, 126
Hostile environment 98–9, 116

Huntington, Samuel 4–5, 16–18, 29, 35

Identity of Christianity 6, 10, 120, 134–44, 156–7
Identity politics 2, 53
Image of God 76, 83, 85, 89, 105–6, 119, 121, 138
Immigration 4, 16, 18, 22–3, 60, 66, 75–6, 80–1, 87, 95–9, 107, 109, 117, 119, 124–7, 134, 136, 143, 150, 153, 187
Imperialism 44, 110, 166
Inter-faith 5, 149, 151
Islamization 23, 26–8, 32, 38, 47, 61, 66–70, 74, 141, 150
Islamism 6, 68–70, 100, 152

Jeanrond, Werner vii, 8, 114, 129
Jesus of Nazareth 7–8, 33, 41, 45, 49, 56, 60, 65, 77, 79, 81, 84, 87, 93, 106, 112, 120–3, 136, 138, 140–4, 150, 156, 161, 196
Judaism 7, 24, 27, 43, 45–6, 56, 59, 64, 86, 114, 138, 140, 149, 159, 164, 167, 196, 197
Jihad 27–8, 44–5
Johnson, Boris 95, 99–100, 117, 152
Judaeo-Christian 101, 104, 152
Justice 63

King Jr, Martin Luther 134, 195
Klug, Brian 10, 164, 197

Law 26–7, 33–4, 45, 98, 112–14, 153 (*see also* Sharia)
Leave campaign 94–8
LGBTQ+ 34
Liberation theology 127, 140
Lived religion 7, 163

Love 7–8, 20, 48, 56, 65, 77, 87–9, 91, 106, 111, 114–15, 118, 136, 141–2, 153, 159, 161 (*see also* Double Commandment)
Luther, Martin 57–8, 79, 138

Masculinity 44, 75
May, Theresa 98–103, 117, 152–3
Meir, Ephraim 64, 140, 164
Middle Ages/medieval 7, 29, 44, 47–9, 148, 178
Migration vii, 5, 22, 75, 86–7, 95, 98, 107, 112
Misogyny 30–1, 34, 76, 119–20
Mohammed (the Prophet) 26, 76
Müller, Jan-Werner 67, 128–30, 139
Multiculturalism 4, 18, 21, 28, 42–3, 47, 86, 100

Nationalism 2, 23, 95–6, 109
Nativism 85, 104
Neighbour 6–8, 12, 22, 48, 77, 87–9, 91, 95, 105–11, 116, 118–23, 130, 132–4, 141–3, 153–5, 158–60
Neutrality 14, 32, 69, 74, 107, 123, 126, 128, 140, 142–5, 154–5, 158
New Racism 4, 11–15, 18, 20–5, 36–7, 40, 49–50, 56–9, 64, 67, 71, 78, 89, 93–4, 97–8, 117, 126–7, 130, 138, 147–55, 158 (*see also* Racism)
Nostalgia 84–5

Openness 10, 14, 52–3, 57, 65, 140–2, 158

Patriarchy 44
Paul 114
Peaceful Revolution 67, 71–2, 150, 177

Pegida 66–77
People of God 46, 85
Populism 11, 62, 66–7, 69, 71–2, 83–91, 94–6, 122, 128, 150–2
Power 20, 28, 47, 57, 66, 74, 77, 89, 94, 104, 106, 110, 114, 124–5
Prejudice 5, 12, 48, 52, 56, 70, 91, 130–4, 141–2, 155, 157, 194
Protestantism 44, 57, 67, 72, 78, 83, 90–1, 114, 122, 135–6, 151, 160
Purity 42

Qur'an 27, 64, 70, 76, 82–3, 114, 119–20, 127, 136

Racism 4, 12, 15–16, 18, 20–5, 31, 46, 63, 65, 68–9, 86, 91–3, 96–7, 99, 104, 107, 117, 130, 140, 149, 151, 153, 155, 158, 166 (*see also* New Racism)
Radicalization 26, 41, 69, 148
Reddie, Anthony 109–10, 140
Refugee 60, 66, 71, 75–8, 86–7, 90, 95–6, 112, 120, 134, 160

Secular 6, 12, 17, 19, 31–2, 43, 73, 124, 170
Semantic struggle 10, 14, 59, 61, 64–5, 91, 118, 120, 134, 137, 149, 152, 156, 158
Sharia 26, 30, 68, 112–13
Siddiqui, Mona 114–15
Solidarity 54, 64, 87, 116, 130
Spencer, Robert 28, 39, 42–7
Stereotype 23–4, 35–6, 71–2, 75, 82, 107, 132, 147, 158, 187

Terror 1–3, 6, 11, 13–14, 23, 26, 29, 38–41, 45, 48, 51–9, 61, 65, 67, 69–70, 75, 82, 86, 89,

INDEX OF NAMES AND SUBJECTS

90–1, 92, 97, 100, 117, 148–9, 159, 163
Tradition 7, 10, 15, 40–1, 44, 55, 58–9, 71, 74, 76, 78, 83, 87, 103–7, 110–11, 125, 133, 135, 139, 141, 146, 150, 157, 184, 197

Unity 23, 46, 108, 116–17, 122

Values 26–7, 31, 33–4, 43, 45, 51, 53, 61–2, 69, 80, 95, 101, 103–4, 110–13, 117–19, 140, 152, 170
Violence vii, 1, 6, 9, 13, 23, 28–30, 33, 40, 44–9, 61, 64, 67, 70, 82, 86, 90, 96–7, 100

Virtue 80, 95, 106, 110–11, 117–19, 140
Vulnerability 51, 62, 66, 74–5, 84

Welby, Justin 110–15, 118, 136, 190
West, the 17–18, 27, 35, 43, 45, 133, 147
Windrush scandal 99

Ye'or, Bat 27–8, 39, 126

Xenophobia 92–3, 108, 117, 178

www.ingramcontent.com/pod-product-compliance
Lightning Source LLC
Chambersburg PA
CBHW021947290426
44108CB00012B/981